James John Hissey

On Southern English Roads

James John Hissey

On Southern English Roads

ISBN/EAN: 9783337420260

Printed in Europe, USA, Canada, Australia, Japan

Cover: Foto ©Andreas Hilbeck / pixelio.de

More available books at **www.hansebooks.com**

On Southern English Roads

BY

JAMES JOHN HISSEY

AUTHOR OF
'ON THE BOX SEAT,' 'ACROSS ENGLAND IN A DOG-CART,'
'A HOLIDAY ON THE ROAD,' 'THROUGH TEN ENGLISH COUNTIES,' ETC.

'*Hisce rotis patrias juverit isse vias*'

WITH SIXTEEN FULL-PAGE ILLUSTRATIONS BY THE AUTHOR
AND A PLAN OF THE ROUTE

LONDON
RICHARD BENTLEY & SON
Publishers in Ordinary to Her Majesty the Queen
1896

All rights reserved

TO

Richard Bentley

THIS VOLUME IS INSCRIBED

BY HIS FRIEND

Jas. Jno. Hissey

PREFACE

IN the present age of rushing to and fro at steam-haste—not the slow post-haste of old—when "globe-trotting" has become quite commonplace, this simple chronicle of a leisurely driving-tour of only a few hundred miles "On Southern English Roads" may seem almost an anomaly. On behalf, however, of quiet-loving tourists like myself, who do not measure beauty by the mile, and who from pure pleasure choose to travel by road and behind horses, just as our pre-railway forefathers did, I may quote a dictum of Ruskin's, "A fool wants to shorten time and space, a wise man wants to lengthen both."

How many of those who rush over different lands and seas, as fast as railway-train or steamboat will convey them, really know anything of the countries they hasten through, or are cognisant of the charm of deliberate and desultory travel? wherein one has full command over one's time, conveyance, route, and luggage, and so can stop at any point on the way as wished—this is true travelling; the railway simply takes you from place to place, by it you merely depart and arrive! The distance traversed in a given time never appeals to me: one man may actually see more in a quiet walk round his garden than another who has "done" his thousands of miles; the traveller who goes the farthest and journeys the fastest does not therefore see the most. So, even in these days of rapid transit and magnificent distances, I trust that this unvarnished record of a restful, health-giving holiday, spent in driving about the peace-bestowing English country, may help to show how much of beauty and interest lies at our own doors, and prove the needlessness of going abroad to discover the picturesque.

For many summers now past have we taken driving expeditions through some portion of Old England, our aim being, as much as possible, to keep away from the crowded and well-beaten tourist track; and this volume contains a simple account of the last of these most enjoyable outings in search of "fresh *roads* and *taverns* new."

To Mr. Pearson my thanks are due for the pains he has taken in engraving my drawings. It seems to me only consistent that the story of an old-fashioned journey like this should be illustrated in the good old-fashioned way by wood-cuts.

J. J. HISSEY.

1896.

CONTENTS

CHAPTER I

Road travel—A real holiday—A pleasant pilgrimage—Old coaching inns—An early start—The South Downs—Seeing and thinking—Windmills—An architectural dream—A lesson in patience—A relic of the past   1

CHAPTER II

Distance the enchanter—Country towns—"A shoemaker's holiday"—Our country towns—Toy rivers—The Sussex iron age—"Hammer Ponds"—Dry sermons!—Local pronunciation of place names—A town beyond railways—Out of the beaten track—The Pelham buckle—A chat by the way—A serious mistake—A Sussex proverb—A curious bequest—A haunted hill   17

CHAPTER III

Halland House—Old buildings and their uses—Laughton Place and moat—An ancient tower—The South Downs from Laughton—A sea warrior of "Great King Henry's dayes"—A picturesque village—English wild-flowers—Exploring a fresh country—A well-wooded land—Old traditions—Facts or fables—Isfield—Useless directions—A mystery—The world as others see it—A quaint old home .   . 36

CHAPTER IV

Isfield church—The Shurley Chapel—An ostentatious tomb—Old brasses—A eulogistic inscription—Wooded Sussex

—Old-time roads—A wandering artist—Buxted—An old ironmaster—Sussex cannon—A family rebus—A quaint brass epitaph—Invented facts—Haunted? . . 53

CHAPTER V

A wild district—Changes of scene and climate—English landscapes—A gipsy encampment—A grand panorama—The romance of the road—Left to the imagination—A windy height—A lonely inn—Unrecorded legends—"Blowborough"—Curious notices—Crowborough Beacon—Modern miracles—Old-fashioned country folk—Ghost lore—The Red Cross Inn—A lovely country—A modern village—Tunbridge Wells—An elevated hostel 73

CHAPTER VI

The much-abused English climate—An old moated house—An old-world garden—Poor amateur photographer—Rural England—A picturesque farmstead—Old houses and new—An ancient hostelry—A deserted mansion—A mystery—"Sussexian"—A satirical traveller—Cyclists' inns—The evolution of the spire—Ashdown Forest—Sketching from nature—Forest Row—Visitors' books at hotels—Ruins of Brambletye House—An old coaching inn . 89

CHAPTER VII

At East Grinstead—Sackville College—"Modern Gothic"—"Ye Village Cage" at Limpsfield—A new reading of history—Old houses—A tip declined!—Fine altar-tomb—A tradition—Too good for this world—Old chained Bibles—Benefactors—A picture in building—Crowhurst church—Oldest yew tree in England—A smock-frocked clerk—Crowhurst Place—A legendary house—A quaint and interesting interior . 112

CONTENTS

CHAPTER VIII

An ancient home—A million years old !—Sussex lanes—Haste the curse of the century—Nature's cathedral—An Anglo-Saxon church—A curious font—Worth Forest—Balcombe —A Sussex tarn—Cuckfield—The charm of old country towns—The "doom tree"—A weird custom—An old-fashioned ghost—A poet's license . 133

CHAPTER IX

Haywards Heath—Scaynes Hill—East Mascalls—A ruined manor-house—An ideal village—A picturesque home— Motto over doorway—Chat with a miller—Sussex names —A quaint brass and an interesting tomb—Old helmets —Ruins of Slaugham Place—An estate extending from London to the Channel—A long parish .   152

CHAPTER X

St. Leonard's Forest—A local tradition—The "Capital of the Weald"—Where Shelley was born—Knepp Castle—A wayside cross—Steyning—Curious panelling—A Norman church—Mysterious carving—" Sir Harry Gough's house " —" Heathen burials"— Wiston — Storrington — Parham and its treasures—An historic home—Old armour—A picture with a story to tell—Hiding-holes—Where Queen Elizabeth dined—A natural sun-dial . 172

CHAPTER XI

"The Wild Brooks"—Amberley Castle—" Four good things of Sussex"—A church hour-glass stand—Lost on the Downs—A case of "Hobson's choice"—A river ferry— Arundel—The Fitzalan Chapel—A brace of anecdotes— Swanbourne Lake—A Sussex "hanger"—A famous view —Nature and art—Slindon—A ruined priory—Boxgrove —An interesting interior—Chichester 194

CHAPTER XII

An old prophecy fulfilled—Chichester market cross—An old-world village—Traditions—The legend of the bells of Bosham—An historic church—Old words and expressions —An English Holland—The invention of ox-tail soup— Sea and land—Porchester Castle—Fareham—Church towers—Titchfield Place gateway—Bursledon Bridge— Southampton—Ferries old and new . . 215

CHAPTER XIII

An old-fashioned inn—The money value of a view—The river Test—The New Forest—Stoney Cross—The Rufus Stone —Possible origin of an old saying—The valley of the Hampshire Avon—Ringwood—Anglers' inns—Wimborne and its minster—Old customs—The curfew—A curious tomb—A library of chained books—Sign-posts—Poole Harbour—A peculiar inn sign . . 233

CHAPTER XIV

Wareham—A town within its ancient Roman walls—A deserted Saxon church—The Isle of Purbeck—Corfe Castle—A quaint village — Picturesque houses — Swanage — Old customs—A professional invalid—Pure air!—Durlston Head—The world in stone—A grand cliff walk—Tilly Whim caves—" Wesley's Cottage " 254

CHAPTER XV

Curious inscriptions—An amusing blunder—" The Bloody Bank"—Hills and heather—A haunted manor—Wool Bridge—Bindon Abbey—Winfrith—Roadside acquaintances—A primitive interior—The story of a pew—Maiden Castle—Dorchester—An evening ramble . . 271

CONTENTS xiii

CHAPTER XVI

PAGE

A Dorsetshire poet—Uncertain weather—The restorer in his glory—A ghastly sight—A lovely valley—Godmanstone—The art of seeing—Cerne Abbas—Old legends—Cerne Abbey gateway—The Cerne Giant—A deserted mill—A grand mausoleum—Long Burton—A picture for a pilgrim   287

CHAPTER XVII

Sherborne — House names — Bell inscriptions — An ancient abbey conduit—Sherborne Castle—A wild and hilly drive—Bruton—A church with two towers—King Alfred's Tower—A monastic pigeon-house—Somerset hills and scenery—Frome—Bishop Ken's curious tomb—An easy stage—Westbury White Horse—A charming village—Trowbridge   307

CHAPTER XVIII

An uninteresting town—A quiet spot—Seend—God's garden—"Shane's Castle"—A hill-climbing canal—The "Bear" at Devizes—The glamour of a name—A curiously-inscribed market cross—"The Island"—A wayside monument—Another white horse—An ancient earth-work—Upavon—Benighted on Salisbury Plain—An oasis in a desert   .   326

CHAPTER XIX

A grand playground—Wild England of to-day—Adventures—Ludgershall Castle—Herring-bone masonry—A decayed town—An interesting market cross—Weyhill—Andover—An old rhyming proverb—The upper Test—Nature's music—Scenery and character—A wooden church—Two old inns—A Roman road—Winchester—A reminder of the plague—The valley of the Itchen—A curious church—Saxon sculpture?   .   .   .   346

CHAPTER XX

Itchen Abbas—Alresford—Epitaphs and Burial Boards—A greenland solitude—The fascination of the far-away—Rogate—A fine brass to an Agincourt hero—A "leper's window"—Latin or English—A wild heath—Peat-cutting in a southern county—The ruins of Cowdray House—Queen Elizabeth as a sportswoman—"The curse of Cowdray" . . . 367

CHAPTER XXI

Cowdray Park—Petworth—Nineteenth-century ecclesiastical architecture—Bric-á-brac hunting—A novel title—"The Wastes of the Manor"—Happy travellers—The blessing of scandal!—An artist-haunted hostelry—A quaint conceit in inn signs—Stopham Bridge—Washington—Over the Downs—The helmet of "the great Earl of De la Warr". 384

CHAPTER XXII

Sompting—A unique church tower—Disappointed cyclists—"The Sussex Pad"—Old Shoreham—Picturesque Lewes—A castle with two keeps—Mystic symbols—Round-towered churches—A Saxon sun-dial—Seaford—Friston Place—The end of the journey . . . 399

APPENDIX: Itinerary of Journey . . 419

INDEX . 421

ILLUSTRATIONS

BURPHAM FERRY . . .	. . *Frontispiece*	
"A HAUNT OF ANCIENT PEACE" .	. To face page	44
IN MID-SUSSEX	,, ,,	74
A MOATED HOME—GROOMBRIDGE PLACE	,, ,,	92
A DECAYED MANSION—CROWHURST PLACE .	,, ,,	126
A RUINED MANOR-HOUSE—EAST MASCALLS .	,, ,,	156
THE SOUTH DOWNS FROM NEAR STEYNING	,, ,,	178
AMBERLEY CASTLE FROM THE WILD BROOKS .	,, ,,	196
BOSHAM, LOW TIDE	,, ,,	218
THE VALLEY OF THE HAMPSHIRE AVON, NEAR RINGWOOD	,, ,,	240
ST. MARTIN'S CHURCH, WAREHAM . . .	,, ,,	256
HAUNTED! WOOL BRIDGE MANOR-HOUSE .	,, ,,	278
CERNE ABBEY GATEWAY .	,, ,,	298
SALISBURY PLAIN, NEAR EVERLEY .	,, ,,	348
THE RUINS OF COWDRAY HOUSE .	,, ,,	380
LEWES . .	,, ,,	404
MAP OF ROUTE	*End of Book*	

ON SOUTHERN ENGLISH ROADS

CHAPTER I

Road travel—A real holiday—A pleasant pilgrimage—Old coaching inns—An early start—The South Downs—Seeing and thinking—Windmills—An architectural dream—A lesson in patience—A relic of the past.

SAYS William Hazlitt in his delightful essay "On going a Journey" anent the charm of freedom in travel: "The soul of a journey is liberty, perfect liberty, to think, feel, do, just as one pleases . . . to be free from all impediments and of all inconveniences." He was discoursing about a walking tour, which has its special delights counterbalanced, however, it seems to me, by certain decided drawbacks; for on a pedestrian expedition you can take but very few things with you, otherwise tramping all day long with a heavily-laden knapsack strapped to your back is apt to turn what should be a pure pleasure outing into one of positive toil, the more especially should the day be hot and the way be hilly; besides, it requires a certain amount of training to set forth on a lengthened walking tour, so as to be refreshed and not fatigued by the unaccustomed exertion.

There is, of course, cycling to be considered, but with all its charms as a pleasant exercise, cycling is also open to the foregoing objections as regards the limited amount of luggage available on tour and the training needful; besides, it entails the additional disadvantage of your having to look after and clean a possibly muddy machine at night when perhaps sufficiently tired with a long day's work; for, as I have found from bitter experience, the task of tending to the steel steed is one not lightly to be entrusted to the average and probably unsympathetic ostler. Moreover, your companion, unless you go alone, must necessarily be a cyclist too; and then there are the considerations of pace and distance to be done each day to be carefully taken into account beforehand; otherwise disagreements might arise on the way, and what should be a health and pleasure-giving outing might easily prove, by over-exertion, a hurtful experience.

Now the essence of a true holiday (especially to those not over-strong) is to enjoy a change of scene and air with as little fatigue or worry as possible; and so far as I have been able to discover, the best way of securing these supreme advantages is to take a driving tour, for travelling thus you are enabled to have with you a reasonable amount of baggage, including all things needful for health or comfort, besides sundry luxuries, such as a few books by favourite authors to beguile a wet evening at a lonely country inn, an ample supply of sketching materials, as well as perchance a photographic outfit, to say nothing of wraps, overcoats, or waterproofs in case of bad weather; for the English summer, delightful though it be, is like a fickle maiden, uncertain and tearful at times. And who would wish it otherwise? Not I, in truth. Variety is the salt that lends zest to the pleasures of life, and shower—ay, and even storm —as well as sunshine are needful to bring out to the full the picturesque qualities of the landscape. Where would be the peculiar charm and the poetry of the majority of Turner's pictures without the changeful sky scenery he introduces? A glance through his illustrations to *England and Wales* will show what I mean. Sometimes, indeed, during our wanderings the skyscape has even been more interesting and noteworthy than the landscape.

A driving tour is the very luxury of travelling. Whether you be the fortunate possessor of a carriage and horses, or have to hire them for the occasion, it matters not; nor in face of the fact that no further expenses are entailed for railway fares, cabs, etc., and that the charges at the rural inns are the reverse of extortionate, can it be deemed a costly form of spending a summer holiday, especially taking into consideration the constant change of scenery and air, the varying incidents and feast of loveliness such an expedition provides.

The driving tourist, too, is in an enviable position of delightful independence; time-tables trouble him not, and having no one's convenience to consult but his own, he need never be in a hurry; he is happily free from the worry of looking after his luggage or the risk of losing it, for his belongings go with him and are ever at command (even on the way if required); he can breakfast at his leisure without the fear of missing a train, can start on his day's stage when he will, can loiter on the road or speed along just as his mood at the moment dictates. He can pull up for rest and refreshment at any wayside hostelry that may take his fancy, or should he so prefer, may picnic in a shady nook or grassy field, for he can carry his lunch in his conveyance and a bait for his horse besides, all that is really needful for him being to reach an inn at the end of each day's pleasant pilgrimage. For a happy combination of comfort with independence, what form of travelling can compare with a driving tour? And who would not be light-hearted having such an expedition in immediate prospect, full of untasted pleasure, with all fair England before him to explore?

Having thus sung the praises of our special mode of travel, though not, I trust, having sounded the horn too loudly, let me bid you, kind reader, in imagination to mount the box-seat of our roomy and comfortable four-wheel dog-cart, and as we roll pleasantly and peacefully along the quiet country roads in spirit together, allow me to note to you the varied beauties and characteristics of the mellow home-like scenery we pass through, to point out from time to time the interesting architectural features of the ancient churches, stately halls, or moated granges —haunted or otherwise—we may come upon, and to talk over the traditions which that rare old romancer Father Time has gathered round about the latter, to show you the quiet charms of sleepy medieval market towns and remote old-world villages that have never known the hand of the modern builder, nor heard the sound of the rushing railway train, to call your attention to the simple poetry that exists in many a peaceful farmstead and rural cottage home.

Now and then, too, our eyes will be charmed by the vision of a genuine old coaching inn standing in dignified solitude by the side of the erst turnpike road, with its weather-stained front, and storm-beaten sign swinging as in times long past at the top of a post, so that all who pass by cannot fail to notice it. Such ancient hostelries appeal strongly to one's sympathies by the associations they arouse of departed days, too often, alas! also of a departed prosperity, and the pictures they inevitably bring to the mind's eye of jovial hosts, jolly Jehus, rollicking post-boys, and, by no means least, of our hail-fellow-well-met, port-wine-loving ancestors—peace to their ashes—who, beheld through the mellowing influences of the glass of Time, appear much more interesting and desirable company than their unpicturesque descendants who travel by railway in the same carriage with you for hours at a stretch and say not a word. Why the railway should be so conducive to unmannerly and chilly reserve I cannot comprehend; however, it may not be wholly to blame, for in America sociability reigns in the cars, and if you be so minded you may chat with your fellow-travellers all the while you journey on, with merely rests at meal times. But after this digression to return to my subject and Old England, permit me furthermore to discourse from time to time during our pleasant progress of quaint rural customs, curious folk-lore, local legends and wise sayings that still linger in the land, and to crave you not to fail to observe the sundry odd characters that, even in these conventional days, may yet be encountered when travelling out of the beaten track, and generally permit me to do the honours of the charmingly beautiful and interesting line of country we shall traverse during our tour.

On previous journeys we had made London our starting-point. This, however, involved, both on the first day's outward stage and the last stage homeward, a tedious, intensely uninteresting, and unprofitable drive through the mean and "long-drawn-out" suburbs of that mighty province (or county, is it?) of smoke-begrimed bricks and mortar. This time, by way of change, we planned to start from Eastbourne, so that practically we could at once commence our drive in the real country. We had agreed that we would spend our holiday of three or four weeks exploring some portion of Southern England; as to our route we had formed no precise plans, we merely had a sort of hazy notion that we would drive first northward to East Grinstead, and then on through Sussex, Hampshire, and Dorsetshire, find our way possibly into Somerset, and so home through Wiltshire, returning by a different line of country, to be arranged when the time came. How we carried out our plans the following pages will show; we were purely on pleasure bent, and declined to be bound by any precise itinerary. Judging merely from the map, our course may probably appear without much plan or purpose. I will not here anticipate our exact route.

The day we set forth upon our expedition happily proved to be all that we could desire; the Fates smiled on us, and we felt duly grateful. Following the excellent example of that famous pre-railway traveller, the worthy Samuel Pepys of Diary renown, we "awoke betimes" to find, however, the sun already up before us shining cheerfully down from a fine summer cloud-dappled sky; moreover, a rising barometer promised a continuance of such satisfactory conditions. Had we the ordering of the weather, it could not have been more to our liking.

Early in the morning the dog-cart was at our door in full travelling order (we had packed it overnight), a list of everything that could possibly be required for use or comfort on the journey having been carefully thought over some time before, so that nothing was forgotten in the hurry of departure. Our farewells said, there was no further cause for delay, we were quickly in our places, the word was given, the traces tightened, and we found ourselves without any loss of time traversing at a brisk trot the tree-lined streets of Eastbourne. We "got away" (to use an expression in vogue in the good old coaching and posting days) by the Lewes road,— a rather hilly one at first it proved to be,—and in a short time the prosperous-looking yet withal unpicturesque domain of modern villadom was, with small regret, left behind, and we reached the fresh and free open country.

Our road led us at a considerable elevation alongside of the smooth sloping Downs; these flanked our way to the left in stately rounded masses; to our right a great expanse of level land was spread out map-like beneath us, dotted here and there with sleepy hamlets and lonely farmsteads; the silvery sparkle of still water in sluggish dykes, and a long white trail of evanishing steam from a passing train—speeding along in the feverish nineteenth-century haste—enlivened the restful monotony of green and gray which was bounded in the far distance by a low uneven line of faint blue hills.

Glancing southwards and seawards the fine rounded sweep of Pevensey Bay (where the war-like Normans landed of old) came into view, with the many martello towers marshalled in orderly array along its shore, the white foam of the breaking waves being traceable far far away in curving parallels with the pebbly beach; and beyond the bay, hazily indistinct, could just be discerned the bold cliffs above Hastings, the town itself being half hidden by a blue veil of its own smoke. We called a short halt to enjoy the wide panorama of land and sea. Through our field-glasses we could make out Pevensey's ruined castle, a dark spot in the sun-steeped landscape, and the uplands by Battle, where the Normans won them a kingdom: we looked upon historic ground!

It is refreshing to the eye of the town-dweller, after his usual limited and unlovely vision of house-lined streets, to be enabled thus to range unrestrained over vast spaces of open and beautiful country like this. The man whose vision is for ever cramped is but too apt to have his mind cramped also. To see broadly is a great help to thinking broadly; it expands one's ideas. Looking down from some commanding height upon a far-reaching expanse of country, over hill and dale, and rock, and wood, and river, how poor and trivial seem even the greatest affairs of man, how paltry his ambitious aims, his strivings and struggles for more or less transient fame—but I am moralising, and that is a task best left for the priest in the pulpit.

Here and there in the landscape we noticed with delight several windmills plainly showing in the bright sunshine, their sails busily revolving round and round in the freshening breeze, now white in light, now gray in shade. It is curious how small a thing in a distant prospect will at once arrest attention if it only moves, that were it merely motionless would in all probability escape notice altogether. Windmills at work always give a cheerful feeling of life and movement to a landscape, and one can only regret that they are not more general features of the country-side, but nowadays, what with steam (which is so much more dependable than wind power) and farmers finding that cattle-raising is more profitable —or shall I say less unprofitable?—than corn-growing, I am sadly afraid that the picturesque and artist-loved windmill is doomed to gradual extinction; certainly during our road travels for years past in various parts of England, covering altogether some thousands of miles of ground, we have come upon many such mills deserted and going the way of all uncared-for things, whilst during all that time and in all those many miles we have seen only one windmill in the course of erection, and this exception to the rule was impressed upon our memory by the rarity of the proceeding.

As we drove on we had a fine panoramic prospect of the long lines of the Downs rising and falling in apparently endless succession. This famous range of chalk hills has a subtle charm of curve, a dignity of modelled mass, and a grandeur yet grace of form all its own. The South Downs are "majestic," as Gilbert White has truly remarked, though some people who fail to realise that grandeur belongs to form as well as to size have sneered at the term as applied to their modest elevation. The Downs possess the majesty of mighty masses and of grand sweeping unbroken outlines; they impress the artistic beholder by the expression of spaciousness and the idea of vast distances they convey; the prospect looking along their level summits seems infinite; ridge succeeds ridge endlessly, fading away in colour from green through gray to tenderest blue, till in the far horizon their outlines become dim and dreamy, and it is hard to distinguish between land and sky. Surely there is a majesty in such vast, far-reaching visions of earth, and air, and sky, quite as much as in mere height? There is a poetic glamour in the mystery of the far away, where all things seem possible, that appeals to me even more than the uprising snow-clad peak, and that makes the guide-book statement of so many thousand feet above sea-level seem vulgar, boastful, and absurd.

You cannot measure grandeur by feet, any more than you can purchase true art-work by the square yard.

There is a breadth in the bold golden-green slopes of the Downs viewed in unshadowed sunshine that contrasts most effectively with the soft purple-gray shadows of their vast hollows, and the shadows themselves possess a peculiar quality that I can only liken to a deep bloom, a something that cannot be defined in words, and can hardly be given in paint, and that is quite different and apart from the broken shadows of a steep mountain or fell side.

The Downs possess a gentle grandeur—they are impressive, but never gloomy or forbidding, and owing to the gradual curves of their hollows, there is no abrupt transition on them from light to shade, such as is caused by rugged rock, crag, or cliff on the hills of the sterner North Country. The light upon the Downs softly merges into shade, and shade again imperceptibly merges into light, without the beholder being able to point to any decided bounding line. But though it has the happy and rare combination of grandeur with gentleness, and is so delightful to look upon, this wild yet not barren Downland is a difficult country for the artist to deal with successfully because of the want of good and varied foregrounds, so abounding in Wales and most other favourite sketching grounds. A rutty chalk road, some rugged gorse bushes, and rarely here and there a few ragged, twisted, and wind-blown thorns are available, with perhaps a sunburnt, gray-cloaked shepherd, crook in hand, and straggling sheep for life, but such foregrounds become monotonous by constant repetitions, yet the artist, if he paints the truth and what he sees, is sadly limited to these.

Up and down hill, with gradual rises and falls, our road now took us through the somnolent village of Willingdon and past one or two windmills, close at hand or in the near distance, till it brought us to the intensely uninteresting collection of mean modern-built cottages yclept Polegate, an unhappy nineteenth-century product, apparently begotten of the railway junction there of that name. It is sad to think how man can spoil such fair spots by his purely commercial needs without a thought or consideration of mere beauty. The green fields around and the fair Downs beyond are a setting surely worthy of something better, but the needful railway is the sworn enemy of the picturesque. It seems inevitable that we should pay the price of ugliness for the undoubted blessings of speedy and cheap communication, though why it should be so of necessity I cannot comprehend ; but facts are unanswerable arguments ; we have simply to accept them with as much grace as may be. Had the locomotive been invented in the picturesque medieval times, I wonder whether the railway would then have been so aggressively a scenic spoiler. Fancy a medieval railway! Well, perhaps it would be as easy to imagine a medieval cathedral built not *ad majorem Dei gloriam*, but cheaply by contract at the lowest tender, art-work and stone-carving included, with stained glass windows an extra as per separate estimate!

Apropos of my remarks I may here relate a little history, which, though it sounds somewhat like a fable, is, I believe, strictly veracious. When the building of the Roman Catholic cathedral of Southwark was first mooted, the elder Pugin was commissioned to prepare plans of an edifice that should rival those poems in stone of the ancient days. Pugin was in his glory, the work was a labour of love to him, and after some considerable time he completed his plans and elevations and duly submitted them to the Council for their approval. As shown on paper (and how delightful a thing is it to idealise on paper) the designs were worthy of any century. Pugin had produced a masterpiece, greatly was it admired, the Council were enthusiastic over it to a man, the architect was delighted, and everything promised to flow on as smoothly and as certainly as a river to the sea. Then the Council asked Pugin how much he estimated his scheme would cost to build, and how long it would probably be before completed. These were purely commercial questions, needful without doubt, but they elicited from Pugin a crushing rejoinder, "How can I rival medieval work," exclaimed he, "if I have to consider time and cost? How can I tell how long it will take to build? No one has, or ever could, build nobly thus. If you merely wanted an ordinary big church, a building roofed in capable of holding so many people comfortably, or more uncomfortably, with an altar, tiled floor, and a series of windows, why did you not say so?" Whereupon the dream in architecture remained a dream, like so many others have done, and a simpler edifice, that this century can produce to order, took its place.

Our thoughts wandered thus whilst we were kept waiting at a level crossing at Polegate during the progress of some shunting operations—the only thing that a railway appears to do slowly. However, at last the gates were opened, and, our unacceptable lesson in patience over, we proceeded onwards, the greenful country before us appearing doubly beautiful after our unwelcome detention amongst such ugly surroundings. There is one thing to be noted about the railway that is a negative virtue, it does manage to attract and keep to itself much of the unsightliness there is in the land; the cheap tripper—one of its peculiar offsprings—never ventures very far therefrom, the speculatively built "desirable villa" makes a virtue of being within easy distance of the station, the hideous manufactory and kindred eyesores all cling as close as they can to it. Old England beyond the modern iron road is, however, Old England still, fresh, and green, and mellow, with the bloom of ages upon it, restful to the eye and peace-bestowing to the jaded mind weary of the stress and strife of modern city life, whether that stress be society's monotonous mill, professional cares, or business worries.

A short distance beyond Polegate we pulled up for a time and wandered across some fields in search of a spot marked as Otham on our map. Here, adjoining an old farmhouse, is the desecrated chapel of St. Laurence, all that now remains of a former abbey. An artist friend had told us of the existence of this ruin ; he had accidentally come upon it whilst tramping and trespassing about the locality in quest of subjects for fresh pictures. The red-tiled roof and chimneys of the house peeping above surrounding woods showed us our destination, which we reached without more difficulty than climbing over two five-barred gates. Here we found before us a picturesque old farmstead of the homelike Sussex type, with a tranquil pond in front. The building was long and low ; one portion of it we discovered was supported by strong buttresses that gave the dwelling a quaint appearance, and conveyed the pleasing impression that the old home was considered one worthy of being preserved and cared for, rather than one to be ruthlessly pulled down in parts when these showed signs of weakness. Even the humblest home that has existed long enough possesses its own little unwritten history, perchance also its lowly romance, and mutely appeals to be allowed to exist if possible.

We found the farmer himself leaning over his wicket gate apparently studying the weather. We apologised for our intrusion, and asked if we might be allowed to inspect the ruined chapel that we understood was somewhere close at hand. His reply, smilingly given, was, however, somewhat enigmatical. "What! two all in one day," said he. We could not fathom his meaning, so we merely expressed our regret at disturbing him. "Well," he exclaimed, "there's surely room enough for you both, you're very welcome to wander about where you like." The mystery of his original remark was soon solved ; it turned out that an artist had already arrived there that morning before us, had set up his easel, and was busily at work (the artist proved to be our friend, as happy chance had it), and the farmer, seeing us come also armed with sketching materials, thus jokingly expressed his astonishment at the unwonted appearance of two artists coming on the very same day to paint his old place, the tranquillity of which was seldom disturbed by the presence of a stranger the whole year long. So near to, yet so remote from the outer world lived our Otham farmer. We soon made excellent friends with him, by dint of taking an interest in his interests, and gaining thus ourselves some insight into the life of a small tenant-farmer in these parts. He courteously invited us into his house for a rest, an invitation we accepted in order to obtain a glance at the interior, but there was nothing within that arrested our attention or called for comment.

The chapel, of which we had come in special search, we found doing duty as a stable; there is an Early English window in it, the stone-work crumbling fast away, and the remains of some buttresses externally, and that is all that is now left of the ancient "Abbey of Otteham" founded by Ralph de Dene and Sibilla, his wife, in the middle of the twelfth century, who

> . . . thought it would have canopied their bones
> Till doomsday—but all things have their end.

CHAPTER II

Distance the enchanter—Country towns—" A shoemaker's holiday —Our country towns—Toy rivers—The Sussex iron age— " Hammer Ponds"—Dry sermons!—Local pronunciation of place names—A town beyond railways—Out of the beaten track—The Pelham buckle—A chat by the way—A serious mistake—A Sussex proverb—A curious bequest—A haunted hill.

WANDERING back over the fields from Otham, we regained the dog-cart and resumed our driving, the horses, refreshed with their short rest, going gaily along, as though they entered into the very spirit of the journey.

We had now an undulating stretch of road that led us through a pleasant enough country, though its scenic attractions were not remarkable. After a short time the thriving market town of Hailsham came into view, rising out of the wooded weald, and looked quite a charming place with its houses gathered irregularly around its ancient fane, the tower of which formed a conspicuous feature in the landscape.

I am afraid, though, that Hailsham gives point to the poet Campbell's dictum that "'Tis distance lends enchantment to the view." Not that Hailsham is a dirty or an ugly town; on the contrary, as we passed through, it struck us as a specially clean and neat place — two excellent virtues, certainly, — but the fronts of the houses and shops had manifestly so suffered from the usual modernising mania as to become monotonously uniform, and therefore void of interest; though, if I remember aright, one old home of the Queen Anne period that we caught a glance of in a by-street was a notable exception to the rule.

I think the reason why Hailsham and some of our other country towns appear so picturesque when seen on a near approach, and prove so disappointing on actually arriving therein, is that whilst the street fronts of the buildings have been improved—save the mark!—more or less up to date, the rears of the same have been fortunately left much as originally planned and constructed by their first owners, and show consequently an interesting irregularity of form, design, and colour, combined with an accidental grouping of gable, roof, and chimney, that is so delightful to an artist's eye. One house may be of red brick, the adjoining one of flint, the warm tones of the brick and the cool tints of the flint forming a charming colour contrast; still again, another house may have its walls weather-tiled, yet another may be of half-timber and plaster; their chimneys too may vary agreeably in shape and size, their roofs also both in pitch and material, and even a blue-slated roof may be pardoned when set amongst a wilderness of ruddy tiles, for ugliness, in small doses, has its uses as a foil to beauty.

About one mile out of Hailsham we crossed the Cuckmere, one of those delightful Sussex toy rivers that wind through such restful, pastoral scenery, so essentially homelike, and so thoroughly English. Most of the Sussex rivers might by a good pedestrian be explored from source to sea almost within a summer's day, and certainly with ease in two. And a very capital pretext for a rambling expedition would such an exploration make. I throw out the hint for the benefit of any of my readers who may be inclined at any time to take a short "shoemaker's holiday," as Goldsmith quaintly has it, and thus see a portion of picturesque and sequestered Sussex seldom visited by strangers. Besides the Cuckmere (that, by the way, leads the wanderer along its quiet banks to the remote old-world village of Alfriston, with its sixteenth-century hostelry and pre-Reformation Priest-house) there is the Rother, the Ouse, the Adur, and the Arun, all purely Sussex rivers that have their birth and run their course down to the English Channel wholly through that rural county; and where can you find a sweeter valley than that through which the Arun flows, so beloved by painters and bepraised by poets?

But to return to ourselves, we crossed the Cuckmere at Horsebridge, where some picturesque cottages were gathered round its banks, besides an old whitewashed mill, whose wheel is turned by its waters. Here we turned to the left, bound for East Hoathly, "and beyond," as we jokingly remarked, for as to where we should go next we had at that moment only a very hazy notion. Sufficient for us was the pleasure of the hour. There would be time enough for us to consider our next stage when we arrived at our inn and could study our maps and discuss the matter at our leisure; just then the scenery monopolised our attention. This was our usual free and haphazard mode of touring; yet there was perhaps some wisdom in our indecisiveness, for on arriving at a fresh place—if a town—a glance over local views in a photographer's shop, a chat with a chance acquaintance at our inn, or with the landlord, landlady, or even the ostler thereof, might (as it often did, in fact) reveal to us some point of interest in the neighbourhood, such as a fine old church, a moated manor or other characteristic old-time home, a ruined castle, a fine view, a bit of beautiful scenery, etc., that might determine us to drive that way; for perfect freedom was the essence of our expedition; our route was unfettered by any precise or prearranged plans. Happily independent travellers we! In fact, we never knew in the morning with any certainty where the end of the day would find us. The old roads lead everywhere, unlike the despotic track of the rail that goes its own course, which may not be yours. We might get on somehow without the railway, but without the highroads, by-ways, lanes, and footpaths we could not manage at all.

Some distance beyond Horsebridge our excellent road—excellent as to surface, not as to immediate scenery, that is—led us across a bare and almost treeless stretch of country known by the not very euphonious title of "The Dicker." This desolate-looking district erst formed portion of a vast forest, but was denuded of its timber during the Sussex iron age in order to make charcoal for smelting purposes. It is difficult now to realise that this peaceful, agricultural, and pastoral county of Sussex was from the fourteenth down to the seventeenth century in truth the Black Country of England, busy with manufactories, and abounding in flourishing ironworks, but such was the case. The iron ore is still there, but the proximity of coal with that mineral in the North ruined the southern iron industries, all of which is a matter of history, though the history seems to have passed wholly out of the minds of the many. Old-time writers, however, make frequent mention of the numerous and important Sussex ironworks, of which many relics still remain in the shape of large "cinder beds" and "hammer ponds." Camden says: "Sussex is full of iron mines . . . where, for the making and founding thereof, there be furnaces on every side, and a huge deal of wood is yearly burnt; to which purposes divers brooks in many places are brought to run in one channel, and sundry meadows turned into pools of water that they might be of power sufficient to drive hammer mills, which, beating upon the iron, resound all over the places adjoining."

During our drive in various parts of the county we frequently came upon some of the old "hammer ponds," many of which are doing duty to this day to drive more recent, though still ancient, water mills, only they grind corn instead of forging iron; besides, we noted numerous names that unmistakably recall the busy days of the long ago. A few of the names we jotted down from time to time.

These I give here, and they speak for themselves: "Hammerwood," "Cinder Hill," "Cinder Banks," "Furnace Field," "Steelforgeland," and sundry others of a like nature—but of this subject more anon.

Close to "The Dicker" is a long straggling village, ending with a place of worship that proclaims itself by large lettering thereon as "Zoar Chapel." Adjoining the chapel is a public-house called the "Potter's Arms"; for there is a pottery in the neighbourhood, though what are the precise armorial bearings that belong to the potter, I know not, for they were not shown upon the sign-board.

Here we chanced to meet a talkative native, who remarked, "The Bible and beer are pretty close neighbours, but seem to agree very well together. Bless you, sir, that chapel be mighty popular with the people around; they drives for miles to it on Sundays; wet or dry, they don't miss the preaching if they can help it. Then the public-house profits by their religion, the folks as drives puts up their horses and traps there. I've counted twenty or more traps a-standing outside the Arms of a Sunday morning, and the parties mostly has a drop of something before they goes back home. It strikes me somehow as how the sermons must be mortal dry. I've not sampled them myself, though," and he chuckled to himself as he proceeded on his way; and we went ours.

Shortly after this we inquired our way to East Hoathly of a lad, and found that it was not so easy to make ourselves understood as we should have imagined, owing to the curious local pronunciation of the names of places. "East Hoathly," he repeated in reply to our query, "there bain't no such place hereabouts—leastways I never heard tell of it"; then with a sudden enlightenment he exclaimed, "Maybe it's East Hoäd*lie* you want," giving a very decided emphasis upon the last syllable. We guessed it was so, whereon he directed us the way thither. Writing of the stress the country folk in these parts put upon the ending of the names of places, we afterwards came upon a curious Sussex couplet, which I give as follows :—

>Helling*ly*, Chidding*ly*, and Hoath*ly* :
>Three lies, yet all true.

Now a long and gentle incline through thick woods, whose cool shade was very grateful that warm summer day, brought us to East Hoathly. We had selected this little town to drive to first for the simple reason that, looking on our map, we found it set away in a district far removed from railways, reasoning to ourselves, from former experiences, that on this account it would possibly prove to be a place retaining an old-world flavour and picturesqueness, and either in itself or immediate surroundings we might perchance come upon some interesting "find," to use an expressive term much favoured by archæologists ; nor were we disappointed. It was one of the chief aims and delights of our journey to explore little-known and out-of-the-way places that possess all the subtle charm of freshness and the unfamiliar. We rejoiced to make our own discoveries, and not be guide-book led; we felt in some measure like imitators of Columbus, humble though our explorations were, for did we not propose to cruise about the new world (to us) of Old England in our staunch and well-tried ship, the dog-cart? It had already weathered thousands of miles of storm and sunshine, and was fit to weather thousands more.

East Hoathly promised well. It greeted us with pleasant-looking cottage homes, each with its well-tended and flower-decked garden; then as we proceeded on, we passed the "Yew Tree" inn, that earned its title from two tall clipped yews that flourished on either side of its doorway, but as the "Yew Tree" appeared to have no stables attached to it, we drove on in search of a hostelry that had, for in a district where all who travel must needs go by road, we felt certain that we should come upon one so provided.

Passing the rural-looking church, the approach to which was through a picturesque lich-gate, we espied and pulled up at the "King's Head," whereupon the landlady came out to greet us in the good old-fashioned way. Having seen our horses comfortably stabled, we next sought refreshment for ourselves, for the fifteen-mile drive from Eastbourne in the bracing country air had given us healthy appetites; however, when on the road we always make it a point to see first after the welfare of our "cattle" before considering our own; this was a pleasurable duty, though, even from the lowest and most selfish point of view, it is wisdom to give primary care to your horses, for upon their well-doing depends much of the pleasure and prosperity of a driving excursion.

At the "King's Head" we were ushered into a cool, low-ceilinged parlour, where an excellent repast was in due course set before us. Our parlour, we noticed, was partially panelled with painted deal, which gave it a cosy appearance, a sense of snugness that a merely papered wall can never convey; the window here was deeply recessed, and the recess was made gay with flowers, the cheerful colours of which were set off by a big pot of flourishing shamrocks. In one corner stood a genuine old grandfather's clock, not one of your expensive Wardour Street imitations made to look ancient to the inexperienced eye, of which the supply is ever equal to the demand, and that profits nothing except the dealer's pocket. This clock amused us by reason of two curious figures on the top that took the place of the usual revolving moon and dial showing, generally wrongly, the days of the month. The figures were manifestly intended to represent Adam and Eve, clad in somewhat European dress however, but that is a trifle. Between the figures was a tree unknown to modern botany, and round its stem wound the serpent; the reptile, as shown, one would imagine hardly likely to tempt any woman, but let that pass. As the clock marked the minutes, Eve at every tick, with a most mechanical movement, offered Adam a very sour-looking apple that even a schoolboy would have thought twice about before accepting ; then just as Adam should have taken it, away it was jerked from him, to be re-presented again, and so on *ad infinitum*. It was a most irritating clock that—the story never progressed.

Our modest though enjoyable meal over, we sought out the landlady, for the purpose of having a chat with her before exploring the place, in order, if possible, to gather if there were anything locally worth seeing, and we learnt that there were two old historic homes within walking distance, which, from description, we deemed likely to prove of interest.

Having thanked the landlady for her information, we set forth, with our map as a guide, in search of the old houses she had described, at the same time affording our horses, after their long stage, a lengthened and well-earned rest, determining on our return to proceed to Uckfield, and there to spend the night, unless we should be unduly delayed with our walk, when we felt quite content to stay in our present comfortable quarters, as hurry was no part of our programme.

One remark our landlady made struck us. Said she, "We are five long miles from the nearest railway, and that is the charm of this place, though some people would like to have one close by. But we get on very well as we are." To which remark we merely added, "Long may East Hoathly remain railroadless!" But then we did not reside there.

The two old and one time stately homes we went in search of were those of Halland (called Holland locally, we noted) and Laughton Place, both built by the ancient and warlike family of the

Pelhams, and both now converted into farmhouses. Our way led us at first through the churchyard, from which there is an extensive view looking over towards the South Downs. We found the church doors carefully locked, and not feeling inclined just then to go a-clerk-hunting, the interior remained unseen, but on the ancient and weather-worn tower we observed the famous Pelham buckle cut in the drip-stone on either side of the doorway, and in the spandrels above were shields bearing three boars' heads, the arms of the Lunsford family, who had extensive possessions at East Hoathly in the seventeenth century.

The Pelham buckle was proudly assumed as the armorial badge of the family of that name immediately after the battle of Poitiers in commemoration of the surrender of the King of France to John de Pelham during the fight, it being intended to represent the sword-belt buckle of the vanquished French monarch; and thereafter, wherever the Pelhams built themselves a home or endowed a church, they caused this badge to be conspicuously engraved thereon. Old traditions are oftentimes written on our ancient walls. Walls have their stories of the past to tell, as plainly as any printed page, and are more lasting; it only needs one to be able to read them aright. Our ancient churches are chapters of history in stone. At one window of the church we noticed a curious and to us a novel arrangement: from the sill at the foot of this a miniature stone gargoyle projected, so that the small amount of rain water that drained from the glass, and collected there, was thrown off from the wall beneath, instead of running down it in the ordinary course. It is a most excellent thing to keep all walls as dry as possible, especially when, as in this case, they face the west, but this arrangement did certainly suggest an excess of precaution, or else a too manifest striving after quaintness.

We found that a pleasant footpath across green meadows led directly from the churchyard to Halland House. Half-way there, in a secluded hollow, we came to an extensive sheet of water surrounded by woods that doubled themselves on its stilly surface; possibly in past times this formed a pleasure lake appertaining to Halland Park. Here we observed a man, clad in a faded tweed suit, and wearing leather gaiters, lazily leaning over some rails complacently doing nothing, in a fashion that, I think, only a country-bred man can, or a sailor on shore. There is an acquired art in absolutely doing nothing, and not seeming bored thereby. We imagined that this individual might be a tenant-farmer or a gamekeeper, for both dress much alike; only the former is, as a rule, the more reserved in his speech of the two. However, it is not always safe to judge by outside appearances in country or in town. Once on this journey we innocently mistook a horsey-looking butcher, loitering in the stableyard of our hostel, for the ostler thereof, and, alas! addressed him as such— terrible blunder. I shall never forget the fine fury we aroused within him (in rural England, class distinctions are very nicely drawn). We had committed an unpardonable sin in taking a butcher for an ostler! He was "a gentleman butcher," he loftily informed us, "who kept his own trap and horse, not an ostler who received tips." I do wish people who play their parts on the world's stage would dress their parts. Not even a profuse apology would calm the wrath of that "gentleman butcher"; an offer to shake hands with him was scorned. There was no doubt about it, we had hurt that good man's feelings and vexed ourselves besides for having done so. Still, only to think of the various kinds of personages I have been taken—or mistaken—for, from time to time, on the road, and how heartily I have enjoyed, and fully entered into the spirit of, the situations so caused.

I have, whilst being busy with my camera in the field, been accosted as a peripatetic photographer, and commissioned to take sundry "likenesses," which I have sometimes, though not always, done just to please the good-natured country folk; I have been taken for a commercial traveller (but failed unfortunately to keep up my presumed character as long as I could have wished), a theatrical "gent" on tour, a guide-book writer, an engineer surveying a line of country for a new railway or some other scheme, an architect, thrice at least for a newspaper correspondent, once even for a "real live" lord, and this in spite of my protestations to the contrary, and I have forgotten for the moment what else besides. These have been my precious opportunities for engaging in conversations, more or less confidential and interesting, with the various parties of different classes, with their diverse religions and political opinions, chance threw in my way, gathering thus much information that it would have been impossible otherwise to have obtained, and learning besides to see the world through fresh eyes.

But to return to the even tenor of the chronicle of our tour. Never letting slip the opportunity of a friendly chat with any one on the way, we accosted the man in tweeds, by way of a variation on the somewhat unoriginal and overdone topic of the weather, with the remark, "It's a pretty spot this." Responded he, "I don't know much about that at this time of the year, but it's a lovely place in the winter time after a hard frost; there's grand skating on the pond then." It was ever so. People mostly see the country from their own narrow point of view or self-interest; the charm of a landscape, after all, rests in the eye of the beholder. Dr. Johnson— whom it is the privilege of all Englishmen to quote —confessed that he saw no beauty in the country, "only a succession of trees and green fields," barren and unprofitable after his beloved Fleet Street. The farmer, as a rule, looks upon the country as so much soil, poor or rich, as the case may be; he measures the loveliness of the land by the crops it is likely to grow; the sportsman looks upon the country as to how it lends itself to his special sport, the engineer as to how it will suit his schemes, and so forth; only the artist, much-to-be-envied being he, looks upon it purely for its beauty.

We chatted on about many things with the man in tweeds, who turned out to be somewhat of a character, well up in local doings, traditions, and sayings, and by no means adverse to imparting what information he possessed. In fact, he was just the very sort of person we delighted to meet. He kindly offered to walk with us as far as Halland House, and as we went along, the inevitable topic of the weather did arise, after all; there is no suppressing it in England, for, as a friend of mine once remarked, "What's the good of having such a climate if you cannot talk about it?" Our self-appointed guide was looking in a wise manner towards the Downs, then *apropos* of nothing remarked, "The weather will keep fine for a bit." "How can you tell?" we asked, for there was a plentiful supply of suspicious-looking clouds about that might mean rain before the night. "Well, you see, sir, we've a natural and infallible weather-glass here in Firle Beacon, that round-topped hill you see over yonder," pointing at the same time vaguely into space, "and I've never known it fail yet. There's an old proverb about it which I can give you if you would care to hear it." We replied that we should very much, and here it is :—

> When Firle Beacon wears a cap,
> We in the valley gets a drap;
> When Firle Beacon's head is bare,
> All next day it will be fair.

Observing us write this down carefully in our note-book, our informant remarked that we seemed to take an interest in it, and volunteered another old weather proverb, of which we also made a memorandum; it runs as follows :—

When old hens scratch the ground and clouds have tails,
'Tis time for ships at sea to shorten sails.

Of this we heard later on a slightly different rendering from a Dorsetshire native, his version being :—

Mackerel scales and mares' tails
Make lordly ships carry low sails.

The first proverb appears to be a near relation of many others of a similar nature that prevail in most hilly or mountainous lands. The precise wording of the different proverbs varies considerably, and the names of the hills or peaks necessarily do so, but their purport is the same, namely, that if the nearest height be cloud-capped, rain is probable, but if it be clear, there is a prospect of fine weather for the next twelve hours or so, more or less, according to local conditions.

Our companion was becoming decidedly interesting, and as we strolled slowly on we endeavoured to extract from him any further sayings or proverbs he might know, but in this we failed. Arriving at Halland House, he pointed out a large flat field in the hollow below. "That," we were told, "is called 'the Devil's Race,' and there is a curious story related about it. A gentleman—so the tradition goes—was returning on horseback late one winter's night from feasting at Laughton Place (that's the old road there, the long green track before you, close alongside of the meadow). Just as he got opposite the field, the Devil suddenly appeared all flaming red, and set to work to chase the belated traveller round and round it. The gentleman eventually got home, half dead with fright, his horse being covered with foam and blood, and ever since that field has gone by the title of 'the Devil's Race.'" "Possibly the gentleman was drunk," we unromantically suggested, for tradition has it that there were frequent high festivities and wassails held at Laughton Place when in the fulness of its first estate, and that it was considered a point of honour that no guest should leave there quite sober, otherwise it would be deemed that he had not been hospitably entertained! Even the parson, we are told, was not permitted to make himself an exception to the rule, but this must surely be scandal!

Our chance acquaintance was turning out trumps. We found that we had not nearly exhausted his mine of good things; moreover, to our delight, he appeared to be in a communicative mood, nor seemed displeased to have a good listener, so we lighted our pipe to keep him company, and let him do the talking, and here follows a summary of his remarks. "Oh yes, there's lots of queer stories told of the people and places round about, and of the strange happenings that occurred in times past—not that I credit them all. There's a wood over yonder called Breeches Wood, and I've heard its name originated like this. Long ago the parson in these parts was a very poor man and used to dress very shabbily, one portion of his garments being especially noticeable for their general want of repair, so the owner of that wood, taking compassion on him, left the rent of it to provide breeches for the parson. It's funny history, but true." Then our friend pointed out a rounded hill to the right. "That's called Tarble Hill," he exclaimed; "maybe you'll find it marked on your plan." Thereupon we consulted our map, and found a hill marked in the direction shown as "Terrible Down." Now when a "Reduced Ordnance Survey Map" (the one we used on the journey) marks a hill with such a name, it is only probable to suppose that there is some genuine history attached to it, and we confidentially expected to hear something strange, if not weird, in keeping with the suggestive title; and this is what we gathered. "Yes, there be strange stories told about that hill. Some folks will drive miles round rather than cross it at night-time, for there is a way over it. It is reported to be haunted by a woman in white, with long flowing hair, fiery eyes, and skeleton arms, with which she seizes all travellers who dare to cross the hill after midnight. They do say as how some lady was murdered there, and this is her ghost. Other people have it as how she was invented by the smugglers, who had a hiding-place for their contraband goods on the hill, and found it convenient to keep the country folk away at night. Still others believe that the hill was called as it is because the road over it is so terribly steep and a number of accidents have happened on it. Yes, that's the way to Laughton. It's about two miles there if you don't go wrong. Good day, sir. Thank you very much." This in return for a small silver coin of the realm which changed ownership, and for which we thought we had received more than the value in the shape of the information given. At first we felt a little uncertain whether this were a case for tipping or not; it is sometimes a delicate matter to decide, but we acted upon the principle—When in doubt, tip!

CHAPTER III

Halland House—Old buildings and their uses—Laughton Place and moat—An ancient tower—The South Downs from Laughton—A sea warrior of "Great King Henry's dayes"—A picturesque village—English wild-flowers—Exploring a fresh country—A well-wooded land—Old traditions—Facts or fables—Isfield—Useless directions—A mystery—The world as others see it—A quaint old home.

OLD Halland House, we found, had been mostly pulled down, and the rest of the structure converted into a humble, though pleasant, farmhouse. The tenant kindly gave us permission to look round the place, and we gathered something of the original scope of the ancient edifice from the wall that surrounded the large farm garden and orchard of gnarled old trees; this had apparently formed the boundary of the mansion, and had been left a few feet high to do the duty described. Inside the garden wall, at intervals here and there, were arched recesses and ruined fire-places, with their broken moss and ivy grown mantels, that told plainly enough the old moral of departed greatness and the mutability of things.

Over the entrance door of the farmstead we observed a weather-worn stone, having the date 1575 cut on the top; below this was a shield, bearing on the left hand a representation of the famous Pelham buckle, and on the right, of a peacock proper, that is at least what we made it out to be. We further noticed a string-course of stone with a running ornament of Pelham buckles; these ornamented stones were probably relics of the old Halland House worked up into the building.

Rambling about the farmyard, we discovered there a high structure of brick with well-designed stone-mullioned windows, mostly blocked up; this, now employed as a barn, we imagined might possibly have been the stables of the mansion, the height being accounted for as providing sleeping-rooms for the men above, such an arrangement being not uncommon in the sixteenth-century homes of the nobility. One of the farm hands we questioned, however, told us that it was called "the old granary," and as in country places the original names of outbuildings are frequently retained for generations following, though they have outlived their first uses, it may possibly have been one, though why a simple granary should have been built so needlessly high, and have been provided, moreover, with a number of large stone-mullioned windows, was not easy to explain.

To prove how tenaciously the ancient names of buildings are preserved in rural parts, even when for many more recent years they have been put to other purposes than that for which they were at first intended, I here give the following authentic little experience of mine. Whilst staying at an old coaching inn, I overheard the landlord tell a servant to go to the packhouse and fetch some article. Being anxious to know what a packhouse was, I took an opportunity of glancing in it, and discovered a harness room; so, never losing an opportunity of gaining information, I asked of the landlord if a harness room was called a packhouse in that locality. "No," replied he; "I don't wonder the title puzzled you. The fact is, long even before turnpikes, there was an inn here, and that is the only part of the old building now standing. Travellers then, I've been told, often used to go about country on horseback with their things in packs; these were stored in that place, and it has ever since gone by the name of the packhouse, and it always will, I expect, till it tumbles down; then if we put up a fresh building in its place, it's a hundred to one but that they will call it the new packhouse." By which it would appear that John Bull is of a very conservative nature when the names of places and things are concerned. Even on the modern railway the old terms that prevailed in the coaching age are preserved: the engine sheds are professionally known as "stables," the railway carriages are called "coaches," and the ticket office is still labelled "the Booking Office," the last in spite of the fact that nowadays one takes tickets and does not book places.

Our walk on to Laughton Place took more time than we expected; the two miles, even though they led through a pleasantly wooded country, seemed over-long ones. When we reached Laughton village, which we came to first, we found on inquiry that Laughton Place was still another mile on the other side of it, and we had to make our way there over a narrow, rough, and very rutty road that wound about in a provokingly indirect manner. However, as we trudged along we could see the tower of the ancient house standing prominently forth out of the extensive level plain, showing a dark and telling spot in the sun-suffused landscape; all else around was charged with radiant light, wide and open as it was to the summer sky.

Arriving at some cottages, we deserted our uneven road for a field-path that led direct to the remains of the decayed mansion, and passing over one or two rickety wooden foot-bridges that spanned some stagnant dykes, we arrived at the side of the broad moat that surrounds the present diminished building and its garden.

The tall tower is nearly all that is now left of the once stately and fortified home of the Pelhams, but the extensive amount of ground, possibly three acres or more, enclosed by the moat attests the former size and importance of the place. The tower is now incorporated with a lowly farmhouse. This latter, though modern in comparison with the ancient structure that rises so picturesquely from it, is by no means of yesterday, judging from its time-stained appearance. The farmhouse, with sundry out-buildings, besides gardens and orchards, are all within the moat, which is crossed by two bridges, the one a slight wooden structure, the other of arched brick. Let into the chimneys here we observed several stones carved with the Pelham buckle.

The tower is of much interest, and has terracotta ornamentations, a very rare thing to find in old English buildings, although made great use of in the grand and unique gateway of Layer Marney in Essex,[1] one of the very few structures of the kind and period in which this material was employed, and suggestive of the Italian craftsman. The tower of Laughton Place is of brick, possibly owing to the want of any good stone within reach, though flints might have been procured from the Downs only a few miles off, but flints did not seem to commend themselves to the builders. We noticed that the tower was of a very dark gray—with age, we imagined, though it may have become darkened thus by the smoke of years from the farmhouse chimneys below it. At the side of the tower, which is a tall square structure of considerable size, there projects an octagonal building, evidently containing the staircase. The ancient English architects, it may be noted, took no trouble to conceal the interior arrangements of their edifices; indeed, they seemed rather to glory in revealing them; their exteriors were the simple outcome and expression of interior requirements, so what they lost in uniformity they gained in convenient planning and picturesqueness. The tower is now supported by tall buttresses; though these now look old enough, they are probably of a later period, added to uphold a weakened structure. An inscription on the front of the house, done in raised letters, round the initials "W. P.,"

[1] Described very fully in *A Tour in a Phaeton through the Eastern Counties*.

and ornamented with the inevitable buckle, informs us that " Lan de grace 1534 fvt cest mayson faicte." So that there can be no mistake as to the date of the original building.

Strolling around to obtain the best point of view of the old place in order to make a sketch, we found a picturesque group of out-buildings rising directly from the moat that appeared to us to be coeval with the tower, but the bricks of these had become a whitey gray, contrasting greatly with the dark tone of the tower.

Laughton Place was built in the early part of the sixteenth century by Sir William Pelham, "a righte doughty knighte." His son, Sir Nicholas Pelham, no less a valiant warrior on sea than his father was on land, defeated the French in a determined descent on Seaford, a feat that is recorded on his mural monument in St. Michael's Church at Lewes, above which is placed the helmet he possibly wore in the encounter. This helmet still retains traces of gilt and colouring.

> His valrs proofe, his manlie vertue's prayse
>   Cannot be marshall'd in this narrow roome :
> His brave exploit in great King Henry's dayes
>   Among the worthyes hath a worthier tombe :
> What time the French sought to have sack't Sea-Foord
> This Pelham did repel 'em back aboord.
>   OBIIT 15 *Decembris, Anno Dni.* 1559,
>   *Aetatis suæ*, 44.

In the reign of Elizabeth it appears that Laughton Place was deserted for the then newly erected mansion at Halland. Possibly the family had become tired of the flat, marsh-like country around the former spot, albeit there were fine and far-reaching views of the South Downs to be had from Lewes stretching south-westward to the sea, but our ancestors had not learnt the refined value of a view; neither had the poetry and romance of an Estate Agent's catalogue been imagined. Most probably the Pelhams erected their fortified home at low-lying Laughton owing to the ease of establishing there the needful moat for defence, which, from its position, could not be drained dry during a siege. "Every Englishman's house is his castle" had an actual and pregnant meaning in those far-off days. I feel sure, from the numbers of moated homes I have seen in this historic old England of ours, that low-lying positions were so generally selected by notable medieval families in which to erect their residences on account of the water-supply for the moat, and not because they sought out or desired sheltered spots, as has been imagined by some authorities. Fancy a rough, bold knight of old considering for a moment such a thing when he was selecting a site whereon to build an abode. Verily, it is enough to make such a one turn uneasily in his grave beneath his marble effigy for anything of the sort even to be whispered of him.

I have remarked upon the fine and extensive view of the Downs from Laughton Place. It was this view that aroused the enthusiasm of White of Selborne, and, as aforementioned, caused him to term them "this majestic chain of mountains." This saying of White's has been the cause of much comment and cheap criticism by those whose chief knowledge of the Down country would appear to have been derived from the railway ride to Brighton ; yet strangely enough, as I was looking at the Range in question from near Lewes one cloudy day in June, when the silvery sea mists were rolling in stately masses along the continuous summits of the Downs, lifting and drifting now and again so as to reveal their vast undulations, a friend who was with me (a true mountain lover) remarked, " How mountainous they look." It is much a matter of sentiment and how you see things. My friend considers Snowdon to be far more impressive than Mont Blanc, because of its fine peak-like form that uprises from its broad base at such a pointed angle, and is so sharply defined against the sky, "just as a mountain should be."

Retracing our steps, we passed again through the pretty little village of Laughton, in the church of which lie past generations of the Pelhams. Some of the cottages there looked very picturesque, especially the old Post Office, whose roof was partly thatched and partly tiled, the structure below being a happy combination of brick, half-timber, rough casting, and weather-tiling, the manifest outgrowth of a long life, giving to even so humble a building its own little history, and therewith a dignity that no modern cottage could possess. The variety of material, too, gave a variety of colour and quality that made the old Post Office a tempting subject for a sketch, though we never made one, for the longest day comes to an end, and we had two good miles to walk and several more to drive before we reached our proposed evening's destination. Moreover, had we attempted to draw or paint even a small portion of the picturesque old places and scenic gems that presented themselves to us on the way in such endless profusion, we should have required quite a bulky stock of sketch-books, and had we not hardened our hearts from time to time we should very soon have exhausted our supply of photographic films.

Here I may remark, though the statement may sound somewhat paradoxical, that we did a good share of our driving tour on foot. Not only did we oftentimes make digressions, like the present one, from our main route, but for the pure pleasure of the thing we frequently got down from the dog-cart and walked considerable distances, besides most of the hills; from driving to tramping was an agreeable change, and the reverse was equally so.

When on foot we took the advantage provided of exploring any tempting path or pretty lane that suggested a rewarding ramble, or being likely to lead us to any "haunt of ancient peace," besides ever and again indulging in the pleasure of gathering sweet nosegays of wild-flowers from the tangled hedge-rows that they love so well. I would not exchange an old-fashioned nosegay culled from the country side for the finest bouquet of hothouse flowers that highly-paid gardeners produce with so much cost and care, for to me the first is so much the more beautiful, and the more lovable from old associations.

Why our wild-flowers are so lightly esteemed

"A HAUNT OF ANCIENT PEACE."

except by boys and girls, who gather them but to throw away again, I cannot understand. Take, for instance of their beauty, the hardy daffodils that need no tending, but simply beg to be let alone, brightening the earth with their tossing yellows like moving patches of sunshine; the poppies, with their burning reds (the very acme of colour). But I will not enumerate them in this catalogue fashion, or I should fill a page; they are all familiar enough, only it is their beauty we do not see. I must, however, beg space to mention the glorious foxglove that rises up so stately from the ground with its many rich crimson bells. What perfect tints, modelling, and grace of form! Were this truly splendid flower delicate and rare, only to be produced in a hothouse at great expense, how we should all admire and rave about it! But, like a glorious golden sunset, it is commonplace. Who would rave about the beauty of a thing that all can see, and costs nothing?

These little impromptu explorations were our special delight. When travelling through a fresh country—even though it be a portion of your own—what delightful surprises, scenic and otherwise, may be in store for you! There is ever a certain fascination about the unknown. Throughout our tour we were always kept in a charming state of expectancy. Each day was stored with good things for us. The true beauty of the land is only revealed to the leisurely road traveller, who takes his own time as he jogs on and his ample ease at his inn. We happily combined all the advantages of a pedestrian outing with the comforts of a driving tour. When we were tired of walking and exploring there was always a rest and a comfortable seat within hail, or if a comparatively uninviting stretch of country had to be traversed, we could pass through it at a good pace without causing ourselves any weariness. We walked unencumbered, but with everything that we could possibly want, even down to little luxuries, at command.

Arriving back again at East Hoathly we set forth for Uckfield, and so along "by-paths and indirect crooked ways" that led us through a country made beautiful with gentle hills, shady dales, and far-spreading woods, we found our way to the little village of Isfield. We had driven thither, though slightly out of our direct road, because we had heard of an interesting old moated house near by, and wished, of course, to see it. An old moated house (I never saw a modern moated one, so the adjective is hardly needed) is to us much as the proverbial red rag is to a bull, we must go after it at once—"if not sooner," as my wife has it. What a number of moated homes still remain to us in England, which plainly proves how plentiful they must have been in times past—and what unwritten histories and unrecorded romances may not be theirs! I have gathered during my various driving expeditions quite a host of more or less curious, and in some cases even thrilling, traditions connected with these old homes. The relating of these stories and traditions is a delight to some of the old-fashioned country folk; they really seem to believe in them, weird and wonderful though they be. What a mine of wealth lies here for a novel-writer of the old romantic school! Harrison Ainsworth confessed that he availed himself of the local traditions he had picked up of various ancient homes and worked them into his books. These "old wives' fables" are out of fashion now; even the Christmas numbers of the illustrated papers have given up the haunted house, the ghostly chamber, and the like; steam and electricity have almost ruined romance and made the world so convenient and commonplace, yet withal so dull, that the query has been seriously asked—by the wealthy and leisured, not by the poor—" Is life worth living?" It has taken generations to perfect these old crusted traditions, and now even a schoolboy laughs them to scorn. To-morrow other traditions may follow the same fate; the scientific man will ask for proofs, and of some things no proofs can be given.

It struck us as we drove into Isfield (which seemed a somewhat rambling village) that possibly the church might be worth seeing, for former experience has taught us that where there has existed a fine mansion belonging to an ancient family there is frequently to be found in the church some more or less interesting record of it, whether in the shape of private chapel, stately monument, quaint brass, or curious inscription. Once we were shown one of these private family chapels, and to our astonishment noticed that there was a well-filled library attached to it, so, should the sermon be tedious or prove too long, the select worshippers, hidden by a screen from the common congregation, could retire unseen to the library and read a while, though I must confess that the ancient and ponderous tomes gathered therein had all a theological basis, and appeared to me as dry and dull as any discourse could be, and perchance as unprofitable.

Seeing an intelligent-looking lad loitering by the roadside much occupied in doing nothing, we asked him the way to the church, and also if he knew whether the door were open, and if not where we could get the keys, and this was the lucid reply we received. "If you wants the church you'd best go straight on till you comes to ourn house; there be a gate alongside it and a pathway from there as leads you direct to the church. The key be kept at Mr. Dash's, the churchwarden as is; you'd best call and ask him for it." Now this is an excellent specimen of the way some country people (bless their dense heads) will innocently direct you. As we had never been in the place before that day and knew no one there, naturally "ourn house" and "Mr. Dash's" did not convey much meaning or help to us.

In another little country town we were directed to a certain place thus, "Just you go down the street till you comes to old Barabbas's and the first turning past his house," etc. Now the name Barabbas struck us, and on further inquiry we found that the unfortunate man's real name was, say, Jones, "but we all calls him Barabbas because . . ." Here came an awkward pause. "Well, why?" we asked, but, after all, no explanation was vouchsafed. This was tantalising, for our curiosity was aroused, but we had to form our own conjectures.

Not knowing the whereabouts of Mr. Dash's abode, we concluded that it would save time and trouble to make a contract with the lad to go and get the key for us—this we concluded for the sum of sixpence. The lad jumped at the offer, and at once started off at a run, shouting back to us to "keep straight on until you comes to ourn house, and I will meet you there." We drove slowly along, and eventually pulled up at a neat little cottage, by the side of which we observed a footpath which led towards the church, the tower thereof being plainly visible above some woods some distance away. "This must surely be 'ourn house,'" we both simultaneously exclaimed. So we waited there, and in a short time the boy, key in hand, duly made his appearance, a little out of breath in his eagerness to be speedy. He offered to walk with us to the church and take the key back without any further fee, so we closed with the offer. He was a bright, civil lad, and interested us. As we trudged along the fields we questioned him about himself. It appeared that his father had been a carter, but was now a gardener; he (the lad) was eleven years old, and worked at tending sheep, and sometimes as a carter's boy. "And how much wage do you get?" "Well, not too much, sixpence a day is what I gets, and I have to walk a mile to my work. I'm out of work just now." We learnt, moreover, that the height of his ambition was to take a long railway journey "as far as Brighton. We can hear the trains in the valley at ourn home. There's the breakfast train, the dinner train, and the supper train. Railways is very useful as clocks, I don't know how we should do without ourn." It is instructive as well as interesting to see the world sometimes with other eyes. It moreover struck us as a grand testimony to the punctuality of the unfrequent trains on this branch line, that they should serve the purpose of a clock—so, however, did the mail coaches in the old days, the country folk setting their watches and time-keepers by them. Provincial people are, however, not always particular to a few minutes. I remember well, whilst waiting for an arriving friend at a small station on one of these sleepy Sussex lines, observing a ruddy-faced farmer running up to the platform just after the train (a good five minutes late) had started. "Well, you're mighty particular," exclaimed he irately to the solitary porter, "I bain't more nor a bit behind!"

On our way to the church we suddenly and unexpectedly caught sight of, a little to our right, the ancient mansion of Isfield Place, which we had come to see. I shall not readily forget the thrill of pleasure the first vision of this gave me, enclosed as it was by its curious and massive outer walls and restored watch-towers at each corner. This fine old home has manifestly been much modernised, but it still retains a look of genuine antiquity, and sufficient of the original structure remains to make it exceedingly interesting and attractive to the antiquary, archæologist, and artist.

Isfield Place was formerly the residence of the Shurleys, an ancient Sussex family of note, and their coat of arms and motto still exist, boldly carved in stone over the entrance doorway. This small, though important, part of the building, and this only, suggests classical work; but the pillars support nothing, and are purely decorative, as was frequently the case in mansions of the period; all the rest of the fabric is essentially English in feeling.

It would appear that the house was originally erected in the centre of a considerable-sized plot of ground of some acres in extent; this was surrounded by a high wall for defensive purposes; from this wall watch-towers rose at intervals, the lower portions of which are still intact; beyond the wall was the wide moat, so that Isfield Place must be considered to have been a strongly fortified home. The arrangement of a surrounding high outer wall and watch-towers is very unusual in England, and the two towers, though merely restorations, give the place a delightfully quaint and picturesque appearance. The buildings as a whole make a most effective group, and seen from a short distance, the old and the more recent blend well together. The modern alterations and additions are not too aggressively apparent, and except to the experienced eye would probably not be specially noticeable.

We observed a clipped yew hedge bordering the entrance court, or garden, and some time-toned outbuildings beyond, apparently unaltered; we judged these to be the original stables. A rookery at the farther end of the place added to its charms; a moss-encrusted sun-dial, and some peacocks proudly strutting about the terraces, would have been pleasingly appropriate, but one cannot have everything.

The present owner deserves the thanks of all lovers of the picturesque and never-returning past for having preserved so far the ancient character and features of the old place.

Having sketched and photographed this unique old-world home, we proceeded without further delay to the church, for the day was growing old, and we wished to make the most of the light that was still left.

CHAPTER IV

Isfield church—The Shurley Chapel—An ostentatious tomb—Old brasses—A eulogistic inscription—Wooded Sussex—Old-time roads—A wandering artist—Buxted—An old ironmaster—Sussex cannon—A family rebus—A quaint brass epitaph—Invented facts—Haunted?

STRANGELY enough there is no carriage-road to Isfield church, it stands alone surrounded by fields, and well away from the village; the only approach thereto is by footpaths. At the porch we noticed a huge iron scraper, and close by, what the lad called "foot-brooms"; these consisted of big bundles of twigs (somewhat resembling small faggots) set on end at the bottom of wooden posts "for people to wipe their feet on. You gets mighty muddy a-walking to church in wet weather." Fortunately for us the day was very fine and the field-paths fairly dry, but we could easily imagine a very different state of affairs in the winter time: then possibly the big scraper and "foot-brooms" are necessary.

Entering the church we discovered that it contained a private chapel on the south side, known as the Shurley Chapel; the walls of this are partially panelled with old oak finely carved with the linen pattern (that is a design intended to represent folded linen decoratively treated); there were also some old private family pews of oak similarly carved, but alas ! much worm-eaten. The rest of the walls are covered with brasses and monuments to the Shurley family, one being a magnificent, not to say ostentatious, altar-tomb with an exceedingly laudatory inscription to Sir John Shurley, but of this anon.

The more ancient brasses claimed our first attention ; these are fixed on the walls, and not set in stone slabs on the floor as was the general custom. The earliest brass is to John Shurley, deceased 1527. Another sixteenth-century one is to Edward Shurley, who "depted this mortall lyfe ye XVI day of Marche Anno MCCCCCLVIII . . . . & Iohanne his wyffe deptyd ye   day of Anno   whose souls God p'don & bettwen them God sente them essue thre sones & one daughter." This brass has, over the inscription, a representation of the said Edward Shurley standing upright and in full armour; his wife is shown standing opposite to him. It is noticeable that whereas the date of the husband's death is duly inserted, that of the wife—or wyffe— is left blank. Presumably this brass was engraved after the death of this Edward Shurley, but before his wife's decease, hence the date of the latter event was left vacant to be filled in hereafter.

On many of these ancient brasses similar spaces may be found blank ; sometimes this was due from neglect, more frequently from the want at the time of a skilled craftsman, for, putting aside the art required to form the lettering thereon, the genuine old brasses were of a composite metal, very hard and enduring, and consequently most difficult to engrave; many of them, as may be proved by trial, will resist the blade of a pocket-knife so successfully indeed that it will not make even a scratch thereon, try you ever so hard. Possibly most frequently of all, re-marriage would account for the spaces remaining vacant.

Still another interesting brass is to Thomas Shurley; this bears the date of 1579. A modern brass of 1867 that is inserted on the adjoining wall contrasts very unfavourably with the ancient work of a like kind, the wording of it is even now hardly so legible; the letters of black, varied with red, look mechanical and feelingless, they sadly want character; the brass fails because of being too perfect and precise in the cutting, and from a want of spirit and boldness in treatment; there is such a thing as inconsistent refinement; the colour of the modern metal, too, is dull and cheerless, it is entirely devoid of the deep rich tint of most old brasses.

The art of making the composite metal for what is known as "brasses" appears to be a lost one. During the period when this form of memorial to the dead was in its prime—all the best metal for brasses was manufactured in the Netherlands and imported into England. In those pre-patent days the process was kept a profound secret; the demand then for the metal in this country outran the supply, and sad to relate, as many a palimpsest brass will show, the already engraved brasses were uplifted from their places on tomb-slabs to be engraved on the other side afresh, in some cases even the original figure was audaciously left as it was, or but slightly altered to suit circumstances, and merely a new inscription placed beneath. Oh for the honest days of old!

The monument to Sir John Shurley is a very different affair from the unassuming, yet effective, brasses that sufficed for his more modest ancestors. His memorial is truly magnificent, it is of finely carved marble, and occupies considerable space in the chapel; beneath a canopy this knight is represented in a recumbent alabaster armoured effigy of full life-size with his two wives, one on each side of him; below are the sculptured figures of his two sons and seven daughters in long array. The inscription on this monument is quite a curiosity in tomb eulogy. The particulars of Sir John Shurley, his wives, family, ancestors, and his many personal virtues appear on a space at the top, and are complete in themselves; beneath, in another space divided from it, is the record of this great man's death. We judged from the foregoing and from other details that this monument with its laudatory inscription was erected in the lifetime of Sir John Shurley, and doubtless was ordered and approved by him. There is one thing to be said on behalf of this exemplary knight, if he praises himself he does not begrudge the meed of praise to his second wife. Here is the inscription: note that some of his children were "called into Heaven," and others "into severail mariages of good quality." This caps another inscription that we came upon later on to the memory of a brave squire whose six daughters "all found themselves husbands."

That ye Fame
    Of Sr Iohn Shvrley of Isfield,
   In ye Covnty of Sussex, Knight,
 May be pretiovs in ye memory of all Men
    Till ye change of ye Last Man.
 Be it delivered to Posterity that Sr Iohn Shvrley was of
An Avncient Family, of a Magnanimous Hart, of an exemplary Industry,
Of a Ivstnes beyond exception, & that he was stovt in good cavses,
         Yea & Good in All Cavses.
His First wife was Daughter vnto Sr Thomas Shirley of Wiston, Knight,
By whom he had 2 Sonnes & 7 Daughters, ye sonnes and 2 Daughters
      Are called into Heaven, and ye 5 Living
         Into severail Mariages of Good Qvality
    .   .   .   .   .
 His second wife was widdow of Sr Henry Bower of Cvckfield,
       In ye Covnty of Sussex, Knight.
    She was a Merite Beyond Most of Her Time, for her
  Pvrse was open to a Prophet's Name, Her Pitty was ye
  Clothing of ye Poore, Her Piety ye Mother of her Practise.
Her Devotions were her Daily Offrings to God, Her Mercy sure against
Condemnation, and all Her Minutes were bvt steppes to Heaven.

Beneath this inscription in another space we learn that this paragon of all the virtues " Deceased at Lewes ye 25th of Aprill, Anno Domini 1631." At the foot of the monument the two sons and seven daughters are represented in carved alabaster; they are all shown as kneeling, and have their hands together in the attitude of prayer, with the exception of the two sons and two of the daughters, who each hold a skull in their hands, a rather gruesome way of showing that they were dead at the time. The dress of the daughters struck us as being most artistic, and I only wish that so graceful a style of apparel for girls could be revived, it is sensible and decidedly picturesque. Over the heads of the children their names were inserted in numbered order thus:—1, Anne; 2, Thomas; 3, Iohn; 4, Iane; 5, Cicelie; 6, Elizabeth; 7, Charitie; 8, Hannah; 9, Mara. I do not remember another instance where the names of children are recorded on a monument to their parents thus.

We noticed a large "squint" at the side of this chapel, so that "the quality" as represented by the Shurley family could see the altar and officiating priest without being themselves seen by the mere vulgar worshippers in the nave. But proud knight and plain plebeian are now one common dust. As another Shirley — that grand old lyric writer—so finely puts it :—

> The glories of our blood and State
> Are shadows, not substantial things;
> There is no armour against fate—
> Death lays his icy hand on kings,
> Sceptre and crown
> Must tumble down,
> And in the dust be equal made
> With the poor crooked scythe and spade.

Charles I. used often to repeat this verse aloud when in prison, and whilst repeating it how sadly he must have felt the truth expressed therein! Charles I., if he failed in the pose of a tyrant, succeeded to perfection in that of a martyr.

From Isfield to Uckfield our road led us through a thickly-wooded country, which in the gloaming looked enchanting with all its leafy beauty. We observed, as we went along, a quantity of sturdy oaks amongst the trees. In the days of the old three-deckers this district was famous for the quantity and quality of timber it supplied to the dockyards. A last-century traveller, Daniel de Foe, proceeding from Tunbridge to Lewes in 1724, and who passed through this locality, thus writes of it in *A Tour through Great Britain*:—" The timber I saw there was prodigious, as well in quantity as bigness, and seemed in some places to be suffered to grow, only because it was so far off any navigation that it was not worth cutting down and carrying away. In dry summers, indeed, a great deal is carried away, and sometimes I have seen one tree on a carriage drawn by two-and-twenty oxen, and even then it is carried so little away that it is sometimes two or three years before it gets to Chatham, for if once the rains come on, it stirs no more that year, and sometimes a whole summer is not hot enough to make the roads passable." Writing of the bad state of the Sussex roads in the past the following extract (which we took from an old volume we came upon during the journey) may be interesting, it tells its own story :—" In the year 1728 a Sussex lady, dying in Kent, left directions in her will for her interment at Brighton ' if she should die at such a time of the year as the roads thereto were passable.' Her death occurring in June her wish was complied with." Well, perhaps, there is the reverse to the medal of the good old road travelling days, at any rate in Sussex, for the bad ways and the sprinkling of highwaymen must have taken a good deal of the pleasure away from a driving tour in these parts then. There are many advantages in being born late in the nineteenth century! Time ever throws a halo of romance round the past; even in the heyday of the coaching age there were writers who looked longingly back to "the merry times gone by," and so it may come to pass that in a century or so hence our descendants will sigh for "the good old railway days."

We arrived late in the evening at Uckfield, just as the light was fading out of the landscape, and the sky was growing from gold to gray, the very hour when all places look their best, but even so Uckfield did not impress us. It is of the order of one-streeted towns, whose thoroughfare is "long drawn out." Possibly it may have been owing to the sharp contrast with the lovely country and picturesque spots we had seen that day, but Uckfield struck us as an ugly little town: nor when viewed by the garish light of the following morning was our first impression changed. What fails to please the critical eye in the tender, poetic gloaming, seldom profits by the searching sunshine.

The somewhat singular title of Uckfield is probably evolved from Oakfield, at least we saw the name of the town spelt "Oakefield" on an ancient map; and oaks, "that weed of Sussex," still abound in the country around.

Truth to tell, Uckfield is, at the best, an intensely uninteresting town set in the midst of a charmingly pretty and well-wooded country. We turned our footsteps towards the church, trusting that there we might find something to interest us, some bit of medieval work made doubly beautiful by the weather-tinting of centuries; but even the church failed us, suffice to say it was rebuilt from the foundations in the year of grace—but truly not of taste—1840. However, one of the worthy inhabitants of the place, at least I presumed he was a worthy one, said he considered the church a very beautiful building, quite an ornament to the town, " I 'ate your high hart churches, I do." This quite settled us, we had not a word to say, we did not worship there, what affair was it of ours? But exactly what a high art church is he failed to explain, simply muttering as he turned away something about "musty, fusty, damp, dirty old buildings, I can't abide 'em." As we never asked whether he could or not, his remarks were scarcely polite or to the point; but one meets strange characters on the road, sometimes crusty ones too : but they all interest us. It is the people, as well as the places one comes upon, that lend a special charm to such devious wanderings as ours, out of the beaten track of tourist travel. Such quaint and original characters are a blessed relief after the monotony of multitudes that throng our modern cities, and are as refreshing to the town-tired eye and brain as is the summer shower to the parched and thirsty soil.

Perhaps I am a little unjust to Uckfield, in truth I must acknowledge that at the foot of the long street there does stand a real old cottage (Bridge Cottage it is called) with a small garden and big tree in front, and this cottage might even form the subject of a passably pretty sketch, granted a little "dodging"—but one cottage does not make a town!

I really think that the best bit of Uckfield, in a

picturesque point of view, was the stable-yard of our hotel; the buildings ranged round this were old, irregular, and time-painted with various hues in pleasing harmony; moreover, these little-considered outbuildings grouped well together, they were happily too unimportant to be considered worthy to be improved or altered "up to date." There is a great safeguard in humbleness, so the cottage escapes unharmed, whilst the grand cathedral and old historic church is restored out of recognition. The fatal gift of fame has been their undoing.

On the evening of our arrival this stable-yard looked quite charming, as partially revealed by the lights from our carriage lamps, which caused deep mysterious shadows, and just afforded a suggestion of odd gables, bent roofs, and crooked chimneys. Things half seen thus lend such scope for the imagination; the mind, delighted to be free a while from positive facts, conjures up to itself all sorts of pleasant and picturesque possibilities, regardless for the moment of the disenchantment that it knows from past similar experiences is almost certain to follow. If our poetic dreams could only be converted, by some magic, into realities, what a lovely world this might be!

On going to look after the welfare of our horses in the morning we discovered an artist in the stable-yard with his easel set up in front of him, busily at work on a picture of a horse (the landlord's horse, he told us); the ancient buildings formed an excellent and effective background to this. Now we can never see an artist at work without being attracted to him. Some painters resent such intrusions, others are only too delighted to have the opportunity of a chat with a kindred spirit, and of the latter sort was our artist, so we had a long and pleasant chat together. We gleaned from our conversation that he had begun his career in London with much promise, but loving the country much, and hating town and its ways still more, and lacking the refined art of pushing his wares upon the public, nor caring to curry favour with the picture-dealers, he elected to enjoy his life according to his own ideas. So, provided with a goodly supply of canvases, colours, and a little cash, he set forth one fine summer morning on a country outing, determining to paint his way along somehow. He would rather live on the proverbial crust of bread and cheese in the country than fare sumptuously in town, so he tramped hither and thither, chance led, accepting such commissions as he could get, now painting a gentleman's hunter, his house, his cattle, "or anything that was his," or a pack of hounds, or a farmer and his wife, or whatever else might offer, frequently getting his quarters free whilst at work, and so one way and another he managed to get along very well in the summer time: he luckily never failed to get commissions—at a price. Then he thoroughly enjoyed his wandering life; nor envied he his fellow Academy student who had remained on in London striving and struggling after fame with such worldly success that he had built himself a fine studio with a house attached (we liked that remark, it was fraught with meaning) and had even become a real live R.A. He mentioned the familiar name of this Fortune's favourite to us, but it is needless to repeat it here. Our artist friend enjoyed excellent health, the free country life just delighted him, his wants were few, he had all he needed, and was thoroughly happy—and even a R.A. with commissions galore, and a fat balance at his bankers, could not be more than that.

Having consulted our maps and road-book overnight, we decided to proceed next to Tunbridge Wells, going first to Buxted, then on by Crowborough and Eridge to our destination. The morning turned out gloriously fine, so, as usual under such favourable circumstances, we made an early start in order to have a long day before us for our explorations.

A short and pleasant drive of three miles or so brought us to Buxted, a sleepy little village, but erst a busy centre of the Sussex iron industry; now the country around is quite Arcadian in its pastoral peacefulness. Here, adjoining Buxted deer park, stands an ancient building, once the residence of the Hogge family, and still retaining their rebus, a rudely sculptured figure of a hog over the doorway, with the date 1581. This ancient home is locally known by the not very euphonious title of " The Hog House." It is recorded that a member of this family, one Ralph Hogge, an ironmaster, made the first cast-iron cannon in England at his furnace some three miles away; this spot is still marked on the Ordnance Map of to-day as " Huggett's Furnace." Prior to this all English cannons were constructed of iron bars put together in the form of a tube, and bound round by strong hoops of that metal. The name Huggett is said to be a corruption of Hogge. Whether tradition be right or not in this respect, I cannot say. An old Sussex couplet has it :—

> Master Huggett and his man John,
> They did cast the first can-non.

Another edition substitutes the name Hogge for Huggett. Still another reads :—

> Master Huggett and his son John
> Between them cast the first can-non.

During this period, and for long afterwards, Sussex manufactured a quantity of excellent cannon, so excellent that it was much desired by our enemies ; and there were men unpatriotic enough, even in those patriotic days, to sell and smuggle a number of them to our ancient foes, the French. When one of the Sussex ironmasters was taken to task for knowingly supplying cannons for this purpose, he exclaimed, " Whatever does it matter? We get the Frenchman's money, and when we fight we get the guns back again " !

Whilst taking a photograph in the village we noticed a clergyman coming along the road, and it struck us that we would take the opportunity to ask him if the church were worth seeing. As Buxted was an important place of old, it seemed probable that the church might reflect some of its past prosperity. " There's nothing of special interest in it," he said in reply to our query, "but it is worth the walk there through the park for the sake of the view from the churchyard. If you care to see inside, the key is kept at the Post Office, but I do not know whether they will let strangers have it." We thanked the clergyman for his information, and as the Post Office chanced to be close by, we thought it worth the trouble of asking for the keys, even at the risk of a refusal; as a matter of fact, however, we have never once been declined access to any church in any part of England or Wales that we have desired to see during many years of home travel. Indeed, sometimes I think that as utter strangers we have been more than once rather rashly entrusted with the keys of certain ancient fanes, wherein were rare old brasses, some small and loose and easily to be removed by the daring collector, whose ideas of *meum et tuum* are not always quite what they should be.

Inquiring at the Post Office, not only were the keys at once handed to us, but an apology was made for keeping the church doors locked. "You see, sir, were we to leave them open the children would get inside and play there." This did not speak well for the Buxted children, and it seemed to us a curious remark, considering the fact that in so many parts of England we have found the church doors always open, and the buildings nearly always forsaken even by worshippers: Englishmen keep their religion strictly for Sundays. Why should it be safe to have the churches open all day long in some portions of the country and not in others?

This question naturally occurred to us, but we could not answer it.

Buxted Park is a fine demesne, with glorious old trees and broad sweeps of green turf suggestive of vast spaces; set in the midst of it is an ugly classical mansion of the style that a former generation deemed in such perfect taste for a noble country residence. A countryman we met told us that there was a window in it for every day in the year, and this fact—if a fact—seemed to impress him, and he even appeared astonished that it did not impress us likewise; but we have heard this story of so many houses that it has become rather stale. Fancy estimating the merit of a building by the number of windows it contains! I wonder whether the window tax was in existence when this mansion was built. Still to this day one may occasionally note in rural places windows built up to escape this iniquitous tax on air and light, and that since its repeal have been allowed to remain so. I was looking over an old rambling farmhouse one day, and the farmer pointed out to me two blocked spaces where windows were before this now almost forgotten tax was imposed; these were not replaced, on account of the cost, and because "we've learnt to do without them very well, so we don't bother about the matter, though maybe I'll put them in again some day when farming is a bit more profitable. My father made a little fortune at farming, but I can barely get a living at it."

A footpath across the park led us to the church, which we found situated on an elevation, surrounded by the pleasant park, and divided from it by a low stone wall, over which the tame deer peeped at us, as though wondering what a stranger could be doing there. From the churchyard, in which is a very fine and flourishing old yew tree, we looked down upon a richly wooded prospect, though the view was of no very great extent. Here we found some children playing a noisy game of hide-and-seek, and others chasing each other merrily over the tombstones, unmindful of the underlying dead. The thoughtless gaiety and joyousness of youth recked little of the solemnity of death. Perhaps, after all, it was well that this church was not left open, for as the God's acre appeared to form a sort of village playground, the sacred edifice itself might be invaded in time.

Coming to the north porch, our attention was arrested by its time-worn appearance. In the gable over this is a curious bit of sculpture representing a woman with an old-fashioned churn, with small doubt the rebus of the Alchorne family, who gave largely to the church, and may very probably have built this very porch. In the spandrels below on either side is an armed figure carved in stone and holding in his hands a shield. A recess on the shield would lead one to imagine that a coat of arms was originally inserted there—possibly of iron, for we saw one thus *in situ* on a former journey. This is, however, a somewhat rare arrangement, for coats of arms were generally carved direct on the stone, and the departure from such a usual and convenient custom is hard to account for. The figures are much weather-worn, and their age is difficult to estimate.

Entering the church, we discovered some interesting old brasses but no altar-tombs; the wealthy ironmasters appear to have been contented with modest memorials to themselves. We were surprised to find no iron tomb-slabs here as exist at Mayfield, and in many other parts of Sussex that boasted of foundries. This struck us as singular. Just beneath the chancel arch we came upon a quaintly worded brass, unfortunately without a date; the lettering of this is puzzling and difficult to make out, a difficulty that was added to by the bad light at the time we were there. I believe, however, the following to be a correct rendering of it:—

> Here lyeth graven under thys stoon
> Xffore Savage both Flesh and Boon
> Robert hims sone was person heere
> More than XXIIII yeere
> Chryst Gody's Sone borne of a Mayde
> To Xffore and Robert hims sone give aide
> That owt of thys worlde being passed fro
> Grante thy mercy and to us also.—Amen.

"Xffore," is, I believe, short for Christopher. It is curious that there should be no date to this inscription—at least we could find no trace of one. "Person," of course, should read parson. The priest in old times was often known as the person of a place, possibly because he was often the most important dweller therein. Another ancient brass in the chancel has the representation of a coped priest in the top of a fine foliated cross; there is, close by, also another foliated cross of less interest. A stone slab on the floor, with a deeply-cut matrix, has apparently contained an important brass—gone who knows whither? I am not aware that Cromwell's soldiers were ever at Buxted, so that I cannot suggest that they were the guilty parties. An old clerk, in a confidential mood, once confessed to me that when at a loss to account for the disappearance of a missing brass, or the disfigurement of a tomb, he just put it down to Cromwell; it saved a lot of trouble, and people never questioned such a reasonable explanation! This might be a convenient way of making local history, but scarcely an honest one ; however, clerks and vergers are by their nature anti-Puritans and bear no love for the memory of " brave Oliver." Remarked that innocent and truthful man by way of excuse, " You see, sir, people who comes over our church wants to know the exact particulars of everything, and they will have them, so I has to supply them as best I can. I had an antiquarian gent a-over one day ; says he to me, 'I shall tip you according to what you can tell me.' Now I calls that a-tempting a man. You see I've a wife and big family to keep, and a good tip is not to be despised." Was this a hint for us, we wondered? " Well, that gent was so anxious to know all about everything, that I obliged him, though I nearly got out of my depth once or twice. However, he took it all down in his note-book, and when he left said as how I was the best-informed clerk he had ever come across, and praised me up for my store of information." So facts are sometimes invented, and history ready made to order on the spot. Why such unsought-for confidences should have been reposed in me I cannot say, but it was by no means a singular case of the kind during our driving tours. On one of my early journeys by road, in a remote country village I came upon a modern manufactory of genuine old carved oak furniture, spinning-wheels, grandfather's clocks, and ancient curiosities generally; the proprietor appeared to think he was carrying on a perfectly legitimate business. "People want old furniture and things," said he, "and I supply their wants at a moderate price, and make them happy. I consider I'm a public benefactor; besides, I do use real old oak, and I copy the best patterns of old furniture." Some people have easy consciences.

There was not much else of interest we discovered in Buxted church, except an old carved oak pulpit and a rather curious and much worm-eaten muniment chest, likewise of carved oak. We noticed that the chancel ceiling was of enriched plaster, which gave it a very unecclesiastical appearance; this unusual arrangement we observed later on obtains at Lindfield church, of which anon.

Just as we were leaving we heard a long and curious series of noises in the church. There was no one but ourselves within, and until that moment the silence of the interior was almost painfully profound. Was the church haunted? Did some of the dead men turn in their graves below, indignant because we had—however reverently—trodden over them and taken rubbings of their ancient brasses? But we had done such things before without disturbing the sound sleepers of departed generations. Nor am I aware that the dead dream and have nightmares, so on calm consideration, and in the true spirit of a materialistic age, which is sceptical about ghosts who do not subject themselves to scientific inquiry and proof, we put down the sounds to either rats romping down below, or to rooks in the rafters above. For the moment, in such a place, the sudden, unexpected, and unaccountable sounds were somewhat startling; for there is a leaven of superstition left in the minds of most men, inherited from remote ancestors, so hard is it to break entirely with early traditions and the impressions caused by the fabled stories of childhood. The sounds only lasted a minute or two, and then all was solemn silence again. It is a rather gruesome idea, but I am inclined to attribute the mysterious sounds to rats scampering about in the vaults below. Rats have often before now played the part of ghosts in ancient mansions with great success.

In the churchyard we observed some finely cut old tombstones. The lettering on these was raised instead of being incised as usual. Two especially well-carved ones bore dates of 1696 and 1698 respectively. On another ancient tombstone we found Buxted spelt "Bukstede," which may possibly point to the origin of the name, "stede," of course, being Anglo-Saxon for a station, "buk" perhaps meaning beech, but this is a matter for the learned antiquary, versed in name origins; however, the ancient spelling of Buxted is worthy of note. Tombstones have sometimes their stories to tell beyond the enumerating of the virtues of the dead.

CHAPTER V

A wild district—Changes of scene and climate—English landscapes—A gipsy encampment—A grand panorama—The romance of the road—Left to the imagination—A windy height—A lonely inn—Unrecorded legends—"Blowborough"—Curious notices—Crowborough Beacon—Modern miracles—Old-fashioned country folk—Ghost lore—The Red Cross Inn—A lovely country—A modern village—Tunbridge Wells—An elevated hostel.

OUR road on to Crowborough led us through a wild, well-wooded, and sparsely populated district; it was, more or less, on the ascent all the way of about six miles. There were green grassy margins to the road that gave a pleasant idea of space, as though the ground were not enclosed to the uttermost yard. These grassy margins make delightful walking, as we proved by tramping at least three-quarters of the distance, stopping here and there to admire the picturesque prospects and peeps of far-off country as seen between the trees, to say nothing of the delays caused by making pencil sketches, taking photographs, and gathering ferns and flowers. No one need be dull on a country road, if he only knows how to use his eyes. We made slow progress truly, but what of that, we did not set forth to do so many miles an hour, else would we have taken the train and seen nothing, but we set out to enjoy ourselves, and to lay in an ample supply of health and strength at the same time, which we succeeded in accomplishing.

In a health-giving point of view the great advantage of a driving tour is, that it compels you to be out in the open all day long, and that without entailing fatigue—a consideration to the delicate. And you get, too, so many changes of air during a lengthened holiday on the road, now you may find yourself in the sheltered lowlands, next on the breezy uplands, then by the side of the bracing sea; perhaps by way of change you arrive in a district of pine woods and gorse and heather-clad commons or heaths, where the air is laden with soft, balsamic odours; again you may be traversing the open Downs, or a wind-swept moor, where the atmosphere is tonic to a degree, and so the quality and kind of air continually changes, with the scenery, as you journey on. We specially noted the change that day from sheltered Uckfield, where it was almost oppressively hot (even in the early morning), to the top of Crowborough Beacon, where we found the wind blowing refreshingly cool, so much so indeed as to induce us to don an overcoat.

As we rose, so our horizon extended, affording us, from time to time, wide views over a wealth of English woodlands, that in this sunny, southern county have a tender beauty, a rich leafy loveliness, and a grace of form that is a quality apart from the sterner glories of the northern forests.

<blockquote>Oh the blessed woods of Sussex, I can hear them still around me
With their leafy tide of greenery a-rippling in the wind.</blockquote>

IN MID-SUSSEX

Then, for a time, the woods gave place to an open country of wild sandy heaths, with winding rutty roads leading across them and vanishing behind their ridges, ridges that rose round and barren against the sky. The country was now more suggestive of rugged Scotland than southern England; indeed, a Scotsman once told me that, in his opinion, the highlands of Sussex more closely resembled certain aspects of "Stern Caledonian scenery" than anything to be found between the Thames and the Tweed. When will artists discover wild Sussex?

It was a grand sight to watch the mighty cloud shadows sweep across these broad spaces of rough open country: now a flood of sunshine would illumine the sandy waste, giving it a general tint of golden yellow, broken by the blue-gray shadows of its hollows, and varied here and there by the green and paler yellow of the waving bracken, the bright effect of the landscape being emphasised by a few wind-blown Scotch firs, whose dark green gloom no sun could lighten up; anon the whole prospect would be changed in tone by the vast cloud shadows into one mass of mysterious purple-gray.

It is these glorious and changeful effects of light and shade that lend such a charm to the English landscape and cause one to love our cloud-laden skies, and to listen with pity, rather than envy, to the laudation of more favoured (?) climes. A cloudless sky is doubtless a very fine thing—in poetry or romance, it sounds enchanting truly; but constant sunshine, with the dust and heat that are its concomitants, is apt to become wearisome in time, and the glare of light fatiguing to the eye. Poets may rave about the charms of sunny climes to their heart's content, so it please them, and they make good verse; but the grateful and gentle gloom of our English skies has its poetic charms also, and is full of untold restfulness. Our climate is a very poor one for big, smoky cities, I grant, but it suits well the open country. It is a reproach to a scientific age that the atmosphere of our large towns should be rendered dismal, if not poisonous, by being polluted by filthy smoke and gases. Contrast the melancholy look of a smoke-begrimed London house with the weather-tinting of the walls of an old country building!

Continuing on our upward way we reached a land of wood again, only the trees had changed in kind, the tall fir and pointed pine taking the place of the lowland spreading oak and leafy elm. The former trees are true mountain-lovers, and told of an altered soil and climate. Then we came to a wide common whereon we noticed a gipsy encampment, the tent these restless wanderers had pitched, their tethered white horse, the curling film of blue smoke rising from a fire of sticks (over which was a tripod supporting an iron pot that gave forth a savoury odour), the unkempt gipsies themselves, together with their sun-tanned children playing around in childish glee, rejoicing in their wild freedom, formed quite a picture. We should much have liked to photograph the encampment and its surroundings, but former experience has taught us, for some good reasons known to themselves, gipsies strongly object to having their photographs taken, and are apt to rudely resent the advances of the amateur photographer, so we refrained.

From this common, looking southwards to the coast—some twenty-five miles away as the crow flies —there was spread out far below us a far-reaching panorama of continuous woods waving in the summer wind like a leafy inland sea. Even fair Sussex, land of wide prospects and revelations of scenery though it be, has nothing finer within her borders to show the fortunate road traveller: and were there only a silvery river (as in the rival Arun valley) winding, with many a graceful curve, through the pleasant woodscape—if I may be allowed the expressive term—I verily think that this prospect would be second to none in all England, so space-expressing is it in its grand distances; but absolute perfection is rarely to be found in this imperfect world.

The view from this spot, as we beheld it on that lovely summer morning, was simply enchanting; one seldom—in this railway age when trains bury themselves in dark tunnels, or dash through deep cuttings, just when the scenery is best, of course— one seldom has the opportunity of delighting the eye with such visions of beauty: this particular vision was the more impressive because it burst upon us so unexpectedly. The cheap, convenient, and rapid railway has ruined road travel, alas! so that the modern Englishman may go from one end to the other of his lovely land (as he does) by the iron-way (as the old maps called it) and yet know hardly anything of its real beauties. Our ancestors who had to journey up hill and down dale on the old coach-roads, at least had the chance of seeing the countless charms of the country-side, and the scenic gems that those roads ever afforded—then a journey was a succession of pictures. However, "fortune never comes with both hands full," we unhappily cannot combine the advantages of the railway with the romance and delights of the road, for even in these prosaic days there is a flavour of romance about the old roads.

But I have been wandering from my subject. Looking down from our elevated position on the open common, the country in front seemed to suddenly drop down, and the vast expanse of the weald stretched away without a break to the foot of the distant Downs. The many-tinted, waving woods, their foliage all flooded with the warm sunshine, formed a vision of leafy loveliness that no words, least of all any words of mine, can adequately convey. Away beyond this spreading ocean of greenery—over towards Beachy Head if we judged aright, but the distance was so dreamily indistinct that we could not make quite sure—we caught sight of the silvery sheen of the far-off sea. High up in the world as were we, our horizon was high also, besides being hazy that day; and the sea and sky were so blended that, but for the glimmer of sunshine on the water, it would have been difficult to tell which was which. Even the driving tourist does not come upon such a prospect every day; but

I will write no more about it, there are scenes that it is perhaps well not to attempt to describe overmuch, better to suggest the outline and let the imagination fill in the rest. Sometimes, however, too much is left to the imagination, as in a case of a tombstone inscription we came upon in Horsham churchyard, which, after duly recording the name of the deceased, and the date of his death, simply adds, " He was," the rest being left wholly to the reader's fancy. There is a tradition, we learnt, that this inscription was left unfinished abruptly thus of set purpose, and it was not an accidental circumstance. Another epitaph in Ashover churchyard, Derbyshire, though likewise leaving much to the reader's imagination, is more satisfactory; it runs as follows :—

> She lived respected, and died lamented ;
> She was—but words are wanting to say what—
> Think all a wife should be, she was that.

Having got upon the attractive subject of epitaphs, I must find room for one more here, by way of contrast, as to how variously men value their wives; this was sent me by a friend, who copied it from a churchyard in Yorkshire. Here it is :—

> Underneath this stone doth lie,
> Back to back, my wife and I.
> When the last trump sounds so shrill,
> If she gets up I'll lie still.

The wind was blowing keen and strong across the common ; unrestrained it came from the southward and the sea, there being nothing for long leagues to arrest its progress; it was delightfully fresh, sweet, invigorating, but decidedly blustery, so that having enjoyed the view, we did not feel inclined to dally further in such an exposed spot on such a day. Now when we left Uckfield the air was calm, there was not even a suspicion of a breeze, the smoke from the chimneys uprose straight without a suggestion of direction or curve; therefore when it blows a gale in the valley it must be tolerably unpleasant up here. However, if any one wishes to be braced up, Crowborough appears to me to be the very place, and it has the advantage of being a good deal nearer London than Scotland or the Alps.

As we went along we espied a desolate-looking inn, perched all alone on the top of a hill; close to it was a dank, dark pool of water. I know not exactly why, for it is not always easy to analyse one's feelings, but this solitary and forsaken-appearing old hostel appealed strangely to our sentiments, it seemed as though there must be some weird history or romance connected with the building, only waiting to be unearthed; there was, to us, in our then fanciful mood, a flavour of the highwayman, or at least the smuggler about the place. Possibly, however, it has had a very ordinary and uneventful existence. The sign of the inn was a large bird painted black sitting on a white gate. " The Bird and Gate," we presumed, though we did not see the title written up; this was a fresh sign to us, yet not an unnatural one for the country.

We were not quite sure whether we had arrived at Crowborough village or not, and if this were the best or only inn at hand. So we asked of a gentleman, who was struggling along the road against the wind, if this were Crowborough. "This is *Blow*borough," he responded savagely, laying great stress on the first syllable; "there's a good inn about a quarter of a mile farther on." We thanked him for his information, and ventured to remark that it seemed a very bracing spot, to which he made no reply. Perhaps he thought we were satirical in our saying; if so, he was right.

Our road continued on high ground, and took us past a plantation of firs; nailed to one of the trees was the warning, "Beware of Dogs and Alarm Guns." The "alarm guns" is surely a fresh feature on notice boards?—a year before we had seen a board in Lancashire inscribed, "Beware of Man Traps." We thought these to be illegal. All else failing, some little passing amusement may be extracted from the various notice boards exhibited by the wayside. When touring in the eastern counties a year or so back we came upon the astonishing and alarming notice that "Trespassers will be persecuted!" Manifestly the last word was an innocent misspelling of prosecuted, possibly owing to the village painter being unblest with a School Board education. But perhaps the most peculiar notice was one in Hampshire: the landowner was, we presumed, a religious-minded man, for the first thing to be read in large lettering on the board was "The earth is the Lord's and the fulness thereof"; then on a separate board just below was inscribed " Private property, trespassers will be strictly prosecuted according to the law." These notices were repeated at intervals. On one of them some one had painted "land" before "Lord's," and cleverly altered the intention of the reading thereby; the temptation to do this must have been great. Even this notice is capped by one on a sign-post in Kent: "This is a bridle track only to Bethersden, if you cannot read this you had better keep to the Road." A little farther along, to the right of our way, we observed an old cottage with a stone inserted over the doorway and inscribed :—

The Beacon House,
796 feet
Above Sea Level.
—
1838.

We were therefore nearly on the topmost point of Crowborough, the beacon itself being 803 feet high, and so only a very little more elevated. Why a highroad should be carried, with such a long ascent and descent, right over almost the summit of a big hill thus when it might have been kept lower down in the valley, with much easier gradients and less mileage, I cannot say. I venture a random guess that the majority of English roads had their origin in primitive tracks that led through a wild unenclosed country, and that the line that these tracks took was dictated by the necessities of the time, chief amongst these being to avoid swamps, soft lands, and dense forests; high open ground would under those conditions be most likely to afford the best and safest travelling, especially in a thickly-wooded country like Sussex was, and still is to a great extent away from the coast and wind-swept Downs.

Not far from the Beacon House is the summit of Crowborough Beacon, whereon, in the pre-semaphore and pre-telegraph days, signal fires were lighted in times of danger and invasion, which could be seen over a wide extent of country, including goodly portions of the three counties of Kent, Surrey, and Sussex. From here the lights flashed on from Beachy Head the signal that the Spanish Armada was in sight. Stirring times those! there must have been something very thrilling in the watchers and people plainly seeing thus the blazing fires on the lonely heights as they heralded across the country news fraught with the utmost import to the State. Now, in these less picturesque times, the most eventful news is flashed silently along a wire through the heart of peaceful, rural England, and the country folk have even no hint that anything special has happened, or is happening.

I have often gazed on those succession of posts and lines of wire that stretch in long array across the lonely Downs, then suddenly dip into the sea, on the way to the Continent, and wondered what messages were being conveyed by them at the moment over the peaceful country. The modern miracle of the telegraph has become quite commonplace now, that thin line of wire across the vast extent of Downs, and its uses, is not regarded even by the simple shepherd as at all a wonderful thing. " It's just the wires as takes the messages from

France to Lunnun town," was the remark of one of these hardy sons of the soil to me; "I don't see much wonderful about a message a-running along a wire, it seems quite natural like." What the South Down shepherd of to-day considers quite an ordinary thing his forbears would probably have considered as a madman's dream, could they by any possibility have heard of it. We are a progressive race. There is a deal of truth revealed in the proverbs of the people, and one of these proverbs has it, "Familiarity breeds contempt."

The drift of the mind of the rural population has vastly changed in this last quarter of a century. There are here and there a few honest believers in the good old-fashioned ghosts still to be found; once they were quite plentiful, then almost every village had its haunted house, almost as certainly as it had its church. In another generation the age-hallowed belief in ghosts promises to share the fate of the old-world belief in witches and witchcraft. The people have been taught to read, and superstition and intolerance are happily waning before the light of literature, slowly truly, but as surely as the sun disperses the darkness. With the superstitions, a good deal of poetry, which we ill can spare, will go too; old folk-lore, wise sayings, quaint customs and the like, may vanish like the witches and ghosts. Having taught the people what to unlearn, it would be well for our land if we could teach them to love beauty, and strive after it in some way, even in the humblest home and its surroundings, then this fair land of Britain, instead of growing less beautiful as the years roll on, might grow more and more lovely, till it became a veritable Arcadia.

A short descent from the highest point of the road brought us to the Red Cross Inn; here we were ushered into a cool, cheerful room, with a delightful and cosy ingle-nook, that gave the chamber quite an old-time character, together with an indescribable suggestion of comfort. There are two things that go to the making of a perfect room, granted good proportions, oak-panelled walls from floor to ceiling, and an ample ingle-nook, none of your modern builder's paltry make-beliefs, but a little room off a room, with blue Dutch tiles around, and dog-irons on the hearth—a hearth having space for a blazing wood fire, just as in the merry days of old. The room at our inn pleased us greatly, we should like to have taken it away with us, and to have decorated and lived in it!

Chatting with the landlord, whilst watching our horses being groomed, we asked if he could give us any information about his sign, the Red Cross, as it was an unfamiliar one to us, and we thought that just possibly there might be some meaning in it. But all he had to say on the subject was that he believed it had something to do with a battle fought on the hill a long while ago. This was rather indefinite! Still it was all he knew about it, and a man cannot do more than tell you all he knows—unless he invents.

We left Crowborough late in the afternoon, when the sun was getting low and the shadows were lengthening; it was just the hour for driving and day-dreaming; it is an excellent thing sometimes to give rein to one's poetic and romantic imaginings, it makes life brighter to idealise now and then.

We had a glorious drive on to Tunbridge Wells in the warm tender light of the late afternoon. Our way now led us through a hilly and well-wooded country, past sleepy farmsteads it took us, past picturesque old cottages—one with quaintly clipped yew trees in its little garden especially attracted our attention—past green meadows, golden corn-fields, and many-poled hop-gardens, with the hop cones dangling and dancing in the breeze.

It was all downhill for miles at first, and we sped along at a rattling pace, the traces slack and the brake just on; there was an inspiriting feeling of exhilaration in the quick and gliding progress through the cool evening air as the carriage ran on of itself, to the merry accompaniment of the jingle of the harness, the measured tramp, tramp, tramp of the horses' hoofs and the slumberous rumble of the wheels on the sandy road.

On to Eridge Green we drove through a forest of firs, with great rocks peeping out between their slender stems, a stretch of country that called to mind some of the Welsh valleys, only that there were no mountain peaks around. Eridge Green is a pretty model village that, however, has the fault of appearing too picturesque and artificial to be altogether a natural growth; it suggested to us overmuch the scenery of a theatre, so that we almost looked for the inevitable troop of dancers to come tripping forth singing in chorus, dressed all, not in real work-a-day costumes, but in those charming get-ups that country maidens only wear in a play. If you have a model village, to make the thing consistently complete, you need model inhabitants too!

An inn by the road-side here had for its sign a bull and a cannon. According to tradition the first cannon (a banded gun) ever made in Sussex, and possibly in England, formerly stood on this green; this the villagers used to fire off with real shot, that was dug out of the ground after use and so employed again and again, and this went on every high-day and holiday—until the cannon burst. So at least we were told, and this accounts for half of the inn sign, according to the same local authority.

Then driving on through more fir woods the country presently opened out, and our horizon widened from a few yards to many miles. Presently the prosperous town of Tunbridge Wells came into sight, and we soon afterwards found ourselves on its picturesque, rocky common; crossing this we reached and pulled up at the Wellington Hotel, an elevated hostel that boldly proclaims by a painted notice on its front that it stands "442 feet above sea-level." Manifestly our hotel was proud of its high position in the world. The view from our bedroom window looking southwards to the hills of Sussex was fine in the extreme.

Taking an early stroll round the town next morning before starting on our day's pilgrimage we were struck anew with the picturesque appearance and convenience of the old "Pantiles," where ladies can walk and shop in quiet out of the bustle, noise, and crush of the street, and even have shelter in bad weather from the rain, as a past century poet put it here :—

> My lady, without wetting of her shoe,
> May choose her dinner while her gallants woo.

Perhaps we might learn something, even in these days of progress, from this delightful specimen of old-fashioned planning of our forefathers.

CHAPTER VI

The much-abused English climate—An old moated house—An old-world garden—Poor amateur photographer—Rural England—A picturesque farmstead—Old houses and new—An ancient hostelry—A deserted mansion—A mystery—"Sussexian"—A satirical traveller—Cyclists' inns—The evolution of the spire—Ashdown Forest—Sketching from nature—Forest Row—Visitors' books at hotels—Ruins of Brambletye House—An old coaching inn.

AGAIN the weather smiled on us as we left Tunbridge Wells bound for East Grinstead one sunny morning, with a fine-weather, cloud-dappled sky overhead. The barometer was on the rise, so we had no fear or thought of rain; indeed our experience has ever been that it is dust rather than rain which the driving tourist has to dread in English travel. A drier climate would not be nearly so desirable nor so delightful for such an expedition. I once tried—in my younger, more venturesome days—a riding tour in far-off California, where the scenery is so grand and the climate so rainlessly perfect during the summer time, but a very few days' experience of the rough dusty roads or tracks convinced me that, in spite of all that has been sung and said ideally in praise of perpetual sunshine, a long spell of dry weather makes touring by road anything but a delight. At the end of our first day's ride in California of about thirty miles, we arrived at the rough ranche hotel smothered in dust, which impregnated all our garments and permeated to the skin; externally we were as white—or as gray—as millers. Moreover, to add to our pleasure we hardly dared to picnic by the wild forest or mountain-side for fear of rattlesnakes, tarantula spiders, whose bite is dangerous, and other undesirable creatures, to say nothing of the misery of mosquitoes.

This by the way, as so much is declaimed nowadays to the disadvantage of the English climate, with its various samples of weather. However, I like variety of weather as well as of scenery. I do not even object to set out on a rainy morning, provided it is not of a steady downpour type, with no apparent hope of change—that I grant, without reserve, is depressing to a degree. But we have found such unpromising days to be few and far between when on the road; and after rain how fresh and sweet is the country air, and how full of colour the landscape!

Out of Tunbridge Wells we had a long level road at first, with glorious views to the left, over a vast expanse of wooded country, stretching far away to a dreamy distance of faint blue hills. After a time our level road came to an end, and was succeeded by a long and steep descent that required careful negotiating. As we descended we caught now and again, through the tall-stemmed trees, picturesque peeps ahead of a blue country beyond. At the foot of the hill we came upon the peaceful old-world village of Groombridge, gathered irregularly round a rough triangular green. Great was the contrast from frequented fashionable Tunbridge Wells to this sleepy spot, primitive and picturesque with the hush of centuries upon it : we seemed to have driven out of one age into another, to have turned the hand of Time back several generations.

At the end of the village we got down from the dog-cart, and, walking up an avenue of Scotch firs, came to the old moated home of Groombridge Place, built in the seventeenth century, and occupying a portion of the site of a still older castle, once the property of Sir Richard Waller, a soldier of renown in the brave days of Henry V. This Sir Richard took Charles, Duke of Orleans, prisoner at the famous battle of Agincourt on 25th October 1415, and kept him here twenty long years in captivity.

Groombridge Place is situated in a secluded hollow, and with its weather-stained walls, wide, deep moat of clear running water, crossed by an ancient ivy-grown one-arched bridge, and great gateway beyond, forms a truly charming picture of old-world tranquillity; still further enhanced by its terraced gardens with their clipped yews, and enlivened by proud peacocks strutting stately about the lawns thereof. We at once felt impelled to make a sketch of this charming old home, which is reproduced in engraving herewith, and gives a better idea of the place than pages of description possibly can; in this respect the pencil has the advantage of the pen, though, alas! no mere black and white drawing can ever convey the subtle charm of colour or the gathered bloom of centuries.

Many years ago now, when taken on my first driving tour—which tour revealed a new and wholly unexpected pleasure to me — it chanced that my companion knew the then owner of this ancient home, and I shall never forget the intense delight I experienced in coming suddenly upon this romance in building, and of being hospitably entertained therein. What a pleasing and startling contrast it afforded to the intensely modern and commonplace builder's house I was perforce constrained to occupy in smoky London, and that we had left only that very morning. It was midsummer time, and the day was hot, not to say sultry, and the cool, past-time oak-panelled chamber wherein we were received simply seemed to me ideal; indeed, the whole place impressed me with its picturesqueness and quaintness, and for a time held me fascinated. It was one of those red-letter days that live long in the memory, and that only come at rare intervals in a lifetime. Groombridge Place is a picture rather than a house for habitation, a past peace seems to hang over the old mansion like a spell that makes the hurry and bustle of this nineteenth century appear like a dream; but it is a spot to be seen and its influence felt rather than written of. There is an old-world charm about this time-toned home and its mellow restful surroundings quite incommunicable in words. Only in Old England could you find such a spot.

A MOATED HOME—GROOMBRIDGE PLACE

The water from the moat runs into a large tree-surrounded pond, which supplies a gray old mill at its foot with motive power; hither we next bent our footsteps, and begged of the miller permission to photograph it. This was a fatal mistake, we ought to have photographed it first and asked permission afterwards, for though our request was at once granted, the knowledge of what we were going to do brought out the whole family, who thereupon commenced to pose themselves right in front of the mill-wheel to "be took." This was very trying, we wanted a photograph of the ancient mill, not of a family all in a row!

From Tunbridge Wells to Groombridge we had traversed a corner of Kent, though all the views from our elevated road were looking over a wealth of Sussex hills and woods. On leaving Groombridge—a place that will linger long in our memories—we crossed the border of the two counties and found ourselves once again in the sunny land of Sussex, at least it is my impression that Sussex is the sunniest portion of England, and that its skies are bluer than those of any other corner of our land, though it is blessed — or cursed — with an abundant supply of east winds; still these do not always gray the atmosphere as elsewhere. Almost every English county seems to have its advantages and drawbacks; but I love Sussex because, away from the fashionable seaside resorts that fringe its coast, it possesses no large towns with their smoke and untold ugliness—the Sussex country towns are of the clean, sweet, homely order.

First came a gradual rise from the low valley in which Groombridge lies. Reaching the top of this ascent a charming prospect of a fertile and undulating country opened out before us: a spreading land of hill and dale dotted at irregular intervals with prosperous-looking farmsteads, some in the picturesque half-timber style, whose black and white gables showed plainly in the sun peeping above their colony of outbuildings, hay-ricks, and corn-stacks, dotted also with many a humble cottage home, whose russet roofs were often drowned in a very sea of foliage. White winding roads led the eye unknowingly from one beauty spot to another in the scene, roads wandering hither and thither, now lost to view by spreading woods, only to reappear again farther away, and then vanishing in the dim distance into mere thread-like lines, till lost altogether in the uncertain haze of the faint, far-off horizon. Here and there, too, we caught sight of the conical roofs of oast-houses, somewhat suggestive, as seen in the distance, of the towers of foreign châteaux, that give such a characteristic feature to the fair land of France.

. The scenery was, however, intensely English in its perfect restfulness. Eye-delighting and heart-satisfying it was with its mellow homelike beauty—beheld, as we beheld it, under the soft sunshine of that rare summer day. At one spot we pulled up involuntarily, so struck were we with the loveliness of the prospect therefrom. Before and around us were spread out and mingled gentle-sloping corn-fields and verdant meadow-lands, waving woods and sunlit hills, the whole being enlivened by the silvery sparkle and sheen of gliding stream and quiet pool, the waters mirroring bits of the bright blue sky above on the green earth below; this peep of rural England was enhanced, and rendered interesting as well as merely beautiful, by the many mellow-toned homes of man, that told of domesticity, long occupancy, and peaceful abiding. There was nothing to spoil the reposeful harmony of the scene; the landscape had a benign aspect—it was lovable! So gently sloped the hills, it seemed

> As if God's finger touched, but did not press
> In making England—such an up-and-down
> Of verdure; nothing too much up and down,
> A ripple of land, such little hills the sky
> Can stoop so tenderly and the wheat-fields climb;
> Such nooks of valleys lined with orchises.

The English landscape has a heart, it woos you and wins your affections whether you will or no, and having won your affections will not let them ever go again.

About five miles on our way, at a dip in the road, we stopped a while to sketch a delightfully picturesque farmhouse of half-timber with great gables and finely-shaped, clustering chimneys: a farmhouse of the olden time, raised when the yeoman farmer was a power in the land—now, alas! he has almost utterly disappeared, and with him the prototype of John Bull, jovial, prosperous-looking, and abiding. Would we could get him back again!

There is something very pleasing about these old buildings, if only for the solid substance of them, and the absence of any sign, or suggestion, of stint in material, or of any endeavour to make the most of every inch of space. The builders of old, whether of cottage or mansion, were generous to a degree of material, and wanton almost in their bountifulness where space was concerned. And what great high-pitched roofs they gave their houses, supported by mighty rafters, with an ample margin for strength, roofs that would throw off snow and rain, and last for generations. And their chimneys, how big and strong they were : the Englishman of past times ,gloried in roof and chimney, he acknowledged rain and storms, and the need of fires ; unlike the classical architect, who ever seemed ashamed of roof or chimney, and hid them as far as possible.

The look of the strength and solidity of most old buildings gratifies the beholder, although he may not be able to reason to himself the exact cause of his satisfaction. There is one thing that you cannot do, you cannot build substantially and cheaply ; so but too often the modern architect, compelled by circumstances, builds merely prettily and cheaply. This generation carefully considers the cost of everything, it does not seem even to desire the best, it rather demands a building "that answers its purpose at the least expenditure." So we have houses built by contract, generally at the lowest tender; that is, when we do not buy them ready-made of the speculative builder. Haste and cheap production are the curse of the century, when beauty is in question. So we find houses with thin walls, cheap woodwork, puttied and painted over to hide defects; thoughtless planning, and bad designs —for who can design well under present conditions? a man must love his work to do this—and everywhere there is but too manifest a pitiful economy of material. Feeling dissatisfied with the result, as well we may be, we cover this cheap structure with what it pleases us to consider ornamentation, that fails to adorn, for all that, forgetful of the fact that only honest construction should be ornamented. We build mostly houses, not homes; home-building, alas! is almost a lost art in the land. I am writing of the spirit of the age, the trend of modern conditions—not but that there are, happily, many and notable exceptions to the rule.

Leaving the old farmstead that has caused this over-long digression, we arrived quickly afterwards at the humble little hamlet of Withyham, where we found a picturesque and ancient inn by the roadside, with substantial stone-built stabling attached. The old inn looked as though it had been more important and more prosperous erst than now.

The church at Withyham is interesting on account of its Dorset (or Sackville) chapel, which contains several fine monuments to that family, one of these being by Flaxman. Here is buried Charles, sixth Earl of Dorset, celebrated by Pope as

> Dorset, the grace of courts, the Muse's pride,

but this epitaph is not now to be found in the chapel, if it ever were there, as is stated.

A pleasant stroll of about a mile to the southward brought us to Buckhurst and to the remains of the once stately home of that name, built by the first Earl of Dorset in 1560, and acknowledged at the time to be one of the grandest mansions in England. This edifice is shown in ancient prints as possessing eight towers and a large banqueting hall; but of this princely abode nothing now remains but a solitary tower, one of the eight. *Sic transit gloria mundi.*

Early in the seventeenth century Buckhurst was deserted by the family for Knole, owing "to the extreme foul and bad ways, the roads around being little better than quagmires," and the stones of the magnificent mansion were carted away to build other places, and especially the Sackville College at East Grinstead. The badness of the roads was given as the ostensible cause of the desertion and pulling down of this lordly dwelling, but it appears a curiously insufficient one, and rumour has it that the reason must be sought for elsewhere. There is a suggestion of mystery about the sudden desertion and demolition of such a grand place as Buckhurst was. Has rumour found the key? Truly the roads were terribly bad in these parts in those days, but it is recorded that the roads round about Knole were in no better plight. Therefore, it seems that the *real* reason of the abandonment of Buckhurst remains to be revealed, for it is unprofitable to speculate upon mere rumour and tales that vary with the teller. There are chapters of many an old English family history that never will be written, so that plentiful scope is given for tradition.

As to the badness of Sussex roads, all old-time travellers who have left behind them any record of their wanderings thereon agree on this point, a matter I have already briefly referred to. Leland in his *Itinerary* quotes a verse to the effect, "Sowsexe full of dyrte and myre," and even as late as 1750 Dr. Burton in his *Diary* remarks of the Sussex roads: "They are, to explain concisely what is most abominable, Sussexian." He further satirically suggests that "the reason why the oxen, the swine, the women, and all other animals are so long-legged here may be from the difficulty of pulling their feet out of so much mud; as thus the muscles get stretched and bones lengthened." It was hardly gallant of the worthy doctor (I presume he was a worthy doctor) inserting women amongst the animals, and not even giving her first place. Evidently the doctor was angry when he wrote as he did. Possibly, as he was driving across country, he may have got stuck in the mud, and he may have dined badly also at his inn just before filling up his diary. However, nowadays the majority of Sussex roads, especially the main ones, are excellent; some of the by-ways truly are a little loose and stony in dry weather and heavy-going in wet, but one cannot expect perfection in this world.

Strangely enough, in the past days it was the country nobility and squires that opposed any improvement in the Sussex thoroughfares; they dreaded lest good roads should give easy access to the London rogues, and bring down infection upon them. I wonder what these enlightened gentlemen would think could they be brought to life again and behold the railway, the excellent highways, and, not least, the ubiquitous bicycle. Writing of the bicycle reminds me of changed times. Some of the small hostels by the wayside now rejoice in the sign of "The Cyclists' Rest" or "The Cyclists' Arms" (whatever they may be), and I even think that the legend "Good Accommodation for Cyclists" is quite as common to-day as the old familiar one of " . . . for Man and Beast" was of old. In one inn-yard we even saw painted on a stable door "Stands for Cycles." Such notices would surely sorely puzzle our forefathers of the coaching days could they revisit this world again. There is something striking too in the juxtaposition of the old and the new, when you see some of the bright modern steel steeds resting within one of these ancient yards amid old-fashioned and time-dimmed surroundings. The modern generation rides behind the iron horse on the rail, and rides the iron horse on the road. Truly *tempora mutantur, et nos mutamur in illis.*

Leaving Withyham, we passed a small sheet of silvery water overhung with trees, and then a short drive brought us to the very picturesque and pleasantly-situated village of Hartfield, set in the midst of a richly-wooded country; a country charmingly diversified by tree-crowned hill and shady vale. Hartfield possesses some "dear" old cottages, and a quaint and ancient hostelry that would make a capital background for a picture; a hint I throw out, should any artist be this way, and in search of such a subject.

The church here is situated on a prominent knoll, and is famous amongst archæologists as being the first church in England to be built with a "broach" spire : that is to say, the spire does not rise from within a parapet, but is carried up directly from the outer edge of the tower walls, so as to throw off the rain from the building. This, it seems to me, is the most sensible and scientific method of joining a spire to a tower, though perhaps hardly so picturesquely effective as when the base of the spire is enclosed as before described. However, when it is a case of keeping wet out of a building, I think sentiment should give place to common-sense.

There is nothing more interesting in ecclesiastical architecture than to trace the growth of the spire from the mere low roofing-in of the square, and often squat, tower (as at Hastings old church and elsewhere), which became gradually raised to a steep roof, and this in turn grew into a lofty spire soaring to the sky, reaching its apogee—in England—at Salisbury Cathedral, that crowning glory of Gothic daring and genius. The church at Hartfield has a fine old timber lich-gate, with the date 1520 cut thereon.

From Hartfield we drove on through picturesque pine woods, which gave forth a warm, resinous odour; then after a time we came to a long and steep descent; from the top of this we had a fine view northward, over a wide pastoral valley, to the sunlit Surrey hills, and southward over what remains of the once extensive Ashdown Forest.

The steep slopes of the uplands (marked as forest on the Ordnance Map) are either barren, or else covered with bracken, bramble, and long waving grass, though in the distance, here and there, long ridges of firs fringed their summits, and stood out that day sharply silhouetted against the bright summer sky.

Here we rested a while to impress the view on our mind's canvas. Better this, at times, than sketching or photographing, for you can only remember the most important and picturesque parts of a scene; the trivial details, and the commonplaces thereof, are compulsorily lost in blissful oblivion. The difficulty in making a sketch is to know what to leave out—you cannot include all. Sketching, besides being a matter of drawing, is a matter of selection; few people, however, either see or select alike, and what is more refreshing than for an artist to reveal to us an unfamiliar aspect of a familiar place; it comes upon us as a pleasant surprise, and points out unexpected beauties that existed before, but were unperceived by us.

At the foot of the descent we found ourselves in the prosperous and populous village of Forest Row; indeed, it has too much of a prosperous look to be exactly picturesque, though its situation in a sheltered valley surrounded by low hills, and watered by a clear running stream, is most pleasing. Here we pulled up at the "Brambletye Hotel." Even the inn of the village must needs rejoice in the high-sounding title of hotel.

Forest Row is a pronouncedly progressive place,

and promises some day to become a small town. We found very comfortable quarters in the small hotel. There were sweet-scented and colourful flowers on the table of the tiny sitting-room we had, and after a wait—that seemed, doubtless, over-long to us with our keen appetites, engendered with our out-of-door life—an excellent repast was served. Our modest hotel, moreover, boasted, we found, of a "Visitors' Book," and we whiled away the interval until our meal was ready by glancing over the varied contents thereof, in the hope of coming upon something of interest, but though we managed to extract much passing amusement out of the varied entries, we discovered nothing of sufficient merit to deserve transcribing in our note-book. This was a mild disappointment, as, now and then, in such books we have unearthed, hidden amongst a wilderness of rubbish, amusing and even clever impromptu verses, adroit epigrams, odd remarks, skits, and funny sketches; occasionally, very occasionally, we have observed attached to the verses and sketches the signatures of well-known authors and artists (Charles Kingsley's was one, to some short charming verses about how he spent his holiday at the country hostel in whose "Visitors' Book" he had written). We were not quite so innocent as to pin our faith to the authenticity of all the familiar names we saw inscribed beneath sundry productions, notably in one flagrant case where we observed the name of "Alfred Tennyson" appended to some very mediocre verses, in bad imitation of the genuine article. But good things in hotel visitors' books, like quaint epitaphs in churchyards, seem to become rarer and rarer as the years roll on. The present generation takes life and pleasure too seriously to be really witty in everyday life.

Whilst the horses were resting we set out for a stroll, along a pleasant footpath that led across some fresh green meadows, in search of the ruins of Brambletye House, which was made the chief scene in Horace Smith's old-fashioned and once famous novel of that name. This fine house was originally built by Sir Henry Compton in the year 1631. It was deserted and left to go to the inevitable decay of all uncared-for things but half a century later.

Strangely enough, this erst grand mansion shared a precisely similar fate to its near neighbour of Buckhurst, and there appears also to be a similar mystery hanging over it as to the sudden desertion thereof. One rumour has it that Sir James Rickhards, the then owner, was concerned in a plot on behalf of the Orange party, and that, whilst absent from home hunting in Ashdown Forest, his house was searched by the Royal Commissioners for arms, of which a quantity was found secreted away there, together with a large supply of ammunition. A faithful retainer of the family, getting wind of what was happening, went out in search of his master, and fortunately found and warned him of what was taking place, whereupon Sir Rickhards made good his escape to Spain. Another rumour has it that this Sir Rickhards simply married a

Spanish lady of great wealth, and forthwith went to live in Spain (his doing so being the condition of the marriage), and that the story of the search for arms and the flight from England is a mere invention. When antiquaries thus differ, who shall decide the truth or untruth of the rumours? Yet surely the first one should not be so very difficult to authenticate? It is, to say the least, strange how hard it is to arrive at any precise facts as to the desertion of two such stately homes as Buckhurst and Brambletye House.

Traditions, like the clinging ivy, quickly gather round deserted old homes, and are repeated from generation to generation, till they come to be considered as "gospel true." But an unsentimental and utilitarian age seems to take a positive pleasure in demonstrating that most of these cannot be, or are not, true. What but a hard-hearted generation would inquire too closely into the verity of a pretty tradition? Even the charming love story of Dorothy Vernon, so intimately associated with Haddon Hall, has been declared by certain learned antiquaries "having authority" to be purely apocryphal, who maintain that "Dorothy Vernon never eloped at all, but was married after the usual orthodox fashion." These learned men may be right, possibly they are, but they might leave such poetical legends alone; they harm no one and are a source of infinite pleasure to many. There is plenty of matter-of-fact in the world, and a little leaven of romance can do no harm. Romance is as necessary to an old ruin as ivy, moss, and lichen; it seems hardly picturesquely complete without. Life would be unbearable without the relief of fiction.

As we strolled along over the meadows we passed by an old farmstead, and noticed a large stack of bracken in the yard thereof, carefully thatched, as though it were wheat or hay. We had never seen bracken so treated or prized before, but we were told that it formed excellent bedding for cattle, and was much valued for this purpose in some parts of the country.

Then we reached a clear little stream, which we crossed by a gray old stone bridge; on the centre pier of this is cut the date 1613. Doubtless this bridge formed one of the ancient approaches to Brambletye, as much care seems to have been taken in its design and construction, although it only spans an insignificant stream. Now we followed alongside of the bright, gliding, and gurgling water that brought us to a sketchable old mill with a tranquil pool above, one of Nature's mirrors, that reflected the building and trees around, and added to the charm of the scene. Just beyond this mill, and past another farmhouse, the ivy-grown and time-rent towers of Brambletye came into sight.

The ruins of the old seat of the Comptons are very picturesque, and are, besides, pleasingly situated in a low and wooded valley; they consist principally of three towers, of which one alone is in a fairly perfect condition and is capped with shaped stone, instead of being roofed in the ordinary way. There are some remains of crumbling walls connecting these towers, and apart from the main building there is a ruined arched stone gateway, which probably gave access to the main entrance, through an enclosed courtyard. The centre tower—for the three are in line—contains the chief doorway, of arched stone, with bosses above and carved oak leaves on the side for ornament. Over the doorway may still be traced the arms of the Comptons, though the carving is much decayed; above these are two helmets, apparently crestless, and this is all that now remains of stately old Brambletye.

From Forest Row to East Grinstead we had a long uphill stage of three miles or more, with wide views opening out to the left as we rose, over a country of rounded hills and spreading woods. At East Grinstead we pulled up at the old "Dorset Arms," and sought rest and shelter for the night there "for man and beast." Over the entrance porch of the inn we noticed plainly painted the following legend:—

> There is no office in this needful world
> But dignifies the doer, if well done.
> ALFRED AUSTIN, *Fortunatus the Pessimist*,
> Act I, Scene iv.

Mottoes and legends inscribed over doorways thus were quite common in the late Middle Ages, and frequently gave an added interest to a building; it is a pleasant old fashion worth reviving. During this and previous journeys we were glad to see that inscriptions over doorways are coming into vogue again. Over the entrance to a little cottage in the west we noticed, cut deeply in the wooden lintel:—

> Parva Domus Magna Quies.

And a most excellent motto it seemed for that peaceful and unpretending country home. Over the porch of another picturesque but much larger house, known as Old Place, at Lindfield, we observed the following line, inscribed also in Latin :—

Porta patens esto nvlli clavdaris honesto.

Another creeper-covered cottage on the way was happily contented with a simple English motto that all might read, and thus it ran :—

Small, but Large Enough.

Fortunate man : the character of the owner seems expressed in the motto.

The "Dorset Arms" we found in this year of grace 1895 to be an almost ideal inn for the weary traveller desirous of taking his ease. It was clean, comfortable, quiet; our meals were excellently cooked and nicely served; flowers, tastefully arranged, decorated our table ; and all things were well ordered within and without. Great praise this, but it was all warranted at the time we were there. Would that one could only ensure a continuity of such desirable qualities, but landlords come and go, sometimes for the better, sometimes for the worse, and the inn of to-day is not always that of to-morrow. Oh, the restful comfort and home-like flavour of a good old-fashioned hostel, conducted on the old lines, and simply maintained, not modernised and made vulgar! Besides being comfortable, we found that our hotel contained some charming old furniture and decorative china that gave quite a refined look to the place.

The "Dorset Arms" was a noted hostelry in the old coaching and posting days, and many famous men of that period rested and feasted within its hospitable walls when passing this way, and we frequently find mention and praise of it in the diaries of old road travellers. The "Dorset dinners," too, were renowned—trust our forefathers not to forget this important item, as witness the frequent mention of his "good living" in the entertaining *Diary* of the worthy Samuel Pepys, whom it is the privilege of all Englishmen to quote. People who are contented to be simply conveyed from place to place by the railway, careless of all that lies between, could hardly make a diary of their journey, so different in interest are the two modes of travel. Travelling, indeed, in the old sense of the term, is almost a lost art. A driving tour is perhaps the nearest approach now obtainable to the delights and scenic revelations of the old-fashioned posting across country.

From the garden at the foot of the "Dorset Arms" a fine view is to be had, looking down upon and over the district known as Ashdown Forest, which indeed still retains much of the appearance of a real forest beheld from this distant point of view. Our inn garden, besides, afforded us a delightful insight into the charms of past-time building; for if some of the fronts of the old East Grinstead houses that face the main thoroughfare of that town have been to some extent improved up to date (save the mark), no such improvement has happily been considered needful for the rears thereof, and it was these latter that were presented to us, so we obtained a delightful eye-gratifying peep of many unspoilt specimens of old-world architecture, a perfect jumble of odd gables, quaint porches, mullioned windows, twisted chimney-stacks, and the like, in picturesque irregularity—a picture that Prout would have rejoiced to paint. Strange it is how certain subjects recall the work of certain artists; portions of wild North Wales inevitably bring to my mind David Cox, as likewise do parts of Essex, Constable, and so forth. In these cases the artist seems to have caught and transferred to canvas or paper the true spirit of the scene, and it is just this rare spirit that profits and pleases the trained eye and cultivated mind, not the mere topographical reproduction of scenery, the material body thereof, as it were; the camera can give us that, more or less successfully, any day; but any day cannot give us, alas! the soul of the landscape as revealed by the true artist.

It was a delicious ending to a delightful day's wanderings to moon about in that peaceful old inn garden smoking a post-prandial pipe in dreamy contentment, watching the while the slowly-setting sun, whose last rays rested long and lovingly upon the many-gabled houses of the old town, glinting on a restless gilt weather-cock, lighting up the many diamond panes of the lattice windows, and warming up the gray-blue uprising smoke into a film of tender gold—the very poetry of smoke, for in the country even smoke can be beautiful. On the other side the gloom of night was fast settling down upon the woods of Ashdown Forest, causing the whole landscape to assume a mysterious air. We might have been, for aught our eyes could tell, travellers in the days of "good Queen Bess," but our ears revealed to us that we were, beyond doubt, living in the progressive nineteenth century, for we caught, now and again, the shrill shriek of the railway whistle. It is difficult to romance successfully within hearing of the rush of trains and the sounds of shunting operations!

CHAPTER VII

At East Grinstead — Sackville College — " Modern Gothic "—" Ye Village Cage " at Limpsfield—A new reading of history—Old houses — A tip declined ! — Fine altar-tomb — A tradition — Too good for this world—Old chained Bibles—Benefactors—A picture in building—Crowhurst Church—Oldest yew tree in England — A smock-frocked clerk — Crowhurst Place — A legendary house—A quaint and interesting interior.

FINDING our comfortable inn at East Grinstead much to our liking, we determined next morning "to take our ease" thereat for yet another night, and instead of proceeding farther on our direct journey, to spend a day in driving about and exploring the neighbourhood. We learnt that there was in the old churchyard of the small hamlet of Crowhurst, some eight miles away to the north, a fine and famous old yew tree, "the largest and oldest yew in England." We have, by the way, come upon many of the largest yew trees in England, besides six at least of the smallest churches, so this information was accepted *cum grano salis;* however, it was a point to make for, and we determined to drive thither and take our chance of what else of beauty or interest we might discover on the way.

Before starting we took a stroll of inspection round the town, which still retains a good deal of its ancient look. First we sought out the quaint and time-toned Sackville College, a low rambling structure standing on much ground, and built in the form of a quadrangle, round which the various apartments are ranged. This college was constructed from a portion of the materials of Buckhurst (as before mentioned), and is an alms-house for the support of a certain number of poor men and women ; it is set on a height, affording glorious views around, and the whole pile is weather-tinted into a delightful harmony of colourful grays, an indescribable blending of hues that is the priceless dower of age ; its ancient walls are splashed with silver and golden lichen, made green, here and there, with creeping mosses, and stained every imaginable tone with the winter storms of unremembered years. Sackville College would be to me a far more desirable home than any modern palace I wot of. Those men of old, how picturesquely they built ; they romanced in stone, and raised poems in brick and mortar! Now we hear but little else than prose—and poor at that! Shall we ever become an artistic people again ? Possibly, but first we must reconvert our workmen into craftsmen who will take a pride in their work—that is an essential. It was the latter who made the famous old English furniture of Chippendale and Sheraton, that puts to very shame the machine-produced articles of the same class of to-day.

The interior of Sackville College is interesting, and contained some good old carved oak work and fine chimney-pieces. We were told that until of late years the good and almost forgotten custom

prevailed here of bringing the Yule log at Christmas time into the dining-hall, which log blazed and crackled away on the great fireplace thereof, as a Yule log should, having on either side of it one of the fine "fire-dogs," and being backed up by an old Sussex iron fire-back, cast and embellished with the noble founder's arms. On the mantel above, the poor inmates might read in the glow of the burning wood the following inscription, the more easily legible because carved in raised lettering, which raised work takes considerably more time and skill than mere incising, but is infinitely more effective :—
"I pray God bless my Lord of Dorset and my Ladie and all their posteritie. Ano. Do. 1619."

There are many other picturesque and interesting buildings in the town, though of lesser note. One of these, with its mullioned windows and old stone slab roof, attracted our special attention ; it is known as the Judges' Lodgings (a curious name for a private residence, which the house is now, and only shows how obstinately titles are retained in England, even when they are wholly inappropriate, and therefore no longer suitable to changed times or purposes). It is said that amongst other judges the famous—or infamous—Judge Jeffreys once slept there.

Last of all the buildings in the place to be inspected by us was the church, owing to its elevated position a most prominent landmark in the country for miles around, and certainly it is vastly more pleasing when seen from afar (should any of my readers imagine that, for once, I am writing satirically — they are correct). "East Grinstead church is a fine building in the modern Gothic style," remarked a guide-book we found at our inn. We felt grateful for the information. It is useful to know what one ought to admire. It saves some people a lot of trouble—and seeing; they let the guide-book do all that for them. But exactly what the "modern Gothic style" of architecture is, I do not quite know. I rather fancy it to be an utterly feelingless copy of old Gothic work, improved upon to pleasure and made up-to-date in detail by the modern architect, neglecting, of course, such a trifling matter as any attention to proportion; but, of course, I may be wrong. The church was built in 1790 on the site of the old one destroyed by lightning; perhaps, therefore—if one might venture to suggest anything to a guide-book compiler—perhaps a better term for the style thereof would be "late eighteenth-century Gothic"! The church has a tall tower, without a steeple, in perfect keeping with the rest of the edifice, and a Sussex proverb has it:—

> Large town, proud people,
> Big church, no steeple.

I think I have heard something like that before of other places, though in some cases, if my memory serves me aright, it is because the people are poor that they have no steeple.

East Grinstead is situated on high ground, and here and there a road leading down from the town to the valley below is deeply cut through the sandy rock. These shady roads are over-arched with trees, the twisted roots at the foot of their trunks being twined fast around the rugged rocks in picturesque contortion ; road, rocks, and trees forming a delightful picture in the summer time, enhanced by a peep of deep blue distance ahead.

We noticed that East Grinstead was spelt East Greenstede on an old map, so that its ancient name suggests a station in the wood, and doubtless, centuries ago, the country far on all sides was forest primeval.

Our road to Crowhurst began well. Passing by an old wooden windmill on a height, deserted and left to picturesque decay, with its great outstretched arms standing forth dark and grim and gaunt against the sunny sky, our way suddenly dipped down and led us through thick woods into a lovely, lonely country of undulating meadow-lands, dotted with spreading oaks and shady elms, and bounded by a distance of fir-crowned hills. At one point graceful silver birches bordered our pleasant rural road, which we had all to ourselves, for we met not a soul till we reached the pretty and interesting village of Lingfield, which possesses, besides some quaint old half-timber buildings, a remarkably fine church, worthy of a city.

Here by the side of the village pond, overshadowed by an ancient oak, stands a curious structure, looking somewhat like a Lilliputian church, duly provided with a tower to match it in size. We pulled up and got down from the dog-cart, the better to inspect this strange bit of building, and to endeavour to gather what its purpose might be. We observed, upon a closer view, two short and separate inscriptions painted on wood, and placed against the wall of the miniature tower. These read as follows: "Ye Village Cage" and "St. Peter's Cross." The inscriptions only served to increase our curiosity, and so we sought further and more explicit information of an intelligent-looking native who happened just then to be passing. In reply to our query if he knew what the building was, he replied, "Oh, that's the old village cage; it were used for a prison in my grandfayther's time, so I've heard him tell. There used to be then, too, a whipping-post and some stocks outside on the green, and they put the prisoners in the cage o'nights, and placed them in the stocks o'days." "But what does 'St. Peter's Cross' mean on the notice?" we further queried. "Well, I've heard say as how a market cross used to stand on the spot afore the cage were built, but old Cromwell he pulled her down." What a lot of sins of commission that famous Englishman has to answer for, to be sure! There is hardly a castle in the country but (according to local traditions) has been knocked about by his cannon balls. "Are you quite certain it was Cromwell who pulled the cross down?" we asked. "Well, they do say as how he did it; if not, some one else did." This was indisputable but hardly to the point. "Do you happen to know who Cromwell was?" We could not resist the question. "Why, to be sure. He were King of England. Why, I learnt that at school." Well, there is nothing like educating the people; the farmer's daughter can play the piano nowadays, but cannot make butter. I was much amused by a remark that an old farm-labourer made to me one day, as showing his opinion of the drift of up-to-date education. "Lor' bless you, sir," said he to me, "my son he's had a schooling as I never had; he thinks hisself mighty clever, he do; he quite looks down on his poor old fayther, he do. But I'll tell 'ee what it is," this with emphasis, "with all his learning he can't thatch a rick, and I can." That remark gave us food for thought. Surely to be able to thatch a rick and plough a furrow is a legitimate part of an agricultural labourer's education? What profits it if the captain of a ship can read Latin and knows nothing of navigation? Will Latin bring his ship to port?

The most interesting of the old houses in Lingfield is one that now does duty as a butcher's shop, and I think that it is really the only picturesque butcher's shop that I know. This ancient structure is of half-timber with a high-pitched roof, having an overhanging upper story, such a pleasing feature in buildings of that kind and period, combining utility with beauty too, by affording considerable extra space above, where most needed. The corner bracket supports of this shop are finely moulded and carved, and if, as I imagine from certain appearances (though of course I may be wrong in my conjectures), this structure was originally intended for a shop, then such a well-preserved example of a medieval shop is of no small antiquarian interest.

We found our way next to the church, only to discover that the door was "religiously" locked, so we asked a passing workman if he could tell us where the clerk lived. "Yes," responded he, "I can, but I be agoing past his house, and I'll send he to you, if you likes; it'll save you the walk." We thanked the man for his thoughtfulness, and gladly accepted his kind offer. We were about to offer him "the price of a glass of ale" for his trouble, but before we could do so he exclaimed, "It's awful 'ot weather, and I be awful dry, that I be." What a number of dry people one does encounter on a driving tour, to be sure! Having given the man the wherewithal to quench his thirst, we sat on a tombstone in the shade and waited for the coming of the clerk. In due course that individual made his appearance, armed with a ponderous key, and we entered the old church.

I have said the clerk came, though to this day I have my doubts whether he were the clerk or not, for his cultivated speech, refined accent, archæological knowledge, and quiet courteous manner made us suspect that we had not "the genuine article" before us; indeed, had he proclaimed himself an archdeacon we should not have been much, if at all, surprised. It struck us that possibly he was one of the churchwardens, whom the labourer had called on by mistake, and who, nothing loth, entered into the spirit of the thing. However that may be, we felt very awkward when the time for "tipping" arrived, but our conductor by his gentlemanly instinct came to our rescue, suggesting that any trifle we might feel inclined to give for seeing the church should be placed in the box for the building fund, as that was sadly in need of money. Now I have never before in all my experience known a real clerk suggest anything of the kind; they have always accepted my money without a hint about the benefit of any church fund, or even the good of the poor. No, I am convinced that our conductor was not the clerk. As far as I can remember, this is the sole instance that a tip of ours has not been personally accepted, though I have to confess that an American friend of mine owned to a similar experience, which so impressed him by its rarity that he could not help mentioning the strange fact to me, only in his case it was a railway porter who declined a "tip." Well, all I can remark is that wonders will never cease as long as the world revolves.

The first thing that attracted our attention in the church was the fine altar-tomb to the first Lord and Lady Cobham, the former of whom died in 1361. This monument is of considerable interest on account of certain peculiar departures from the usual monumental features of the period. The effigy of "my lord" is shown—carved in alabaster, coloured and gilt—in full plate armour, the details of which are worthy of note as showing the method of wearing the armour. The head rests on a tilting helmet, which has on the top a diminutive figure of a turbaned Turk for a crest, and a garter is shown on the leg. Besides the uncommon crest, a unique feature here is the fact that the two kneeling female supporters are not winged as usual, and there are no signs that they ever had wings; if these figures, as is the case in other similar recumbent effigies on altar-tombs, are intended for angels, then the artist-carver must have considered such ethereal creatures to have no need for wings, therefore differing wholly from the universally - accepted traditions of the medieval sculptor, who always represented them so provided.

Another quaint feature about this effigy is that the feet rest on another figure of a turbaned Turk, that takes the place of the usual faithful dog or fierce lion. Our conductor said there was a tradition that one of the family had served with the Crusaders, hence the Turk at Lord Cobham's feet.

Adjoining this stately monument is a stone slab on the floor, dated 1662, to a certain "William Widnellvs," inscribed with a long Latin epitaph, which we did not trouble to puzzle out. After this comes the following rare panegyric in plain English, so that all may read and understand :—

> Desist those prophane feet, forbeare
> To fowle this hallowed marble, where
> Lies vertues, goodness, honour's heire.
>   .   .   .   .   .
> Cause the world was not worthy him to have
> The great Jehovah shutt him in this grave.

We were careful not to "fowle" the "hallowed marble," but we inwardly thought that it would be hard to cap this vainglorious eulogy. "There is but a step from the sublime" to the contemptible! True worth is ever modest. Such sycophantical inscriptions have oftentimes the effect of making the reader thereof cynical. The inevitable question arises how far the underlying dead are responsible for such fulsomeness. Could we place implicit faith in epitaphs, what paragons of perfection our ancestors must have been, and how commonplace history must have lied! After all, times and manners may change, but the natural man remains now much the same as ever.

In one of the pews we discovered a chained Bible, dated 1682, with the following inscription on the fly-leaf: "This Bible was bought May 10th, A.D. 1683, by William Saxby of the parish of Lingfield in the county of Surrey, Esquire, for the use and benefitt of all good Christians. To remain and continue in the pew he now sitteth in, in the Church of the parish aforesaid." It is possible that such minor gifts as this to the church caused the following satire to be written by Bishop Hall:—

> Whoever gives a paire of velvet shoes
> To th' Holy Rood, or liberally allows
> But a new rope to ring the couvre-feu bell,
> But he desires that his great deed may dwell,
> Or graven in the chancel window glass,
> Or in his lasting tombe of plated brasse.

On a reading-desk not far away was also another chained Bible (black lettered), dated 1603, one of the editions published by Miles Coverdale. This, besides being chained to the desk, was further protected by a cage of brass net-work set over it, so that the modern pilgrim could not even read more than the pages that chanced to lie opened before him. This net-work, we were informed, was absolutely needful to protect the book from the modern vandal, who comes not to read or worship—but to collect. Such a pertinent comment upon changed times needs no emphasis of mine: the Bible of old was chained for fear religiously-minded folk should steal it wholly (a strange thing for such people to do, it always seems to me), now it has to be guarded from the irreligious thief! A distinction with a difference!

Then our conductor led us to the vestry, where he showed us the Registry commencing in 1559, and from that time down to about 1600 we noted that the entries were most carefully made, then they became inexcusably and markedly careless, and from 1653 to 1663 there is a notable void. After 1663 the entries became carefully written in detail again, and continue so to the present day. We were also shown the chalice that, we were informed, was exactly 322 years old when we saw it. And then we took our departure.

On to Crowhurst the country was pretty, though without any special features. Immediately opposite the churchyard gates there, our eyes rested upon a charming old home, having a jumble of red gables, big chimneys, and high-pitched, moss-encrusted roof, with mullioned windows of leaden lattice lights, whose numberless diamond panes sparkled cheerfully in the sun. In the garden between the highway and the house were big box hedges and quaintly-clipped yew trees, that gave the place quite an old-world look. It was a picture worth a long drive to see. This old house, as we afterwards found out, was merely a portion of a former mansion, a relic of one of those ancient and pleasant English homes of good, though not wealthy, families that one may come upon now and again standing in a friendly fashion by the roadside, and not isolated in a park out of sight.

Before entering the churchyard we hunted up the clerk, and found him clad in a smock-frock (the only one we saw during the journey, and looking strangely out of place on a clerk), and he wore, besides, thick hob-nail boots. He appeared to combine the offices of clerk, grave-digger, and farm-labourer.

In the porch of the church we observed a written list of the objects of interest within the sacred edifice, and round about in the locality. This was something of a novelty to us, and was all the more surprising as, one would imagine, but few strangers or tourists would find their way to this remote hamlet. The following is a copy of the paper:—

OBJECTS OF INTEREST IN THE PARISH OF CROWHURST

The church dedicated to St. George is mentioned in the Valor of Edward I. 1304. In the middle aisle is buried Richard Cholmley, Cup Bearer to King James and Charles I.

The yew tree is supposed to be the oldest living yew tree in England. It is mentioned by Aubrey, an Historian in the reign of Charles I., as measuring in his time ten yards round, three feet from the ground : its present girth is about thirty-three feet. Humbolt, in the *Aspects of Nature*, mentions this tree, and states its age, on the authority of Decondelle, to be 1450 years.

The Crowhurst yew was hollowed out about 1820. In 1845 the upper branches were blown off by a great storm. . . . A cannon ball was found in the centre of the tree when hollowed out in 1820.

The house opposite the church is called the Mansion.

Crowhurst Place, an ancient moated house, was formerly inhabited by the family of Gainsford. Henry VIII. is said to have slept a night there on his way to visit Anne Boleyn at Hever Castle, about six miles distant.

Below the church is a spring mentioned by Aubrey, to which he attaches the tradition that it only rises at the approach of any great event in Church or State.

The interior of the church did not interest us much, except for the tombs of the Gainsfords, or Gaynesfords, as spelt on their brasses.

Then we went with the clerk to see the great and famous yew. A door opens from the massive trunk of this, and gives access to the interior, which has been so ruthlessly hollowed out. Stepping inside, we discovered low wooden seats fixed within the badly-treated tree, and the clerk told us there used to be a table in the centre also, and that upon one occasion fifteen people sat round it and dined there. Once they had a band to play in it. All of which seems rather out of keeping with the sacred surroundings. Feasting in a churchyard is surely a very incongruous proceeding, nor does band-playing therein seem much better! We were shown the cannon ball, but were unable to learn any reasonable explanation as to how it originally got where it was found. We suggested the inevitable Cromwell, but the clerk made no response to our remark. Perhaps he had never heard of Cromwell! You can hardly expect a church clerk in a smock-frock to be versed in history.

Taking note of the particulars about Crowhurst Place given in the notice on the church porch, we inquired our way thither, and forthwith went in search thereof. It would never do to miss an old moated manor made historic by a visit from "bluff King Hal." We found the house to be about a mile away, not far from the main road, perhaps a couple of hundred yards, but completely hidden therefrom by a thick clump of trees.

The finding of Crowhurst Place was one of the many delightful surprises of our journey. This was indeed a red letter day for us in the way of discoveries of interesting and picturesque relics of past days. I shall not readily forget the feeling of supreme delight I experienced upon the first vision of that ancient mansion with its wide weed-grown moat, great half-timber gables, gray and brown, and bent with age, mighty chimney-stacks, and humble old wooden bridge that crossed the water—old, but of a much later date than the main fabric. This view of Crowhurst is reproduced from my sketch herewith, and will give some idea of this charming old home, once a portion of the stately abode of the Gaynesfords, for, alas! a good deal of the original structure has disappeared; the rest now does duty as a farmstead. Fortunate farmer to have such a dwelling!

Crowhurst is a spot, both inside and out, to delight the heart of an antiquary as well as the eye of an artist. A glamour of the long ago seems to hang over its time-stained walls, a past presence seems to linger within its ancient panelled chambers.

We made bold to cross the foot-bridge, and knocking at the old oak door, begged permission to sketch and photograph the place; this we did with the ulterior purpose of feeling our way as to the possibility of obtaining a glance at the interior. It happened that the door opened directly into the kitchen. There was a brick-built bridge crossing the moat on the

A DECAYED MANSION—CROWHURST PLACE

further side of the house which gave approach to the front door, but at the time we had not discovered this. The maid who answered our summons, in reply to our query, said she would ask "the missus," and presently returned with a polite permission for us to sketch or photograph the house from wherever we liked, for which we returned many thanks.

So, feeling at liberty to wander where we would round about the exterior of the building, we set to work with sketch-book and camera, and made good use of our time. Presently the genial farmer himself appeared on the scene, manifestly taking an interest in our proceedings. There is, fortunately, something very attractive to the average man about a sketcher at work in the open. I say fortunately, for in some cases, like the present; we have found that if we sit down near a picturesque old home to make a sketch thereof, it generally leads to the owner, or one of his family, coming to interview us out of curiosity; this further leads to a few civil remarks, and frequently to a kind invitation to inspect the interior—not unfrequently to an interesting conversation, with refreshment thrown in! But, of course, much depends upon circumstances—and the sketcher. A pleasant manner opens doors and obtains countless little favours money never could buy. As Seneca says, "He that would make his travels delightful, must first make himself delightful." If you wish thoroughly to enjoy a driving tour, cultivate civility! It is a very cheap commodity, and we always lay in a goodly stock of it before we start forth on our excursions. *Verbum sat sapienti.*

Seeing the interest the farmer took in our proceedings, we endeavoured to take an interest in his farming, and sympathised with him on the bad times. "Whenever do you think that they will get better?" queried he, a trifle anxiously, we thought. Alas! that was a question we could not answer. Would that we could. The end of our conversation was an invitation indoors, "if you would really care to see the old place." Did we not! It was just what we desired at the moment above all. "I'm off to market directly," said he, "but I'll tell the wife to show you round; it's a queer old house." We thanked him profusely for his courtesy, and he bade us good day with a pleasant smile as he drove away. Worthy farmer, may your 'shadow never grow less!

Having finished our sketching and photographing, we elected to knock once more at the kitchen door to beg to see the interior of the house, on the strength of the farmer's invitation. We went to this door instead of the front one purposely because we desired to gain another glimpse of the grand old kitchen, the first peep of which had so charmed us, and it seemed that it could not matter much by which entrance we sought admission. We entered the kitchen and sat down therein whilst the maid went in search of her "missus." It was an ample apartment, with a pleasant-toned red-tiled or brick floor, and great smoke-browned beams above, such vast kitchens as they build not nowadays; it would, we roughly estimated, make at least three ordinary ones of the speculative builder's type. It had besides a huge fireplace of ample proportions to match. What a delightful sensation of spaciousness that old kitchen gave us, after the making the most of every inch of room, that prevails in modern town buildings and cheap country mansions, to say nothing of nineteenth-century villadom. I would far rather dwell in a grandly-built cottage than in a meanly-built mansion or "desirable villa"; a craving for external show is one of the curses of the age, a downward drifting to pretentiousness.

After a short wait the farmer's wife, adorned with "best bib and tucker," came forth to greet us, and kindly offered to show us over the house. First she took us to what she termed the sitting-room, another large apartment, with a delightful old-fashioned inglenook of ample dimensions; this had a quaint little window at the side, so that one might sit before the wood fire on the great hearth and view the country, at lazy ease the while. Here we noticed a comfortable easy-chair set ready, wherein doubtless the master of the house enjoys his last peaceful evening pipe and glass of grog whilst pondering on the prosperous days of the long ago, and wondering when, if ever, they will return. At the back of the hearth we observed a well-preserved specimen of an old Sussex iron fire-back, with the date 1667 thereon. There was oak panelling on the walls of this charming and homelike-looking chamber, which had some excellent and interesting old stained heraldic glass in the deeply-recessed leaden lattice window—a window that appeared to enclose space, not a mere void in the wall, that a big expanse of plate glass suggests. A portion of the stained glass, we were told, represented "the Gaynesford greyhound," that being the family crest. We also noticed there a fine specimen of a carved oak chest, which we were glad to find had escaped the collector's clutches. What an ideal and restful room it looked, at least to us; honestly old-fashioned, with plenty of space and much real comfort, but no pretence—not even an art paper on the walls, only simple panelling! This room once formed the lower portion of the hall, which reached up to the roof-trees of the house, but has been divided by a floor into two stories.

We were shown another delightful chamber on this floor, possessing a fine oak-beamed ceiling with planks between. Here again we have simple construction forming a pleasing decorative feature, vastly more suggestive of comfort and cosiness, as well as more interesting, than a mere vacuity of whitewash. In this room was some more stained heraldic glass, through which the bright noon sun shone, lighting up its ancient walls with a glory of burning reds and glowing yellows. We were tempted to copy some of this glass, on account of the spirited and effective drawing of the heraldic animals, which looked so amiably defiant, like some of the red or white lions that bid you a fierce welcome to your inn. Our hostess informed us that an antiquary (I think she said) who had seen the glass declared that it was all set, or leaded, wrong. How that may be, I cannot say, not being learned in all the precise formalities of heraldry, but I am certain all the glass was genuinely old, and to my inexperienced eyes looked "right" and well. Possibly the ancient families themselves were not so particular as to the precisely accurate display of their crests and coats of arms, according to the strict ideas of modern authorities on the subject, that is; just as certain notable men of to-day I could name, who are far less concerned as to the fashionable cut of their garments than many a city clerk.

Then we were conducted upstairs, and on the first landing we espied a delightfully quaint little stained glass window, the many diamond panes of which were decorated with the device of a grapnel— the badge of the Gaynesford family. According to old authorities (and possibly recent ones, but of this I am not certain) a family may invent for themselves a badge at pleasure, though not a crest or coat of arms. But what especially interested us in this window was the centre ornament, consisting of the Prince of Wales's feathers, with the motto "Hic Dien" below. It will be noticed that "Ich" is spelt "Hic." The feathers may have been introduced into this window to commemorate a visit from a Prince of Wales in the days long past when the old mansion was in the prime of its glory, though there is now no royal coat of arms to commemorate the visit of Henry VIII,—if ever he did stay here on his way to Hever; still they may have existed and been removed. It was a former fashion for the owners of grand mansions who had entertained royalty in their homes to proudly proclaim the fact in this manner, though the window generally chosen in which to introduce the arms of the royal guest was that of the chamber in which the august personage slept. There is a tradition that Queen Elizabeth during her many progresses graciously gave permission to have certain of her visits to noble houses thus to be memorialised, and so the fashion was started.

In one room upstairs we found some linen-pattern panelling very finely carved, and as sharply defined now as when it first left the skilled craftsman's hands —how many long years ago? Another chamber close by was panelled from floor to ceiling, and had a ribbed oak roof; here were the original doors still hanging on their original hinges, and with the ancient bolts and locks *in situ*, the iron-work being of excellent design. After this we reluctantly bade our worthy hostess and picturesque Crowhurst farewell.

Our last view of this interesting old home, that has fallen so greatly from its first estate, was a most poetic one ; the warm rays of the declining sun were tinging its weather-worn walls with a ruddy hue, causing deep gray, mysterious shadows to be thrown from gable, roof, and chimney, and converting the still water of the moat into glowing gold. We should have liked to linger longer there, but the day was drawing to its close, and we had yet some miles to traverse before reaching our inn.

CHAPTER VIII

An ancient home—A million years old!—Sussex lanes—Haste the curse of the century—Nature's cathedral—An Anglo-Saxon church—A curious font—Worth Forest—Balcombe—A Sussex tarn—Cuckfield—The charm of old country towns—The "doom tree"—A weird custom—An old-fashioned ghost—A poet's license.

LEAVING Crowhurst, we returned to Lingfield, and from thence proceeded back to East Grinstead again by a fresh line of country. On our way, just outside Lingfield, we came upon another very picturesque old home, standing close by the roadside, as though set there for the very purpose of being admired. This ancient house is, oddly enough, called "New Place," although the date inscribed over the porch is 1617, with the initials of G. T., presumably those of its first owner. The old house was once, however, new, and doubtless it was then termed "New Place," and so it has remained ever since. The arched stone doorway of this is finely carved, and the oak door itself is studded with great-headed nails, the roof is of stone slabs, and the walls of the building are buttressed up here and there.

Great care has manifestly been taken to preserve this charming old mansion, and the only inharmonious feature about it is that the ancient mullioned windows are filled in with very modern plate glass. Now, whatever else you may do, "you cannot put new wine into old bottles," in an architectural sense, without hurt. Just outside the great iron gate here, with its ball-surmounted piers, stands a "mounting block," with steps to assist ladies in getting on their horses, a good old-fashioned arrangement.

After this our road gradually rose till it brought us to a scattered and uninteresting village bearing the curious name of Dorman's Land. Now the country became hilly and woody, but as the scenery improved, our road, alas! not over-good, grew worse. A steep, rough descent, with glorious views ahead, led us into quite a forest-like land, through which we travelled for some distance; then the country became open again, and eventually we found ourselves once more at the comfortable "Dorset Arms" in East Grinstead, delighted with our day's wanderings and discoveries, and just sufficiently tired to enjoy the luxury of taking "our ease at our inn."

Next morning before continuing our journey we took a final stroll about the town, just to secure another pencil note or two of any architectural tit-bit we might discover. Whilst we were busily engaged sketching a quaint corner of an ancient building, a native of the place came up to us and appeared to take considerable interest in our proceedings. "That be an old house you be a-drafting of, sir, that it be," he exclaimed; "it be a million years old." This remark fairly took us aback, accustomed as we were to astonishing statements. "A million years old!" we repeated after him; "you must surely be mistaken." But we soon discovered that he meant what he said, and, by the tone of his reply, even appeared hurt that we should doubt his word. "No, I bain't mistook; I can show yer what I says is simple truth, I can, for it's cut on a stone right enough. Yonder it be, sure enough, up there," pointing to the date MDCXLIV engraved on a tablet set in the wall. "Now you see, sir, as how I told yer true. 'M' means a million, as you be aware; what the other letters after means I don't exactly know—something over a million, but I thinks as how a few years more bain't of much account when a house be as old as that." What reply could we make? We tried to look serious and interested whilst thanking the man for his information. It would have been useless to argue the point with him. Former experience has taught us that any attempt to set right a countryman's honest misstatements is labour lost; you cannot "convince a rustic against his will." The more ignorant he is, the more hopeless the task; there is no armour like ignorance. In this instance we had come upon a product of the pre-School Board era, and perhaps an example of the truth of the proverb that "a little learning is a dangerous thing." A very little in this case, truly. Such unsophisticated characters are growing scarce in the land, though by no means wholly extinct, and when met with are worthy of a passing note.

Out of East Grinstead our road was uninteresting until we came to the little hamlet of Felbridge, where we turned to the left, bidding adieu, without regret, to the dusty highway. We were bound eventually for Cuckfield, at which little mid-Sussex town we proposed to spend the night—that is, unless for any good reason or mere whim we chanced to change our mind *en route*, a very possible contingency. According to our usual custom, we had planned our probable day's wanderings overnight, after duly consulting our map and road-book, the latter being our faithful old friend " Paterson," published in the heyday of the coaching age, and the last (1829) edition of that useful work. Even in this Bradshaw of the road-traveller there is just one line pregnant of the coming change, that runs "cross the new iron-way."

We did not propose to drive by the most direct road, but, by taking a roundabout course, to explore some of the wild woodland country of the north of Sussex, and to pass, later on, through the heart of the ancient and still extensive forest of Worth—a delightfully picturesque and little-travelled district, that almost reaches the romantic in parts.

Leaving Felbridge, the country at once gave us a sample of its scenic capabilities, which were of no mean order. Coming to a pleasant common, bordered by big, branching, leafy chestnuts that cast a grateful shade around, our road dipped down to a large sheet of water, shown on our map as being about half a mile long by a quarter broad, though not dignified by a name therein, which its size appeared to merit. This quiet little mere, surrounded by rough, heathery wilds and shaggy woods, formed a very pleasing and notable feature in the landscape. It gave expression to it, as does the eye to the human face.

Then our winding road took us between more woods. It was all very lonely and very peaceful. Save for the companionable songs of birds the silence was profound, for not a leaf was stirring in the windless air. We met or saw no one on the way till we reached four cross roads at a spot marked as Copthorne on our map. Here was a lonely inn surrounded by fir trees, with a pool of water in front, and a sign-post that proclaimed it to be the "Duke's Head," but still not a soul was visible anywhere about; even the doors of the inn were shut. Those who have not travelled by road can hardly imagine how lonely some portions of densely-populated England are. The population cling to the railway; the present-time country dweller desires to be within easy reach of a station. Just as we pulled up here to consult our map, a bicyclist hove in sight and halted too. He had lost his way, he said, and used an unparliamentary expression about the "aimless windings" of the Sussex lanes. He was "short of time," he explained. We were not, which made all the difference. Indeed, we rather liked the many unexpected twistings and turnings of the sequestered by-ways, but then when we are in a hurry we take the train; for speed was the railway invented. Haste, however, formed no part of our programme; we set out to see the country, not to be rushed through it. "*La rapidité, voilà le rêve de notre siècle,*" remarks Theophile Gautier, feeling that speed was not everything in life, and that a leisurely existence had its special charms and forgotten advantages.

After crossing a wide, breezy common we dipped down into a country of deep, leafy woods. Our horizon for miles was suddenly limited to a few yards; trees bound our narrow road on either hand, their branches frequently meeting overhead and forming a bit of Nature's Gothic work—a long green aisle, with the trunks of the trees doing duty for pillars, and their branches for groined arches; and through the multitudinous leaves above, the softened sunshine shone, forming changeful patterns of green and gold around us, that made the glories of stained glass seem garish, crude, and unsatisfactory. Nature calls us

> To that cathedral, boundless as our wonder,
>   Whose quenchless lamps the sun and moon supply;
>   Its choir the winds and waves, its organ thunder,
>   Its dome the sky.

How can any "temple made with hands" compare with this? It is comparing the finite with the infinite!

Set in the midst of this green and treeful country, and standing upon a gentle knoll, is the very interesting Anglo-Saxon church of Worth, dear to the hearts of all archæologists and antiquaries. Though this ancient structure has suffered much in times past from alterations and restorations, it still possesses its original Saxon ground plan; the only other church in England that does this is, I believe, the very perfectly preserved one at Bradford-on-Avon in Wiltshire.

At Worth church there is a rude string course of stone, supported in places by pilasters, running partially round the exterior; doubtless this formerly went round the whole building. This horizontal string-course and perpendicular pilasters certainly and very forcibly suggests to me a repetition in stone of the chief features of timber-framing, such as possibly prevailed in the early wooden churches. Indeed, the term "stone carpentry" has been applied to this primitive style of building. The Saxons seem to have been but poor masons. In the north wall we observed with delight a very fine and well-preserved specimen of a Saxon window; it is of two lights, divided by a round stone shaft, increasing in size at its centre; this shaft is of a form more properly pertaining to wood, being suggestive of work turned in a lathe rather than cut with a chisel.

Within the church the massive circular chancel arch of roughly squared stones is strikingly effective. There is a certain barbaric grandeur about the crude solid Saxon masonry; it is substantial, simple, and strong, three excellent qualities, after all, in a building, and one must first learn to construct before thinking of decorating. Saxon work is impressive on account of its massiveness and manifest honesty of purpose, sometimes, indeed, almost reaching to dignity, as in the unique tower of Earls Barton church, Northants, which was erected six years previous to the Norman invasion; but in no case can it be considered beautiful or refined. In fact, during all periods of the world's history, buildings have ever expressed the spirit of the age, and the Saxon structures are a case in point. Show me the architecture of a people, and I will tell you what they were like!

The font at Worth is ancient and curious, being in reality one font placed directly upon another. The reason for this peculiar arrangement is not very apparent, and we could only conjecture that the ruder and more ancient font was made as a base to support the later one, simply because it was found to be suitable in shape and size for the purpose. Knowing the temper of the period, this reason seems sufficient to me; however, I understand it is a matter over which learned archæologists and antiquaries (I wish that there were one word to embrace the two!) love to argue, never, of course, coming to any decision, so that the luxury of a friendly dispute may be left open for ever and ever. Did I not once have to listen to a prolonged and grave discussion between two famed archæologists as to the exact date in which a very unimportant addition was made to an ancient building, conducted in such a serious way, that the fate of empires might have depended on the result! It is well, though, to be enthusiastic in this matter-of-fact age; it gives life an object and an interest! Besides, a cultivated argument is a refined art. Any savage can fight with mere weapons, but to win a victory in words needs centuries of civilisation and mind-training.

The only other points of interest within the

church are the pulpit, a fine specimen of German work, dated 1577, and, curiously enough, coming from Woerth, and an oak gallery of 1610, but these are comparatively of to-day; the real interest of the building is wholly Anglo-Saxon.

Next we turned our attention to the churchyard in search of quaint and old-world epitaphs, deeming it a not unlikely spot for such a quest. The very first tombstone we came to, just outside the porch, had some verses inscribed on it to the memory of one John Alcorn, a former "clerk and sexton of the parish," who died in 1868. These verses we deemed above the average of such literature, so we copied them as follows :—

> Time-honoured friend for fifty-three full years,
> He saw each Bridal's joy, each Burial's tears,
> Within the walls by Saxons reared of old,
> By the Stone-sculptured font of antique mould,
> Under the massive arches in the glow,
> Tinged by dyed sunbeams passing to and fro,
> A sentient portion of the sacred place,
> A worthy presence with a well-worn face.
>
> The lich-gate's shadow o'er his Pall at last
> Bids kind adieu as poor old John goes past,
> Unseen the path, the trees, the old oak door,
> No more his footfalls touch the tomb-paved floor,
> His silvery head is hid, his service done,
> Of all those Sabbaths absent only one.
> And now amid the graves he delved around
> He rests and sleeps beneath the hallowed ground.

Wandering amongst the ancient graves we noticed a monument with an inscription that ended thus :—

> Death set me free when God did please.
> I hope this change is for the best.

We thought the last line rather suggestive of a doubt. A tombstone to a baby bears the following ending to a verse :—

> Such babes as this are Christ's own flock.
> He calls them to increase His stock.

Still another tombstone has on one side the following lines :—

> Husband dear, pray think and see
> Your grave be dug along by me.

And on the other :—

> My dearest wife, the day is come and I am brought
> To lie by you ; it was my thought.

But enough of tombstone literature and versification. Let us away into the cheerful, sunlit country once more.

About a mile or so from Worth we found a sufficiently comfortable rural inn with stabling attached, whereat we made our mid-day halt.

On to Cuckfield we had a most delightful drive, the first three miles being right through the heart of Worth Forest and across what is known as the "Sussex Forest Ridge," a district that, even to this day, deserves the title, on account of the extensive tracts of wild woodlands it comprises. The land is poor, but, as a rule, the poorer the land the finer the scenery, and now that small timber-growing is more profitable than farming, there appears to be a chance of these wild wooded wastes remaining much as they now are, greatly to the delight of artists and of all lovers of natural beauty.

Up and down hill as we drove every now and

then an open glade in the forest would let a gleam of sunshine stream across the road, that otherwise was deep in gray-green shade. We noticed quite a variety of trees as we journeyed on; there were rugged oaks, darksome yews, and gloomy pines, that contrasted with the light and graceful silver birch and tall tapering firs. There were some grand old gnarled beeches too, that would have done credit to Buckinghamshire, that land of beech woods.

From the top of the hill above Balcombe we had a glorious bird's-eye prospect looking right over the forest, an ocean of greenery, that rose and fell with the undulations of the country, till it lost itself in the long level sea-like blue line of the far-away horizon. It was a spot in which to expand one's lungs—truly we felt that we could breathe up there. As we rested a while to enjoy the prospect, a faint musical murmur came up to us on the fragrant air; it was the slumberous rustling of the multitudinous leaves of the waving woods around—not unlike the distant swash, swash of the summer sea upon some sandy shore. Such sounds are eminently peace-bestowing; they are Nature's songs without words— songs that soothe the world-weary soul to rest, and are to be had by the poorest wanderer at the cost of merely listening.

The "Brighton Line" passes through this portion of Worth Forest—rather, perhaps I should say, beneath it—in a long tunnel, so that the unfortunate railway traveller never even gets a glance at all the leafy loveliness around; probably he is wholly unaware of its existence, and therefore of all the scenic revelations he misses.

Balcombe struck us as being a very pretty village, and the country around quite Devonian in character, with its hills and dales so happily diversified by wood, and rock, and water. Low down at the base of the hills, embowered in foliage, we espied the silvery gleam of an extensive and irregular-shaped sheet of still water, large enough almost to deserve the term of lake. Balcombe manifestly derives its name from the Anglo-Saxon cumb, or combe, a valley; indeed, we were struck by the likeness this spot bore to a typical Devonshire combe.

Pulling up here, we dismounted, and set off, armed with sketch-book and camera, in search of the little mere; fortunately we at once struck upon a pleasant footpath on the sloping ground that led us thither, though by rather a devious way. This charming spot, hidden from the outer world by envious hills, we found to be marked on our map simply as "Balcombe Pond." It is quite as large and fully as picturesque (though not, of course, so grand) as some of the Lake District tarns, and I think it really merits a more romantic title than "Pond." Indeed, its title is the only unlovely thing about it; and, let cynics say what they may, there is a good deal of virtue in a name; to set off on a long tramp to see a lake, a tarn, or a llyn is more inspiriting surely than starting forth to view a pond!

We set to work and made a sketch of the lovely lakelet from its reed-bordered and tree-grown banks, looking over to the wooded hills beyond, all goldentinted in the setting sun, with the cattle, as is their wont at evening time, cooling themselves in its limpid waters; and a friend, to whom we showed it, thought our sketch was meant for a bit of Windermere; nor would he be convinced by words or drawing that Sussex had anything so fair to show. Alas! I am afraid that there are a goodly host of Englishmen like my friend, who know hardly anything of the rural beauties of their own land beyond the usual tourist-haunted districts, half ruined by the fatal gift of fame.

Leaving Balcombe reluctantly, we drove down a lovely, tree-girt, sequestered valley, from which, to our right and left, rose gently-sloping hills, dotted here and there with time-mellowed farmsteads and lowly cottage homes, reached by winding roads and climbing footpaths. Again we were reminded distinctly of fair Devon, and had we been taken blindfolded thither and been asked suddenly to name the county from the scenery, we should at once and unhesitatingly have declared it to be Devonshire.

Reaching the foot of the narrow glen, we found that the country once more opened out, and to our left we caught sight of the long Balcombe Viaduct by which the railway crosses at a great height the wide, well-wooded, and watered valley below. For once we were fain to confess that the iron road had added an interesting and picturesque feature to the landscape, a rare thing for it to do truly, so rare, indeed, that we made a special note thereof. Seen as we saw it in the gathering gloom, this fine structure suggested more the work of the ancient Roman builder than of the nineteenth-century engineer, seeking only to fulfil modern and pressing needs in the cheapest way, which is, we are informed by an American authority (Ashbel Welch, to wit), the very essence of good engineering.

Then as we proceeded, before us rose the fir-fringed hills on which the little town of Cuckfield is situated, the setting sun burning a ruddy glow in the west, causing the dark green trees to stand out strongly silhouetted against the luminous sky. We had a long climb up this hill to our night's destination, and pulling up at the "King's Head," found there a ready welcome. In the coffee room of our inn we discovered what appeared to be a newly-married couple alone, and not wishing to disturb their serenity, for once we indulged in a private sitting-room, where a blazing wood fire (for the evening was chilly) gave us a cheery reception.

Next morning, in the course of an early pre-breakfast perambulation, we discovered Cuckfield to be a very pleasant and honestly old-fashioned little town, unblessed with a railway, and delightfully and picturesquely unprogressive. So much did the place impress us, so satisfied were we with our quiet quarters, and so attracted with the scenery around, as far as we had seen it, that we determined to repeat our East Grinstead experiment, to stop over the day at Cuckfield and devote it to exploring the neighbourhood.

Exactly why is it, I wonder, that these old country towns, when they have happily escaped the hands of the modern builder, are so interesting and eye-pleasing, and what an artist would term so "paintable"; and modern towns, or old towns modernised (which comes to much the same thing), are in the main so intensely uninteresting when not actually aggressively ugly? The mellowing hand of age, and the past associations that have grown around their old houses with their weather-tinted walls, have truly something to do with the matter; for a house that has made its history must of necessity appeal far more to our feelings than a new building that has its history to make. Sentiment is a considerable factor in the case, but it is not all; time may tone down the harsher features of an ugly building, but it cannot make it beautiful. I take it that a great deal of the charm of our old unmodernised country towns lies in the varied and picturesque forms of their ancient buildings, and the special character and individuality they each display, whilst our nineteenth-century structures are generally so featureless, or else, going to the other extreme, strive so manifestly to be picturesque, that the eye at once perceives it is not a natural outcome but a purely artificial product, and so these unrestful and assertive buildings fail to give pleasure; they are architectural frauds.

Old work is rarely commonplace; it may be faulty in one way or another, but it seldom fails to interest or to claim our regard. What delightful pictures the old coaching inns make! What could an artist do with a modern hotel—even an artist of a century hence? Men of the past built their homes as best pleased them, not as some one else thought they should be built, nor for changeful fashion's sake; oftentimes they were compelled to be their own architects, but it must ever be borne in mind that they had skilful masons, carpenters, and carvers to work for them, men who were art-craftsmen and rejoiced in their work. Everything then was not sacrificed to cheapness; steam and machinery did not compete with flesh and blood; men who had original ideas had a chance of expressing them; now we have only workmen and mechanics, men who can build a plain wall well and truly, but with few ideas beyond; and mechanics who are practically human machines. What interest can such men take in their work, mostly done by contract? Art comes not so! Can they give us

> The stone that breathes and struggles,
> The brass that seems to speak,

or the quaint conceits of the ancient craftsman? I wot not! The artistic and refined artisan has, alas! departed with the sturdy yeoman and thrifty peasant proprietor; and whilst the healthful country is being depopulated, our manufacturing towns are being over-crowded, big fortunes are being made on one hand, and big workhouses arise on the other, and who can say that " All is well "?

Cuckfield abounds in ancient and picturesque old houses. One known as " Ockenden," erected in 1650, especially charmed us on account of its restful, homelike look and unobtrusive picturesqueness; it seemed to us almost an ideal country home of the modest type, yet withal a home in which a duke or a millionaire might dwell and not be ashamed. We appear to have totally lost the art of building modestly yet grandly. Many an old English farmhouse, and even cottage, I know of are so well designed and built as to put to utter shame the average modern mansion, for they possess a dignity of their own that comes of good proportion and substantial building. At "Ockenden" in the seventeenth century lived Timothy Burrell, who is known as "The Pepys of Sussex," from the very interesting diary that he kept, which throws a curious side-light on the manners and doings of the time, and is quaintly illustrative of the social life that prevailed in England then.

There are many other old houses in the clean little town that also delighted us, but the chief point of interest at Cuckfield is the ancient mansion of the Sergisons, known as "Cuckfield Place," situated in a large and well-timbered park close by. The house is approached from the main road by a fine and flourishing avenue of limes, at the end of which is a gray old gateway tower, that has to be passed before the entrance is reached. This tower gives quite a quaint feature to the approach. The avenue contains a historic relic known as the "Doom Tree," which tradition asserts drops a branch just before a member of the family dies. Cuckfield Place is the original of "Rookwood" in Harrison Ainsworth's romance of that name. Thus he alludes to it in the preface: "The supernatural occurrence which I have made the harbinger of doom to the house of Rookwood is ascribed by popular superstition to a family resident in Sussex, upon whose estate the fatal tree (a gigantic lime with mighty arms and huge girth of trunk) is still carefully preserved. Cuckfield Place, to which this singular piece of timber is attached, is, I may state, the real Rookwood Hall; for I have not drawn upon imagination in describing the seat and domains of that fated family." Besides this, to add to the gruesomeness of the tradition, it was the time-honoured custom of the Sergison family to be buried at midnight. Precisely at that hour the funeral procession, with torch-lights, left the gatehouse in solemn silence, and with slow steps wound its way to Cuckfield church. A weird proceeding truly!

Cuckfield Place too has the honour of being haunted with a good old-fashioned ghost in the shape of a blue lady, who does not confine herself to one chamber, but takes "the run of the house," going where she listeth from midnight to cock-crowing. But as we saw the time-toned mansion on that bright sunny morning, it looked anything but a gloomy or a haunted abode. However, one should view such places in the subdued gloaming or in the mystic moonlight to be in accord with the old-world legends that have gathered round their time-worn walls, as Scott advised people to visit "fair Melrose," though he confessed to a brother poet, Bernard Barton, that he had never "gone a bat-hunting to see the ruins himself," and added in verse:—

> Then go and meditate with awe
> On scenes the author never saw,

Who never wandered by the moon
To see what could be seen by noon.

Well, I suppose poets and painters are allowed a certain amount of license. Scott wrote, and Turner painted poems, but both romanced considerably; and romancing is an art; any one can accumulate facts!

Acting upon our decision, after a morning's very profitable sketching and photographing round about Cuckfield we started forth in the early afternoon upon an exploration of the neighbourhood. We had heard that there was an interesting and quaint old manor-house called East Mascalls some five or six miles away, and we determined to drive thither and inspect it. We found by our map that we could get there by one line of country, returning by another, so as not to repeat our road—always a point of consideration with us.

CHAPTER IX

Haywards Heath—Scaynes Hill—East Mascalls—A ruined manor-house—An ideal village—A picturesque home—Motto over doorway—Chat with a miller—Sussex names—A quaint brass and an interesting tomb—Old helmets—Ruins of Slaugham Place—An estate extending from London to the Channel—A long parish.

FROM Cuckfield we drove first to Haywards Heath, along a level road that took us on high ground, affording extensive views to the right of the sunlit Downs, and to the left over a pleasantly wooded country. We noticed that the footpath running alongside of the highway was in parts roughly paved with stone slabs in like manner to the Derbyshire ones. Many of these stones showed markings resembling "the ribbed sea-sand," and on nearer inspection we imagined them to have been originally formed by ancient waves washing on an ancient sandy shore countless centuries ago. It interested us to trace the markings of the prehistoric seas thus strangely preserved to us by the stratification of old ocean beds; even we fondly imagined that we could faintly make out certain slight tracks that might have been left by crawling crabs or other marine creatures of a species ages ago extinct. So we discovered romance by the roadside and history told in stone to the learned geologist as plainly to be read as any printed page.

Arriving at Haywards Heath, in the good old times a wild waste and a favourite rendezvous of the highwaymen, we found it to be now quite a little town of recent growth, and wholly uninteresting. Haywards Heath stands on high ground, and from the roadway a little to the left of the church is to be had a truly magnificent view looking down upon and over the green Weald of Sussex. I forget now how many church steeples we counted peeping above the spreading woods, and distant hamlets we noted, half drowned in foliage, but revealed by their blue films of uprising smoke. By the way, it is a notable fact that in the wooded parts of Sussex the churches will be found almost invariably to be built with steeples, whilst in the South Downs and more open districts simple square, and often somewhat squat, towers prevail. This would seem to suggest that the medieval builder sought to proclaim his structure in the low woodland districts by a tall steeple that should lift itself above the level of the country, whilst elsewhere in Sussex a tower was deemed sufficient. This is pure conjecture on my part, but whatever the reason, the fact remains.

A pleasant drive through a delightfully pretty and undulating country brought us to Scaynes Hill, a desolate-looking spot with a lonely inn, from which there is a fine view of the Sussex hills; a prospect more suggestive of a Scotch moorland than a portion of a southern county. From here we inquired our way to East Mascalls, and had considerable difficulty in finding it, as the place was not marked on our map and the directions we received were somewhat confused. Sussex lanes, moreover, are as winding, as endless, and as puzzling as ever are those of Devonshire, in spite of their superior fame in this respect; indeed, of the two I honestly consider that Sussex lanes bear the palm for bewildering wanderings. "It is a long lane that has no turning," truly, but what I complain of in the Sussex lanes is that they consist of nothing but turnings!

One man, of whom we inquired our way, incidentally remarked that he had "left America an hour ago." This casual and unsought-for information by no means impressed us with the reliability of his directions; in truth, at first we concluded that he must be an escaped inmate of the Lunatic Asylum — there is a huge one at Haywards Heath, a prominent eye-sore in the lovely landscape for miles around. We afterwards, however, discovered in the course of conversation a reasonable explanation for the extraordinary statement. It appears that there is a little colony of cottages, each having an allotment of an acre for cultivation, established in the ancient wilds near Haywards Heath, and that this colony goes by the name of America. These cottages, together with the land, are let for half-a-crown a week, the whole thing being the scheme of a philanthropic Quaker, who planned and started the colony last century.

At length, after much pleasant wandering along

narrow, hedge-bound, and tree-bordered lanes, we eventually reached the ancient manor-house of East Mascalls, originally built by a family of that name in the sixteenth century. This we found to be in a state of most picturesque ruin, fast hastening, alas! to further decay. It was a sad sight to see such a quaint old home falling, I might almost say, to pieces before our very eyes. Ivy—that ruin-loving creeper—had claimed it for its own. East Mascalls is, or was? a long, low, two-storied structure of half-timber; some of the timber framing was of a curiously curved shape; though structurally of wrong form, the bent wood beams were very effective, and gave the house a special character of its own.

When we were there a man was at work removing some of the falling timbers—better, we thought, to have preserved the house before it came to that. To our questionings he exclaimed, "You see, sir, as how the timbers might fall down and hurt the sheep," for these rambled in and out of its tenantless chambers without let or hindrance, save for a few broken hurdles, which they heeded not. "Of course the sheep might get hurt," we said; "how silly of us not to think of such a thing." This was spoken ironically, but our sarcasm was wasted. Destruction of any kind seems to delight the heart of the English labourer. Remarked a large contractor to me once, "In building up I would prefer to employ foreigners, but at pulling down anything, an English labourer beats the world," and this was said quite seriously. Save for this man and the harmless sheep all was silent and deserted; it seemed the very conception of Hood's "Haunted House."

> No human figure stirr'd to go or come,
> No face looked forth from shut or open casement;
> No chimney smoked—there was no sign of home
> From parapet to basement.
>
> With shatter'd panes the grassy court was starr'd:
> The time-worn coping-stone had tumbled after;
> And thro' the ragged roof the sky shone, barr'd
> With naked beam and rafter.
>
> The flow'r grew wild and rankly as the weed,
> Roses with thistles struggled for espial,
> And vagrant plants of parasitic breed
> Had overgrown the Dial.

After having spent a long time in admiring this picturesque relic of past days we set to work to make a sketch of it, a love task, and we felt what an excellent "motive" the deserted old building would make for a painting of a Haunted House. Our sketch is engraved herewith in order to preserve some slight record of a vanishing home.

East Mascalls is built in the form of the capital letter E. The custom of building houses thus prevailed amongst many of the noble and wealthy country families in the days of Queen Elizabeth, out of flattery to that sovereign; but the fashion was first set in the reign of Henry VIII., when many a country mansion was built in the form of an H, as a similar compliment.

We found the interior of East Mascalls to be even in a more ruinous plight than its exterior suggested: the floors were either worm-eaten or gone to dry-rot, in parts merely the black oak

A RUINED MANOR-HOUSE—EAST MASCALLS

beams, stretching from wall to wall, remained; it was actually unsafe to walk about. I never saw a more pathetic picture of hopeless decay. One structural feature about the old building struck us as novel—at least we had never observed such an arrangement before (perhaps because few houses are in such a state of decay as to so plainly reveal their skeleton plan)—the chimney-stacks are all external; yet in one fine chamber, presumably the hall, the ample fire-place is in the centre of the house; the flue from this communicates with the external chimney by means of an arch, and beneath this arch runs a passage by the outer wall, cunningly devised. I suppose, as was the method of the period, and for long time afterwards, a man must have been sent to climb up that chimney to sweep it, but how he managed to negotiate that arch was a problem we could not solve.

Leaving East Mascalls, we drove back by a different and lower road. In about a couple of miles we noticed another very picturesque home to our right, across some fields. This proved to be a farmhouse, though it appeared to us to have originally been a place of more importance; there was a small sheet of water in front of it, with a tiny wood-grown island to match. This old house made almost as pretty a picture as East Mascalls. We saw a big fish in the water, probably a pike. It has always been a mystery to me how, when not purposely placed there, the various kinds of fish find their way into sundry solitary pools, farmhouse ponds, and old moats. I was once present when a farmhouse pond was being cleaned out. It was a good two miles from any other water, and three huge fish were discovered floundering in the mud at the bottom when the pond was drained dry—a mighty pike, a fat chub, and a big roach, I think they were. The farmer had lived there all his life, and from what I could gather from him, no one had ever been known to stock that pond; the most plausible explanation I can give of the mystery is that probably fish spawn is sometimes carried by birds to distant spots.

In another mile or so our road opened out to a pleasant and wide common, bounded on three sides by field, trees, or woodlands; on the third was a pretty pond, round which were grouped some picturesque cottage homes, with their gardens sloping down to the water's bank; this was the beginning of the charming village of Lindfield, as pleasant and as picturesque a spot of its kind as may be found in all England, that land of pretty villages. From the pond a wide road, lined with old-fashioned houses—clean and neat every one, some even quaint—leads up to the ancient church, with its silvery gray shingle spire. The houses were of all periods, dating downward from the sixteenth century to the present; some, we noticed, were roofed with stone slabs, some with slates, others with tiles; some were built of stone, some of brick, many were of half-timber and plaster; one or two had rough-cast walls, and a few were of timber simply boarded from the weather, a variety of material very delightful to the eye not given to love too much uniformity, and rejoicing in changeful form and colour.

There were trees planted on either side of the road dotted along the grassy margin between it and the footpaths, forming a rural boulevard, and giving somewhat of a continental flavour to the little English village. It is strange, with the inherent love of nature the average Englishman possesses, that we so seldom trouble to adorn our streets with trees. Londoners appear to prefer smoke-stained statues to the fresh green and grateful shade of foliage. Why cannot we honour our great men and heroes by naming our chief thoroughfares after them, and making pleasant the city's highways with woody avenues, placing seats here and there for the tired wanderer? Some of the Lindfield cottages, and even shops, rejoiced in little gardens, gay and sweet-scented with colourful flowers, each enclosed by a wooden railing. One half-timbered building, with a projecting upper story, had roses, clematis, and honeysuckle climbing and spreading over its gabled front; the approach to it was across one of the pretty gardens described, and this was the shop of the "Dairyman and Poulterer." Even the butcher's shop standing beneath a spreading lime tree seemed almost tempting. Happy housewife, thought we, to have to do her marketing under such pleasant conditions. We even felt compelled to stop and make a sketch of the "Dairyman's" shop, it was so picturesque.

The village hostel too, boasting the title of the "Brent Arms," was in accord with its surroundings, and through the wide-open doorway thereof we caught a peep of a green and sunlit garden beyond. So cool, clean, and inviting looked the little inn, that we needed no excuse to stop and "try the tap." A draught of clear, nut-brown ale is a thing not to be despised by the thirsty wayfarer, and this you can generally get good anywhere in rural England; moreover it is a safer drink than water, which, unboiled, unless you are certain of its purity, may not be free from danger.

Duly refreshed, and after a chat with the civil landlord, for which no charge was made, we continued our explorations of the place. Approaching the church, the parsonage is worth a glance; the churchyard is raised on a wall well above the roadway; a tombstone stands there about on a level with the eye, and greets every passer-by thus :—

> Lo! here I lie with my two babes,
> All covered with cold clay.

This mournful statement stares you in the face, so that you cannot help noting it. I think if I lived in Lindfield that tombstone would prove intensely irritating to me in time. When I want to read epitaphs I like to go into churchyards for the purpose, but I do object to have them forced upon me when not in the proper mood; then I resent their trite moralising, and they also fail to raise my sympathy.

Just beyond the churchyard we were delightfully surprised by coming wholly unexpectedly upon a most picturesquely charming and interesting house some part old and some part modern, but the new portion has been built in such loving imitation of the old, that the harmony is complete. From chimney to basement the house is a picture: old forms of English architecture have been faithfully adhered to, even in the smallest details, and the happy result shows that it is not age alone that gives to many an ancient building its beauty, for here we have it in a modern one! A date stone set in the end of a quaint gable bears inscribed upon it: C. E. K. Hoc Opus f.f. Anno Dni MDCCCXCI. The house is appropriately surrounded by a formal garden, with prim walks, clipped trees, beds of old-fashioned flowers, terraces, espaliers, bowling-green, sun-dial, pigeon-cote, and all that goes to make a real old garden so delightful to wander in, and so pleasant to look upon.

Permission was most kindly granted us to make a sketch of the house, which is known as Old Place, and for this purpose we were allowed access to the garden. Whilst strolling about in order to obtain the best point of view for our drawing (there were so many good points of view that the best one was difficult to decide upon) we found our way to the summer-house, and discovered placed away there what appeared to be a disused sign-board of some old hostelry, having a pelican painted on one side, and on the other this legend :—

<blockquote>
Fille the cup
And fille the can
Atte the signe
Of ye Pelican.
</blockquote>

The pelican is a rare sign nowadays, though

once it was held in much esteem by inn-keepers. Why it has so fallen out of favour I cannot say. Can it possibly be, I wonder, because it so readily lends itself to ill-natured jests about the size or length of its bill? The following, amongst other similar effusions, was written by a witty guest of a certain old coaching inn bearing the title of the Pelican, and erst renowned all along the road, and deservedly so, for the excellence of its dinners, as well as for the heaviness of its charges :—

> The famous inn at . . .
> That stands below the hill,
> May well be called the Pelican
> From its enormous bill.

Upon the stone lintel over the doorway of Old Place is inscribed :—

> Porta patens esto
> Nvlli clavdaris·honesto,

which admits of a double meaning. This inscription was, I believe, originally engraved on the arch of the gatehouse of Cleeve Abbey in Somerset, and may still be found there.

A little below Old Place the pleasant village of Lindfield ends at a spot where a branch of the Sussex Ouse is crossed by an old stone bridge ; just above this is an old water-mill, that makes a pretty picture, and we spent a short time in making a sketch of it, and a long time in chatting with the worthy miller —and owner, from what we gathered from our conversation. He showed us all over the mill, and took a great deal of trouble to explain the working thereof. His father, he said, had a *wind*-mill, much emphasis being placed on the word wind, but he preferred a *water*-mill, for you never know when the wind will blow, and oftentimes his father had to be up all night, to make up for lost time, on account of a breezeless day. " You mayn't hardly credit it, sir, but in the summer time it seems somehow to blow mostly o'nights, and to be quiet o'days. You see, a man who has to make his living out of a wind-mill has to consider the weather a good deal, and I think he gets to know more about it than any one else. Now with water power you may run a little short o'times, but you can generally manage to do your work by daylight and get a rest o'nights. Now, sir, take my advice, should you ever go in for milling, you mind and go in for water," and we promised him that we would. And who shall say that one does not pick up much miscellaneous information during the even progress of a driving tour?

Then we returned to Cuckfield by another road, leaving Haywards Heath on the high ground above us to our left; thence we drove on through a hilly, wooded country, with nothing of special interest to attract our attention on the way, though the landscape on either hand abounded in great natural beauty of a restful order. But we had seen enough to interest us during our day's rovings, and were almost glad that the quiet stretch of country we were passing through had nothing exciting about it, so that we could indulge in the luxury of a little day-dreaming.

I have already remarked upon the difficulty of

pronouncing Sussex names aright from their spelling; thus Cuckfield is called locally *Cook*field, and we found afterwards the name of the town spelt in the latter way in an ancient engraving of the place; possibly, therefore, it is the way of spelling Sussex names that has changed, whilst the old pronunciation remains unaltered. So it was on leaving Cuckfield, when we asked the right road out of the town to Slaugham we failed to make ourselves readily understood. "I've never heard of any place of that name aboot here," replied the man; then, after a pause, he exclaimed, "Maybe it's Slap'em you means." We accepted the correction gratefully; it was something to be in the position of asking our way, farther on, with the possibility of being comprehended!

It was a glorious morning, the one on which we left Cuckfield; great white clouds shaded with tenderest gray were slowly sailing across the light blue sky overhead; a delightfully azure blue, not the deep, dark ultramarine of Italy, which, in my opinion, is not half so ethereal or beautiful, though by some strange perversity British poets persist in singing its praises. Curiously enough, it has been left for American writers to discover the loveliness that lies in the soft blue of English skies. Great, surely, is the fascination of the far-away? We were bound that day for a short stage to Horsham, by way of Slaugham. Our road at first led us along a high ridge of ground with wide views to the right over a wealth of Sussex woodlands, bounded by rounded hills, and alternately brightened by gleams of sunshine, and raked by gray cloud shadows; the play of light and shade gave a feeling of restful motion, for there was movement without any disturbing sound.

Staplefield was the first place we came to on the road, a picturesque hamlet scattered irregularly around a wide bit of rough green, though not too rough for village cricket, we noticed. What a delightful feature in rural life are these Sussex commons, mostly of ample size, and what perfect playgrounds they make for the cotter's youngsters! how they contrast with the crowded, dusty, or muddy streets and narrow slums that the working man's children of our large cities have to play in! Would that every hamlet had its green ; the strength and wealth of a nation lies in its health, and these commons are helpful to produce a sturdy race.

Our way now became a narrow lane with high hedges at the sides, that provokingly shut out the view ; then in a short time we reached the village of Slaugham, where we pulled up at the "Old White Horse," with the object of starting forth on foot to see, and possibly sketch, the ruins of Slaugham Place, once the stately abode of the Coverts. The landlord of the inn kindly pointed out the way, but strongly recommended us first to inspect the church, of which he had the key, and forthwith went to get it. Now it is—to me at any rate—a somewhat rare experience to be pressed to go to church by a licensed victualler ; so rare, indeed, that I felt it would be ungracious to refuse such a novel invitation, although it was not for worship that he desired us to go, but for curiosity; at least he told us that was the reason why people visited the building—on week days.

The church proved interesting on account of the brasses and tombs to various members of the Covert family therein. A brass, now fixed on the wall, represents a knight in armour with his head resting upon a tilting helmet; this bears the date of 1506. Another and a very curious brass of 1547 is to a Richard Covert and his three wives; in this Richard Covert is shown as standing up in his coffin, gazing at the figure of our Lord rising from His sepulchre. But the chief monument is a stately one of carved stone (that gives evidence of having been the work of skilful Italian sculptors), with the kneeling figure of one of the male Coverts and (apparently) his two wives, seven sons, and seven daughters. This monument simply has the initials of the family inscribed upon it, with the date 1579. What, however, chiefly interested us in this fine monument was not the sculptured figures (interesting though these were on account of the manifestly correct, careful, and artistic rendering of the picturesque dresses of the period), but the three ancient helmets of the Coverts hanging on iron brackets above the tomb, two of them still having the family crest—a leopard's head — on the top. The helmets were further adorned with modern cobwebs, and we noticed a solitary gauntlet keeping them armoured company, rusting, and half rusted, away. I am no relic worshipper, but I liked to see those old helmets and that one grim worn gauntlet; they seemed suddenly to bridge over the centuries gone, and to make the past more real!

Wandering round the old church we noticed an old jar securely built into a niche, apparently made to receive it, on the vestry wall; this jar, or urn, doubtless has a history, had we been enabled to fathom it; also on the floor there, an ancient iron muniment chest. As we were about leaving the building we observed, hanging on the inside wall of the tower, and close to the porch, what struck us as a very gruesome notice-board, being nothing less than a careful plan of the churchyard, with all the grave spaces shown and the names plainly written upon them of the people buried there. Somehow this would suggest to us a plan of seats of some theatre, so small a step is there in life from the serious to the gay; just as some quaint or punning epitaph seems to rob death, for the moment, of half its terror and all its solemnity.

It was a pleasant change, interesting though the interior of the church was, to get outside into the bright and cheerful sunshine once more. The ancient church showed from its exterior something of its long life's history, not only in its weather-stained walls and changeful architecture, but also from its varied roofing. The steeple was of oak shingles, that had taken on themselves a soft silvery tint very delightful to the eye; other portions of the building were covered with thin slabs of stone, also toned a mellow gray with age and wear of weather; then there were red tiles and, alas! blue slates, the ugliest roofing material in the world, I verily believe, always excepting that most abominable invention (artistically considered) of modern times—corrugated iron. Amongst the tombs in the churchyard we noticed a monument to "Catherine, sister of Vice-Admiral Horatio, Lord Nelson, K.B."

A pleasant footpath from the churchyard that led across some fresh green meadows took us to the ruins of Slaugham Place, which were plainly visible in the wooded valley below, as well as a large sheet of sunlit water near by. It was a pleasant prospect we looked down upon, a ready-made picture such as an artist might have composed: a happy combination of gray ruins, leafy woods, and gently sloping hills, enlivened by the sparkle of tranquil water. A peaceful prospect too, with nothing but the songs of birds to break upon its old-world serenity. An American gentleman once remarked to me, "I would give anything if we could only have a *genuine* old ruined abbey or feudal castle on our side of the Atlantic, with a regular history and the usual crop of crusted traditions." Even ruins have a value, as the managers of the railways that convey tourists to Tintern and other ancient abbeys and castles full well know. Many a good inn lives and prospers on a ruin. Why, when we arrived at our hotel at Arundel our first greeting was, "It's straight up the hill to the castle keep, sir," as though we had come there especially to see that and nothing else, and that we must needs see it at once! In very truth, it seemed to us that the boots was struck at our perfect indifference and our innocent remark that we "supposed the keep would be there next morning, unless an earthquake should knock it down meanwhile." We dislike old historic ruins being turned into peep-shows and besieged by tripper-haunted crowds, who but too effectually put a stop to all quiet romancing.

The ruins of Slaugham Place, though extensive and full of interest, are fortunately not far-famed, nor in the route of the travelling crowd, for they happily stand in a remote valley well away from the tripper-bringing railway. The great extent of the ruins attests the former magnificence of the old home of the Coverts; the mansion proper is surrounded by about three acres of ground, which, in its turn, was bounded by defensive walls with a tower at each corner; round about the foot of the walls ran a deep, wide moat, thus forming a well-fortified residence, fitted to resist a sudden attack, if not a regular siege. It is a notable fact that this house should be so constructed, when such precautions for safety were really no longer needful; the architect thereof manifestly could not escape wholly from past traditions; and thus old forms linger on that have long survived their functions, as witness, in a modified degree, the church towers that still are built with battlements surmounting them, a relic of the ancient feudal keep, and properly pertaining thereto, but scarcely suitable, or in harmony with, a purely peaceful edifice. The motto of the Coverts well might have been, "Every Englishman's house is his castle," at any rate their architect must have been imbued with that idea, and upon that he appears to have modelled his building.

Slaugham Place is now in so ruinous a state that even an approximate conception of the original plan of the house can only be guessed at. The crumbling archways, pillars, and windows that remain show that the mansion was in the Renaissance Classical style, so greatly in vogue amongst the wealthy families of the period. The Coverts were at that time the greatest landlords between London and the Channel, and it was their proud boast that they could ride all the way " from Southwark to the sea " on their own possessions. Doubtless, they had determined to be in the prevailing fashion, and, like many other powerful and influential families, to build for themselves and their descendants a stately home worthy to rank with the finest in the land ; but, alas for the vanity of human ambitions (this is a bit of moralising thrown in, and may be skipped), hardly had the grand mansion been finished or the freshness of the new masonry toned down, before the family became extinct, notwithstanding the number of "sonnes" that appear, from the monumental inscriptions in the church above, to have been born to it.

Though classical in style, with a foreign stateliness, this old home shows undoubted signs that the Coverts would not be bound down in all details to lordly Italian traditions, for in place of the usual decorative scroll-work pertaining thereto, we find that the friezes, spandrels above the arches, and keystones are adorned with numerous shields, each charged with the armorial bearings of the Coverts, and of the Coverts impaling those of the many families with whom they had allied themselves, in all "the boast of heraldry and pomp of power."

The ruins are now overgrown with ivy; brambles, nettles, and weeds luxuriate within the ancient courts and encumber the roofless chambers; sheep and pigs wander in and out of them as they will—all is given over to desolation and decay. Leaving the ruins, we wandered towards the sheet of water we had observed from above, passing on our way an ancient mill, with its wheel gone and roof falling in, quite in harmony with its surroundings. There was a note of sadness all around, and we were not sorry to return to the dog-cart and to Slaugham village— that at least, if not lively, was living.

The village is a very pretty one; the houses there are mostly old, and some are quaint. The landlady of the inn, who greeted us on our return, informed us that artists sometimes found their way to the place, on painting bent; she also informed us that it was the longest parish in Sussex, "stretching away as far as Crawley, eight miles off"; she appeared quite proud of this unique distinction. As we were departing the landlord once more made his appearance on the scene, and we jokingly remarked that we hoped the church was well filled on Sundays by people who did not come there out of curiosity. "Well, sir," responded he with a smile, that might have meant much or little, "it were properly crowded one Sunday when Mr. Gladstone, who was staying at a house in the neighbourhood, came to church here."

CHAPTER X

St. Leonard's Forest—A local tradition—The "Capital of the Weald"—Where Shelley was born—Knepp Castle—A wayside cross—Steyning—Curious panelling—A Norman church—Mysterious carving—"Sir Harry Gough's house"—"Heathen burials"—Wiston—Storrington—Parham and its treasures—An historic home—Old armour—A picture with a story to tell—Hiding-holes—Where Queen Elizabeth dined—A natural sundial.

THE country between Slaugham and Horsham is exceedingly picturesque, with a tender wildness peculiar to the south of England, a tenderness that makes even the ruggedness of Dartmoor seem more beautiful than savage. In about half a mile we came to a gorse-clad common ablaze with a gold glory, and all the air was sweetly scented with the peculiar perfume of the gorse flower. At the farther end of the common was a large " Hammerpond," surrounded by shady woods of beech and pine. Excepting these frequent ponds, the Sussex iron age seems to have left behind it hardly a noticeable trace in the landscape ; there are a number of old " cinder heaps," truly, but so overgrown with grass, brambles, and trees as in no manner to assert themselves to the eye. These artificial sheets of water, formed for driving the wheels of the forging mills (wholly artificial or natural ponds so enlarged as in some cases to approach in size a small lake), have now lost all appearance of being "hand-made," and, scattered about the country, give it a special character.

A mile or two farther on we came to another, and larger, sheet of tree-girt water, marked on our map by the unromantic name of "Hawkin's Pond"; presumably some one of that name was an ironmaster here. On the top of the first rise beyond this we had a charming distant view of Horsham, the roof-trees of the houses just peeping above the surrounding woods, and the tapering steeple of its ancient church rising upwards from the little town; it looked like a cathedral city in miniature!

Now to the right of us we passed by the wild wooded waste known as St. Leonard's Forest, which, according to tradition, used to be haunted by a dreadful dragon or serpent, as well as a headless horseman; they were the terror of all travellers in those parts, and as late even as the seventeenth century people could be found to attest on oath that they had seen them! Likewise, there is a local tradition, still stoutly maintained, that within the forest

    Adders never sting
    Nor nightingales sing.

I have often noticed that the virtue of rhyming sayings seems strangely to impress the rural mind, as though on this account they must needs be "gospel true." A sixteenth-century authority, one Dr. Andrew Borde to wit, writing at that time, declares that "he was assured by a credible person that the nightingale will synge round about St. Leonard's foreste, but never within the precinte thereof." To account for this fact, if fact it be, tradition has it that St. Leonard was disturbed at his devotions in a cell within the forest by the singing of the nightingales, and that thereupon, saint-like, of course, he cursed them, and from that time to this they have fled the district. I believe that there are certain parts of the country that appear to be avoided by the nightingale, the reason for which has caused much dispute between learned ornithologists; whether St. Leonard's Forest be one of them or not, I cannot say. My faith in old-world traditions was rudely shaken in my early youth by being impressed with the statement that a certain gloomy tarn was fathomless which was readily to be fathomed by a rope and a stone. Still the darksome tarn, overhung with huge rugged rocks, with its black-blue waters, looked so weird, that I almost resented the unpoetical action of a matter-of-fact friend who would "test the truth of the tradition." Now, tradition is like a bit of delicate old blue egg-shell china—a very pretty thing, but it won't stand rough handling.

Horsham, that calls itself "the capital of the Weald," struck us as a very pleasant little town, clean and prosperous-looking. A band-stand in the wide main street or square (without a band the evening we were there), surrounded by flower-beds, gave to the ancient market town somewhat the look of a wateringplace, and I must say seemed quite out of harmony with its surroundings. However, " times are changed, and we with them," and in many respects for the best, for on this spot, till early in the present century, bull-baiting was practised. The "sport" was stopped by the Puritans when in power, as Macaulay cynically and unjustly remarks, with a greater fondness for antithesis than truth, " not because it gave pain to the bull, but because it gave pleasure to the spectators."

About three miles from Horsham is Field Place, where Shelley was born; this can be reached by a pleasant footpath across the fields, or by almost as pleasant a road. The house has been much modernised and altered during the present century; over the fireplace here in the chamber where Shelley " first saw the light of day " is, or was, the following inscription :—

PERCY BYSSHE SHELLEY
was born
in this chamber
August 14th, 1792.

Shrine of the dawning speech and thought
Of Shelley, sacred be
To all who bow, where Time has brought
Gifts to Eternity.

From Horsham we decided that we would drive first to Steyning, and then along under the north side of the South Downs to Storrington, sleeping at the latter remote and railless spot, provided there were a suitable inn there, which information we trusted to be able to obtain from the landlord or the ostler at Steyning.

On leaving Horsham, we passed to our left a large undulating park with many great branching oaks, and shortly we came in sight of the fine old stone-built mansion belonging to it; this is approached from the highway by a long straight avenue of limes. The name of this charming domain was marked on our map as Denne Park; we had to consult our map, as there was no one about of whom to inquire. Again and again have we noticed how lonely and deserted are many of the country roads; especially have we been reminded of this fact when in doubt about our way, with not a soul in sight to enlighten us.

We were now in a stone country, as evidenced by a stone quarry in a field, and by the many old farmsteads and barns around, built of that substantial and lasting material instead of half-timber or brick, that we had with us so recently.

Passing by a lonely little inn called "The Cock," with its sign fixed on to the branch of a tree in a picturesquely primitive fashion, we presently found ourselves on high ground, with glorious views all around. Looking northward, our eyes ranged over the vast extent of the Sussex Weald, and to the south they ranged over almost as extensive a tract of woodlands, that rose and fell in vast undulations of greenery, stretching away right to the foot of the distant Downs. Close by the spot where we pulled up in order to leisurely enjoy the prospect stood a large white windmill facing all "the four winds of heaven." It had its name, "Cripplegate Mill," boldly painted on it. If you desire a view, and there be a windmill in sight, make for it; windmills must needs be so situated that there should be an uninterrupted air space all round, and where there is nothing to impede the air, it follows there is nothing to impede the vision.

Our road now dipped sharply down through thick woods, with the blue-looking Downs before us on the high horizon. At the foot of this descent we came to another of those picturesque ponds—in this case it might fairly be called a miniature lake—that abound in certain parts of Sussex, and serve so pleasantly to enliven the landscape with their silvery gleaming and sunny sparkling. A quarter of a mile farther on, standing on a grassy knoll by the roadside, we espied the ruined keep of Knepp Castle. The walls of this are very massive, but manifestly the ruin is a mere fragment of the original building. The only use that the crumbling keep now serves— besides being picturesque, which, however, is a thing not to be despised in an ugly age—appears to be to uphold a weather-cock, that takes the place of the warlike banner of old, which doubtless often floated proudly and defiantly on the breeze here during the first few centuries after the Conquest. The situation of the ruins is delightful, and if one could only imagine that those stern Norman and feudal builders cared in the least for scenery—as one can credit the monks doing—it might almost be fancied that the original founder of Knepp Castle was attracted to this spot on account of its lovely natural surroundings. But, above all, the Norman mind was essentially military; even his abbeys and churches he built strongly rather than beautifully.

At West Grinstead, a small village next on our road, we noticed the charming old rectory, with its fine stone-slab roof, all weather-tinted, moss-grown, and lichen-stained into almost every imaginable hue, and contrasting greatly with the much-restored church immediately adjoining. It seems to me, in the eternal fitness of things, that the church should look older than the rectory.

A little way out of West Grinstead stands a stone cross, close to the roadside, erected to the memory of a gentleman who lost his life there in 1883, but how he lost it the inscription sayeth not. The ditch is wide and high-banked at the sides, and we hazarded a guess that possibly the fatal accident occurred to a horseman whilst rashly attempting to jump it. Wayside crosses are very rare in the England of to-day, but we have come upon one occasionally during our many driving expeditions.

On to Steyning the country still maintained its pleasantly wooded character. Now and again the wide grassy margins to the roadside opened out into long uneven commons, with geese, and ponds, and old cottages thereon, or gathered round about them. Close to a hamlet called Partridge Green we crossed the railway on a raised bridge. From the top of this bridge is a delightful and comprehensive view of the South Down range, with the lowland woods creeping up its sheltered hollows; in the foreground of this picture stands an old black-and-white half-timber farmhouse, just where an artist would have placed

THE SOUTH DOWNS FROM NEAR STEYNING

it for effect. Soon after this we reached Steyning, where we pulled up at the "White Horse," an old-fashioned coaching-house. In the stable-yard we found a gentleman who had just driven from Storrington, and he informed us that there was a very fair hotel there with good stabling; moreover, he further informed us that when he left in the morning "not a soul was staying in it." Being assured of obtaining quarters for the night, we decided to rest the afternoon at Steyning and drive on to Storrington in the cool of the evening ; and to drive through a fresh and pretty country on a fine summer evening, how pleasant a thing it is !

Having the afternoon before us, we started forth for a stroll round about Steyning. We discovered many both interesting and picturesque old houses scattered about the town. There is a quaint bell-tower crowning the Fire Station, that, rising well above a long line of roofs, gives quite a character to the little old-fashioned-looking main street. However quaint and interesting in detail many of our country towns are, they frequently suffer somewhat in comparison with Continental ones, in that they have no one special architectural feature (beyond the church) to form a focus for the eye.

The church at Steyning hides itself away, so much so that during our short perambulations about the town we had failed to discover it, and were fain to ask our way thereto; then, as good-fortune would have it, we met the worthy vicar, who, in response to our question as to where we might get the keys, most good-naturedly not only offered to show us over his church himself, but, furthermore, to make our obligation the greater, very kindly invited us into the vicarage in order that we might see some curiously-carved and ancient oak panelling there. This was quite an unexpected treat to us, and all the more delightful because so unexpected. Our curiosity was aroused!

The panelling proved to be most interesting and deserving of detailed inspection, but we did not like to dally too long viewing it, nor did we venture to attempt any drawing thereof, knowing how fully occupied is the time of a clergyman in the country, and there was still the church to see, and had we once started sketching, there is no saying when we should have stopped. The panelling is covered with many heraldic devices, shields, coats of arms, besides bands of scroll-work and other decorative detail. It is an important piece of work, and the carving is very fine, but what its exact history is, or how it found its way into the vicarage, even the vicar could not say. Amongst the various devices that our host courteously pointed out to us, and explained, more or less fully, their possible meanings, were the following, which I noted down just as they were told to me, and in the chance order given :—

    The Bruce Lion of Scotland.
    The Pomegranate of Queen Catherine of Aragon.
    The Tudor badge of the rose and crown.
    The Portcullis, with crown above, the badge of Henry VIII.
    The royal arms of England and France combined.
    A very fine panel of the arms of the See of London.

Besides sundry dolphins, fleurs-de-lis, spread-eagles,

clusters of grapes, introduced into the various panels, this beautiful and suggestive specimen of old-time carving should delight the heart of an antiquary, and give him something to ponder and puzzle over, possibly also to dispute learnedly about with a friend of similar tastes. Running along the top of the panelling are a number of scrolls, some having inscriptions, and others left blank, as though intended to be filled in at some subsequent time. The centre scroll is inscribed :—

> Da Gloriam Deo Qui Fecit hec omnia
> Anº Dñi Miles Qvincentēs Vicesimo Secūdo.

The carving on one of the panels is left half completed.

Then we were conducted to the church, the vicar kindly pointing out the chief points of interest therein, and they were great. First our attention was called to the fine chancel arch, built, we learnt, in 1096. The pier arches on either side of the nave are enriched with unusually fine carved Norman work—indeed, the finest of the kind and period we have ever seen ; the patterns of each of these differ entirely from the others, and, moreover, show quite original ideas, though essentially Norman in mass and feeling. These arches were manifestly originally constructed of plain masonry and decorated after erection. In proof of this, one remains unfinished, a portion of the arch being carved, the other portion being of plain square-hewn stones, just as first set in place there by the ancient mason. Here one may see the very chisel marks, sharp and clear too, of the old-time carver, exactly as they were left long eventful centuries ago!

Tradition has it, we were told, that there were seven monks here, and an arch was given to each monk to decorate, and it is supposed one of the monks died before he completed his arch, and so it has remained to this day. A little bit of history told in stone, only it had to be translated to us. The north and south transepts, the vicar said, were probably destroyed during the Wars of the Roses.

Then we were taken up some wooden stairs, of deal, I verily believe, into the gallery. "Not Norman stairs these," we jokingly remarked. The vicar agreed with us! Here in the gallery we were close to the capitals of the piers, and our courteous conductor pointed out on one of them something strange and, to me at any rate, inexplicable—something that might well perplex the most learned archæologist, and make him despair of a reasonable explanation, and gave us food to ponder unprofitably over for many days after. On one of the capitals to a side arch is carved, carefully and well, the "Bull and Eagle" of ancient Babylon, and in the true spirit of Babylonian sculpture, not a feelingless reproduction of the same, yet the capital is Norman in shape, and the Eastern device has been skilfully adapted to it. The "Bull and Eagle" of Babylon, as may be known, are curiously combined in one, so that, looking on the carving, we saw, as either of the two mingled forms for the moment asserted its predominance, first a bull, then an eagle, according to the conventional shape of that animal and bird as made familiar by ancient sculpture. But how came this copy of a heathen sculpture, so faithfully rendered, into a Christian church, and that in the early Norman times? How came the Norman carver to know anything about it, or, granting the knowing, to use it there? We learnt that the late Sir Gilbert Scott had made a special inspection of the carving upon one occasion when he was visiting the church, but could not solve the mystery; perhaps no one now will ever be able to!

The church tower is of the familiar Sussex type, added in the sixteenth century, and constructed of chequered flint and stone. The original building appears to have had, or at least to have been designed for, a central tower. The last piers of the nave are partially built into the wall, apparently showing that the nave had formerly extended farther eastward, or else we must conclude that the work was never finished and was abruptly walled up thus. The rector informed us that he believed the original chancel did extend much farther than it now does, indeed as far as the present wall to the vicarage garden, as, when digging graves in the churchyard to the east of the present chancel, huge stones had been discovered, quite white when brought to light; these stones, he considered, were undoubtedly the foundations of a larger structure that had disappeared. The church seems to show that Steyning must have been a place of considerable importance in the early Norman times.

Returning to our inn, still in company with the vicar, we noticed, as we walked along, a small cottage, let into the wall of which was a stone panel bearing this legend :—

> This is
> Sir Harry Gough's House
> 1771.

We asked the vicar whether the inscription had any meaning, or story to tell, as it struck us it might have. " Do you know," he exclaimed, " I have often wondered what it was put up there for, but though I've lived here for so long, I cannot say." Just then a parishioner chanced to come along, and the vicar, taking him by the arm in a friendly way, said, " Penfold, now can you tell us the meaning of that inscription ? " Penfold was equal to the occasion. " I think I can," said he. " You see there were a tenant once there who would not pay any rent and claimed the cottage as his own, and Sir Harry Gough, I've heard say, had a lot of trouble to get him out and regain possession, so after that Sir Harry had that there notice put up to show the cottage were his."

Between Steyning and Bramber we learnt there were some fields known by the curious title of " Heathen Burials," but any further history of them we were unable to discover. The title is, however, suggestive.

Early in the evening we set forth for Storrington, just as the sun was tinging the western sky with a golden glory ; the balmy air too was fragrant with sweet country odours, that seem so pleasantly to assert themselves towards the close of a long warm summer's day. Our road lay along the foot of the Downs, and took us through spreading woods, varied here and there by sweeps of pastoral lands, dotted with peaceful homesteads, from gray old mansion to weather-stained cottage. The whole drive, of six miles or so, was a dream of beauty. The scenery must be enchanting at any time, but its charms were undoubtedly enhanced by the tender warm lights and mysterious shadows of the quiet eventide.

Soon after leaving Steyning we passed Wiston Park, a most delightful demesne, with its placid lake mirroring the glowing sky above, and its wealth of leafy woods showing a translucent yellow green, effectively contrasting with the dark purple gray that the Downs had assumed. Then up and down, with gradual rises and falls and many gentle windings, our road led us from one revelation of loveliness to another—each bend of the way had something fresh to show us. During most of the drive Chanctonbury Hill was in sight, crowned by a ring of trees, but bare to its wooded summit, thus reversing the general order of things, when the base of a hill is generally wooded and its summit bare. Chanctonbury Hill is a noted landmark from far and near, and a striking feature in the prospect from almost any point of view.

Picturesque cottages now and then delighted our vision—really and naturally picturesque cottages that might have come out of some water-colour drawing. The whole country-side had an indescribable look of contentment and long human abiding that was most rest-suggesting; it seemed to us that day a veritable Arcadia. It may be that much of the poetry of the scenery lay within ourselves, and was due to our transient frame of mind, but so it impressed us, and as it impressed us so I write of it.

Then after a time, when near to our destination, suddenly the woods ceased and gave way to an open, heathery, hilly waste—that too had its charms to a vigorous mind. On a prominent knoll thereon stood a solitary and primitive windmill, its four sails slowly revolving and just catching the ruddy glow of the last rays of the setting sun, whilst all around was merged in one mass of cool gray shade. It was a study for a painter, yet possibly did one try to portray it, such an effect would be called by clever art critics forced and unnatural, or an attempt to imitate Turner. If artists must paint for profit, they must paint what the multitude can understand, something that they see every day, and can exclaim when they see a representation thereof, "How natural!" Artists who are able, and content, to paint for future fame may perhaps venture to paint poems, but who can tell what the art standard of the twentieth century may be? Leaving the bit of wild heath, a wonderful splash of deep, dark purple in the landscape, we dropped down into the out-of-the-world village (or tiny town) of Storrington, where at the "White Horse" we found a ready welcome and a smiling landlady, who did all in her power to render us comfortable—and that with much success.

The projecting sign-board of our inn, we noticed, had on one side of it the representation of a white horse, shown as standing quietly and ready saddled at his stable door waiting for his rider; on the other side the horse was represented as galloping wildly away riderless. A little poetical conception, we imagined, of the village sign-painter, and welcome as a spirited change from the even tenor of most (modern) inn signs.

Within a mile of Storrington is Parham, one of the most picturesque and interesting old mansions in the kingdom, notable for its unique collection of ancient armour, including some suits of the Crusaders brought from Constantinople, where they had been hung up in a mosque, as well as for a library of most rare works, that includes a copy of *A World of Wonders*, printed in 1607, and bearing the autograph of Shakespeare on the title-page, and many beautiful, valuable, and curious paintings. Having heard of the wonderful treasures that Parham contains, before starting on our journey we had boldly written asking, as we were driving past there, if we might be allowed just to see the ancient armour, and to our delighted surprise we were most courteously granted the coveted permission, an unexpected kindness that we very greatly appreciated, the more especially as we were conscious that we had no right to beg such a favour. I do not see why any nobleman or gentleman who may be the fortunate possessor of an interesting house with a storied past, and gathered treasures therein, should be expected to admit any curious stranger to view them. "Every Englishman's house is his castle"—even a nobleman's! Nevertheless, for this once we acted as though we had no such delicate scruples; so much easier is it to preach than to practise!

Parham Park is truly forest-like in character, with a wealth of wild woodlands sloping away into shady glens. It abounds in grand ancestral oaks, and boasts of a flourishing heronry. As we drove through the park we passed by many a century-old oak and fir-crowned knoll, then suddenly straight before us stood revealed the gray and ancient mansion of Parham, a very picture in stone, with romance written over all its time-stained walls. The place impressed us, though our impression was not one to be conveyed in mere words; when you attempt to describe poetry the poem vanishes! There are some things beyond the reach of words —feelings too subtle for outward expression.

Parham is approached through a courtyard in the picturesque old-fashioned manner. Truly those Englishmen of old knew how to build a stately home. The house is purely Elizabethan, with the exception of some unimportant portions of an earlier building incorporated into it, and there are not now many genuine Elizabethan houses remaining in England, many of those so considered being of James I.'s time.

To describe Parham and its treasures aright would take a volume at the very least, and I cannot even spare a chapter! It is therefore only left for me to make a brief note of some of the chief features of interest thereof. Entering the fine old hall, lighted by large mullioned windows, and having a flat enriched plaster ceiling, we were at once struck by the grand effect of the ancient armour ranged round the walls in stately chronological order and gleaming array. Many of the pieces are historical, and of exceeding interest. The armour is mostly of the thirteenth, fourteenth, and fifteenth centuries, though some of it is of a much earlier period, one Anglo-Saxon helmet being of the seventh century.

Amongst the helmets one was pointed out to us as being that of Robert Bruce; also alongside, that of Sir Henry de Bohun, who was killed by Bruce on 23rd June 1314. This helmet shows a big dent and a hole on the top where the battle-axe of the Scotch king struck it with fatal effect. It must have been a tremendous blow. Then we saw the tilting helmet of Henry VIII., and an open helmet that had belonged to Little John, and many others, some of rare forms and great antiquity; but space forbids my enumerating these, catalogue fashion; they merit more detailed description.

Amongst all the wealth of ancient and historic armour, what interested us most was the complete chain suit of Sir Thomas de Sandford, who died in 1190. The innumerable rings of the chain mail thereof are all of steel, and each one separately forged! This is reputed to be the most ancient complete suit of chain armour in Europe, and possibly the world. Then there is a finely-engraved suit of armour, once the property of the Emperor Maximilian. Near to this hangs an old German executioner's sword, having the following notice attached: " The executioner was ennobled after cutting off the heads of three noblemen, each at one blow, with this sword (or a similar one) in the good old times." Preserved in another spot is a curious helmet of tin, found at Lostwithiel in Cornwall, and which probably is Phœnician. Against this is a truly ghastly relic of the long ago, consisting of an Anglo-Saxon helmet of bronze with the upper part of a skull still retained in it; this skull has a barbed iron arrow-head through the front that tells its own story. Another helmet close by once belonged to Wihtred, first Christian king of Kent, who died at Dover 726.

Leaving the hall, we were conducted to the withdrawing-room (to use an Elizabethan expression in keeping with the place), and amongst the many beautiful pictures there, a small oil sketch by Raphaelle delighted us, the more especially on account of the surprising freshness of its colouring; it might have only just left the artist's easel. When will modern painters learn the secret of the old masters, whose works stand unchanged for centuries? Here is a portrait of Lady Ferrars, widow of Lord Ferrars, who murdered his bailiff in a fit of temper, and, being a nobleman, had the privilege of being hanged with a silver cord, and I trust he appreciated the privilege! Near to this is a painting of Lady Horton, of whom Lord Byron wrote: "She walks in beauty like the night." The original autographic verses are preserved at Parham.

Next we came to the dining-room, round the walls of which are ranged a number of fine full-length portraits of notable persons. One of these paintings is particularly curious; it is of Sir Ralph and Lady Assheton of Whalley, by Sir Peter Lely. Lady Assheton ran away from her husband, whereupon he promptly pursued and brought her back. In the picture Sir Ralph is shown tightly holding a lock of his wife's hair, with one of his feet firmly placed on the skirt of her gown. This picture is pregnant with meaning manifestly intended. Over the fine mantelpiece in this grand chamber we noticed the coat of arms of the family carved, as was the custom so to place them, with the motto below, " Let Curzon holde what Curzon held."

As we ascended to the top of the house our attention was called on the way to an opening in the kitchen wall; this was closed by a shutter, on opening which the mistress of the establishment could look down below and see what was going on there. What, I wonder, would the present-day servant think of such an arrangement? Our houses show our changed manners.

Reaching the gallery at the top of the building, extending from one end to the other thereof, and some 180 feet long by 20 broad, we admired the wide prospects over the wild park that our elevated position afforded : rich woodlands varied by curved sweeps of greensward, and enlivened by the silvery gleam of water. These long galleries, so placed, are a characteristic feature of all genuine Elizabethan mansions, and would appear to have been originally intended to form dormitories, as otherwise the sleeping accommodation of these old homes would be quite inadequate for their size. Here hangs a large picture, " The Murder of the Innocents," by

Raphaelle, and one that used to hang in his studio. It is done in water-colours, and history has it that the juices of various plants were used as a vehicle to apply them with—possibly an experiment; indeed, such a large and important painting in such a medium, by so famous an oil-painter, seems to point to this.

Under one of the deeply-recessed windows of the gallery the top of a seat lifts up and discloses a darksome hiding-hole, and a very cramped and uncomfortable one it must have been, for there is a degree of discomfort in such places; compared with others, some are even spacious and luxurious! Leading out of one end of the gallery is the chapel, it being placed at the top of the mansion, in accordance with the old (and maybe modern as well, for aught I know) Roman Catholic traditions that there should be nothing above a building consecrated for worship. Here is some fine oak carving and a curious font, purchased, we were told, from some church in Oxfordshire whilst undergoing a thorough restoration. A very thorough restoration, we imagined!

In an ancient bedroom under the chapel, or at least we imagined it to be so, from what we could make out of the geography of the house, is a sliding panel in the wainscot, which gives access to a secret passage closely approaching the perpendicular. This appears to lead to the basement by the side of the kitchen chimney. Down this, we learnt, the priest once made his escape, his priestly office not serving to protect him from his enemies. When will the world learn the oft-repeated lesson : though the priest may save his soul, he cannot by his craft save his body?

Returning to the hall, we had pointed out to us the arms of Queen Elizabeth emblazoned on the top of the wall at one end, with the date 1593 inscribed above, and the letters E. R. below. This, we understood, commemorates the fact of Queen Elizabeth having dined in the hall when on her way to Cowdray, when she sat under the spot marked by the royal arms.

In the garden at Parham we noticed the figures of the hours shown by flowers planted to represent them round an ancient sun-dial, the pillar of the dial forming the gnomon, and telling the time, more or less correctly, by the shadow it cast on the flower figures—a pretty idea.

After this we bade a reluctant good-bye to this picturesque and pleasant old-world home and the grand old park that appears to fade away into the bare blue Downs. The sun, as we left, was lighting up the gray and time-toned walls of the ancient mansion and resting on the woods beyond. The picture was perfect. We lingered on our way with many a backward glance, till at last Parham was lost to our vision, and only a memory of it remained.

CHAPTER XI

"The Wild Brooks"—Amberley Castle—"Four good things of Sussex"—A church hour-glass stand—Lost on the Downs—A case of "Hobson's choice"—A river ferry—Arundel—The Fitzalan Chapel—A brace of anecdotes—Swanbourne Lake—A Sussex "hanger"—A famous view—Nature and art—Slindon—A ruined priory—Boxgrove—An interesting interior—Chichester.

DRIVING out of Parham Park, we found ourselves once more on the highroad, a rather dusty one it proved to be, but the scenery was charming, and more than compensated for the dust. After a slight rise we had a grand view ahead over a long, low, level stretch of country that faded away into a distance of circling blue, and in two or three miles more we found ourselves at Amberley, a sleepy, forsaken-looking, old-world village, with a crumbling castle and an ancient, interesting church — a primitive, picturesque village, that seemed hardly to belong to this century, and that gave us a delightful feeling of remoteness and repose.

Amberley is situated at the foot of the Downs, where the short, dry, thymy turf of the chalk uplands gives place to a great wide stretch of marshy meadow-lands of long waving grasses. This flat district, intersected by numberless stagnant streams, is known as "The Wild Brooks." On some old maps it is, however, marked as the "Weald Brooks," from which, just possibly, "Wild Brooks" may have been evolved. If you wish to discover the origin of a curious geographical name, consult an ancient map. We fondly imagine that we have thus unearthed the source of sundry place-names that have puzzled us by their peculiarities.

In the summer time Amberley is a delightful spot—at least in a dry season; in the winter, however, when the marshes are frequently flooded and damp, and depressing mists hang heavily over the flat watery expanse, suggestive of ague and other evils, it is the reverse of delightful. In fact, the difference between the winter and the summer aspect of Amberley is pointedly signified by a local saying. In winter time an inhabitant of the place is supposed to reply to the query, "Where do you belong?" with "Amberley, God help us," but in the summer the reply to the same question is, "Amberley, where else would you live?" The Arun, that winds through the marsh between earth-banks, is a fishful river, though, strangely enough, there is no angler's inn at hand. Amberley trout are famous, and are one of Fuller's "four good things of Sussex," the other "things" being the Arundel mullet, the Chichester lobster, and the Selsey cockle. Izaak Walton, that prince of fishermen, often indulged in the "gentle craft" here.

The castle is a mere shell, and stands upon a sandstone rock that is just raised above the level of the marsh. Seen from below, with the church apparently incorporated with it, and backed by the Downs, here well wooded at their base, Amberley Castle forms an effective picture, and from this point of view we made a sketch of it. The entrance is on the other (south) side, and is flanked by two round towers. In the grass-grown courtyard of the ruins are the slight remains of a chapel, opposite to which is a pleasant modern farmhouse, built within the walls. The exterior of the castle is more imposing than the interior—in fact, the interior is distinctly disappointing.

A very ancient oak door, that creaked mournfully on its rusty hinges as we opened it, leads directly from the castle courtyard into the grave-thronged churchyard. The church is interesting; the carvings of the south doorway are very fine. The delicately modelled pillars have very beautiful Early English capitals decorated with oak leaves and vines. The art mason who sculptured this must have rejoiced in his work and studied Nature long and lovingly. Within the building we discovered, fixed to the north wall and close to the pulpit, an ancient hour-glass stand in the form of an iron bracket, that plainly spoke of other days and other ways. How often did the rural congregation closely watch the emptying of that hour-glass, I wonder, when the sermon proved wearisome? In the chancel here is a small but very good brass to one John Wantele, who died in 1424. He is portrayed in complete armour, with long spurs on his steel shoes; over the armour is a

AMBERLEY CASTLE, FROM THE WILD BROOKS

surcoat or tabard charged with three lions' heads enamelled green. The chancel arch, we noted, was Norman, with the characteristic dog-tooth mouldings. The font is old and quaint, but we could not judge of the period. On the west wall we observed a "Consecration Cross." The church is flint-built, and has a red-tiled roof, green with mosses in parts; the gray-blue of the flints with the mingling of red and green on the roof formed most effective colour contrasts. It is always well to look out for colour when travelling; those who fail to do so lose much.

Leaving Amberley, we next came to Houghton Bridge, a gray and ancient stone structure of many arches, where we found ourselves alongside the clear-flowing Arun. Here we asked our way to Arundel, and were told we could get there "by keeping to this side of the river, only you'll have to drive over the Downs part of the way, or you can cross the bridge and go by the highroad." We elected to cross the Downs in preference to the dusty roads, and so we sought for more explicit instructions, and were informed to take the first turning to the left, which we did all too faithfully, and found ourselves landed in a chalk pit! So we had to "hark back" again to the main road, and took the next and right turning to the left (no pun intended). Now we had a long and stiff climb uphill till we reached the top of the Downs.

During our ascent we had glorious views presented to us looking right down the wooded Arun valley, bound in by wooded hills on either hand, with the sea-seeking river winding through it, like a narrow ribbon of glistening silver. High up on the far-away horizon we caught sight of the sea sparkling in the sunlight, and about midway between us and it the mass of Arundel Castle stood out dark and gray on a projecting wooded spur of the sloping Downs. It was a delightful prospect, with a special character all its own. I think there is nothing quite like it anywhere else in England; the sea and river combined in one view, the graceful curve of the Downs, the southern luxuriance of the woods, and the fine outline of the castle so happily disposed in the landscape, form a rare picture, yet one that I do not remember ever to have seen painted —a somewhat strange fact, considering that the valley of the Arun has been a favourite theme of artists for generations past; Turner knew and loved it well.

Then we parted company with our road, and drove along the hard, smooth turf of the Downs. It was delightfully easy and noiseless driving, though the carriage rolled about a little on the uneven ground, like a ship at sea. It was perhaps a venturesome proceeding, but we were assured that the route was feasible; moreover, the day was warm and fine, and time was our servant, not our slave; still further, we remembered the fact that we had a friend who had successfully explored the South Downs this haphazard fashion, regardless of the regular roads when these did not tend in the desired direction, and regardless also, I fear, of the law of trespass.

After a time we began a gradual descent to the river, and we had to thread our way between thick gorse bushes; distant hedges and woods now came

into sight, and made us wonder how we were to get
through them, and if we got through them, whether
we should be able to get on farther. There was,
however, nothing for it but to press on and " trust to
luck." Still we could not help wondering what would
be the end of our exploit. It would be annoying if,
after all, we could not find a way out into the valley,
but just as we were wondering what our fate would
be, we espied a gate in a long line of hedges, and made
for it; this led us into a rutty lane that did not look
very promising, and might end abruptly in a farmhouse
or another chalk pit! However, it was a case of
" Hobson's choice," so down the lane we drove, with
a good deal of jolting, and eventually struck upon a
decent road that had the look of leading to somewhere, and it led us into the primitive, out-of-the-
world village of Burpham, pleasantly situated on a
chalk cliff high above the river. We took a glance
inside the church, as we passed close to it, and
noticed therein some Norman arches with dog-tooth
mouldings of rather unusual form; we learnt afterwards that the vicar does not consider the carving
to be strictly dog-tooth, but to be symbolical of the
crown of thorns. The cliff is crowned with a wide
and grass-grown earthwork, that, from its size, we
judged must in prehistoric days have been of considerable importance. In the river below, an
ancient British canoe, scooped out of the trunk of a
big oak tree, was discovered in 1858; this was
buried in the mud. The canoe is now preserved
in the museum at Lewes Castle, where we saw it on
our last stage homeward.

Descending to the river, we discovered a primitive ferry there, and we were *paddled* over to the opposite shore in a large leaky boat for the sum of twopence. We made a sketch of the ferry from the point where we were landed, an engraving of which is given in the frontispiece. An old uncommercial ferry is a pleasing feature in the country; it is such a truly picturesque object therein, and is so fraught with old-world associations and traditions, and dearly loved by the ancient school of romance writers—a ferry with some Roundheads in hot pursuit of hardpressed Cavaliers was the very thing, nor did it come amiss in the case of sundry runaway lovers. Ferries, fords, and stepping-stones are oftentimes inconvenient—very inconvenient in fact, as I can testify from experience,—but I should be sorry, for my part, to have them improved altogether out of existence; there is not so much poetry in the world nowadays that we can afford to lose any! Life is becoming very easy-going—and very humdrum. By some strange, unhappy law, progress and sanitation seem to be antagonistic to the picturesque; the engineer stands supreme throughout the land, and beauty languishes.

From Burpham we had by way of welcome change an excellent, level, and smooth road down the valley into Arundel, passing by many picturesque thatched cottages as we drove on. The scenery was of the restful order that induces day-dreaming, and a soft, soothing, south-west wind tended to this result, and so we rolled along the pleasant country roads till we came in sight of historic Arundel.

Entering the town, we crossed the Arun by an old stone bridge, inscribed on the left pier of which we read, "Be true and just in all your dealings." This is one way truly of preaching to the multitude, but I doubt if of much effect; you cannot make people moral by advertisement! We asked one man if he knew who had placed the inscription there; the reply was instructive: "Noa, I don't, nor do I heed it"!

Looking down the river here, we noticed its smoothly-gliding surface reflected the golden tone of the sky above. Anchored by the bank-side were two coasting sloops and a square-rigged brig, their masts towering above the lowly houses and trees around. It seemed strange to see these sea-going ships anchored and quietly at rest in a narrow river thus, right amongst inland meadows and leafy trees, with the placid cattle gazing at them and the sheep browsing in close proximity. Two types of life were brought into sharp contrast: the weather-beaten salt and the old shepherd. Across the river stand the crumbling ruins of an old Dominican priory. Much of the squared and carved stone-work of this was used to build the bridge, leaving only broken flint walls, which in turn formed a ready-made quarry for the road-makers and menders! The ancient builders could have hardly anticipated such a use for their priory.

We found very comfortable quarters at Arundel, and devoted the early part of next morning to exploring the place before proceeding to Chichester. The Roman Catholic church struck us as a magnificent pile, and nothing more: faultless as to its own special architectural style, yet withal a feelingless production, a purely mechanical, characterless creation; beautifully built, construction merely considered, but as void of all picturesqueness or poetry as a railway station; possibly, but doubtfully, when age has toned and tinted its smoothly-scraped, chiselled, and pointed walls, and winter storms and frosts have crumbled a hard edge here and there, and so broken its too perfect symmetry, and history and tradition have given the structure an interest, then it may be more pleasing to the eye of an artist, and even be beloved by antiquaries yet unborn.

Then we bent our steps to the old church, a solemn-looking building, gray with years, weather-stained and weather-worn, not all of one period or style, but altered here and repaired there; yet all mellowed now into one harmonious whole. The ancient fabric speaks plainly in the present of its chequered past and of the changes and chances of its long life's history, and because of all these it appeals to one's closest sympathies; it is in striking antithesis to the stately and prim Roman Catholic church. Viewing these two buildings directly one after the other brought to our mind Ruskin's remark, "I had almost rather see Furness or Fountains Abbey strewn in grass-grown heaps by their brooksides, than in the first glory and close setting of their fresh-hewn sandstone." From the flint-built tower of the church Waller's cannon plied upon the castle walls, the lead on the roof was melted to make bullets, the Puritans added a chapter to the history of the hallowed pile, and the volume is not finished yet.

Within on the north wall are some remains of ancient frescoes, one of which represents the seven acts of mercy, the other the seven deadly sins, besides which there is a headless figure which fails to explain itself. The stalls of the choir are adorned with the representations of animals finely carved. At the east end of the church, behind the communion table or altar, are (perhaps I had better say were when we were there, for such things change) two large curtains of felt stretching across the archway. Lifting one of these, we found behind a fine old wrought-iron grille that filled up the intervening space from arch to floor, and close on the other side of it a rough brick wall; connected with this is a bit of modern history. The grille was used to divide the chancel (or perhaps, to write more correctly, the collegiate chapel that occupied in relation to the church the usual place of a chancel) from the body of the church. In 1873 the then vicar claimed the chapel as belonging to the church. Thereupon the Duke of Norfolk was advised to build up the partition, which he forthwith did ; a law-suit followed, and it was decided that the chapel was not the chancel of the church, but the Duke's private property, and the vicar and churchwardens, for the time being, were for ever prohibited from entering the same. This is now generally known as the Fitzalan Chapel, and locally called the Norfolk Chapel, and contains many fine, though damaged, tombs of the Fitzalans, the former Earls of Arundel.

Though not generally shown, permission was most kindly given to us to inspect these tombs. They are of great interest. Amongst them is one of Thomas, Earl of Arundel, son of the founder, who died in 1415, and his Countess. Around this are statues of a number of priests with open books before them. On the south side of the chapel is a magnificent altar-tomb to William, the nineteenth Earl, the patron of Caxton ; this is remarkable for its adornments in the Italian Renaissance, and it has an elaborate stone canopy supported by curiously twisted pillars. But perhaps the most interesting monument of all is the one to John Fitzalan, the seventeenth Earl, who died in 1435 from a wound received during the siege of the castle of Gerberoy, near Beauvais, in Normandy, and was buried in the monastery of the Grey Friars at Beauvais. He is shown on his monument in full armour, with hands folded in the attitude of prayer ; beneath this is the representation of an emaciated body, ghastly in its resemblance to a corpse. It was long supposed that this monument was merely a cenotaph, and that the body lay where it was buried in Normandy. However, strange to relate, by the accidental discovery of the ancient will of one Richard " Eiton," a Shropshire squire, it was found that this said squire had ransomed the body " oute of the frenchemennys handes " and caused it to be " buried in the College of Arundell, after his intent," adding, " and so I to be praide fore in the College of Arundell, perpetually." I am afraid, however, that now there is no priest at the College to pray for the soul of the worthy squire, so difficult is it in this changeful world to settle matters "perpetually." Let us trust that he is no worse off for after events he could not possibly foresee or prevent. Space, alas! will not permit any further description of the contents of this most interesting chapel, tempted though I feel to trespass further upon it. To describe the tombs in detail would need a small volume. The difficulty in writing upon a tour in England is to know what to leave out! I feel like an artist painting a landscape from nature : it is impossible to put on canvas or paper all one sees. It matters not whether the brush or pen be employed ; in each case it comes to be a matter of selection.

At Arundel we made the chance acquaintance of a communicative gentleman, and had an interesting conversation with him, some of which is perhaps worth repeating. It appears that at one time the old castle keep was the home of certain favoured owls imported from Norway ; these were the especial pets of their noble owner. These owls and owlesses were curiously named after famous persons, regardless of sex, one of the lady birds boasting of the unsuitable name of Lord Thurlow. It happened at a time when the real Lord Thurlow was seriously ill that the owless called after him was ill also, and one morning a servant came to the Duke and exclaimed, " Please, your grace, Lord Thurlow's better and has just laid an egg"!

Another story we were told concerned an agricultural authority who had been employed to lecture to an assemblage of local farmers on improved modes of agriculture. Having finished his discourse, which had apparently been attentively listened to, the lecturer invited any of his audience to make remarks or to ask questions, whereupon one of the number got up and exclaimed, "Mr. Lecturer, what we knows, we knows; and what we don't knows, we don't want nobody to tell us," which was plain but scarcely satisfactory.

This was related to us as showing the conservative stubbornness of the English farmer. Still, perhaps there is something to be said on the side of the farmer, who has an inherent objection to be lectured by people who talk so glibly as to how he should carry on his business, and yet who have never farmed an acre. Said one of these irate agriculturists to me one day after reading an article in a daily London paper as to the advantages of deep cultivation, "It's all very well for clever folk who lives in towns to write like that. Course you'll get better crops with deep cultivation, but the better crops won't pay for the extra cost of such cultivation; that's where those clever folks go wrong. It's a lot easier to get a living at lecturing upon how to make farming pay, than to set to work to farm and make it pay." And we rather sympathised with the enraged farmer; there was point in his remarks, not to say a moral.

Our road out of Arundel led us at first along by the foot of the castle, a building grand in mass but poor in detail, below which is the tidy ducal dairy, built on the site of an old and artist-loved mill, a most picturesque structure, judging by the old paintings of it. The stream still turns a wheel, but it is employed to force water up to the castle, a useful purpose truly, but if only the dear old mill could have been left *externally* as it was, to delight future generations of artists! Just above the dairy is Swanbourne Lake, a very pretty and secluded sheet of water, and clear as crystal; this charming spot is bosomed in wooded hills, rich in green foliage below and fir-fringed high above. A scene of greater tranquillity there could hardly be, nor would it be easy to find a cooler or more pleasant retreat on a hot summer's day.

Proceeding up the valley from Swanbourne Lake, we presently passed by the side of a typical Sussex "hanger," the steep hillside to our left being thickly covered with trees, and forming quite a wall of wood, more overhanging than perpendicular. A little farther on we espied a primitive wayside inn with the uncommon title of the "Black Rabbit." From this spot, looking back, we had a fine and quite fresh view of the castle; it is astonishing how the appearance of a place sometimes changes with the point of view, so much, indeed, as not infrequently to invest it with quite a new character. The driving tourist should not neglect occasionally to give a glance behind; many a scenic surprise may be secured by so doing. The whole beauty of a landscape does not always lie ahead!

Now our road entered Arundel Park, and we had a stiff and rather rough uphill climb for a mile or more, the climb being amply rewarded by the magnificent prospect revealed to us from our elevated position—a prospect of vast reaches of undulating sward, broken by beech-clad slopes and deer-haunted hollows deep in shade; in the middle distance stood the castle, looking like a real ancient castle by virtue of its comparative remoteness, and beyond stretched forth a vast extent of level country, with the Arun meandering through it to the sea, which in turn was visible as a silver streak over Littlehampton.

This view has been rendered famous by Turner's drawing of it engraved in his *Rivers of England*, and is perhaps the finest of the series. Turner has taken certain liberties with the local topography, but less than usual with him, possibly because the scene naturally composes so well; still he has made the grand, though gentle, slope of the Downs abrupt and bold, he has perched the castle up above the valley, a good deal more than it actually is, and has modified the distance to a certain extent. Turner's drawing is a charmingly poetic vision of the scene—it is true to nature, if not to topography. It is a romantic impression of a lovely prospect, not a mere collection of hard facts; to the material landscape he gives a soul, as a sculptor gives life to the inanimate marble—the similitude is not very good, but it will do. Turner never produced pure transcripts from nature—that is not the true artist's province; he employed selection to secure only the worthy and the beautiful, not as certain schools of modern painters appear to do, to get rid of them and to show how cleverly they can paint the commonplace.

Turner's topography is not to be relied upon ; his aim was picture-making, and this needs composition, but his natural effects are always absolutely true. Look at the ribbon-like form he gives the flash of lightning in that wonderful drawing of Stonehenge (see his *England and Wales*). Till then, and long afterwards, even to this day, painters made their lightning forked—it was the accepted form. Yet Turner was right, as photography has since conclusively proved by the marked resemblance of the lightning flash taken on a photographic plate to the drawing of Turner of the same. Only the other day I was closely comparing the streak of lightning in Turner's " Malvern," engraved in the same work, with a photogram of a lightning flash, and the latter might have been " a crib from Turner," so striking was the similarity of the two.

Emerging from the park, we struck upon the old coach road to Chichester. We were on very high ground. The road was unenclosed, with a wild common in front, bounded by open woods of beech, and larch, and pine. Looking over the woods, we caught a glimpse of Chichester Cathedral spire and of the shining sea beyond. Then we had a long and delightful run downhill through shady woods, followed by a gentle rise into the charming village of Slindon, a collection of pretty creeper-covered cottages, mostly with little gardens in front ablaze with colour, and wafting sweet perfumes on the languid summer air. Many of the cottages were thatched and had a look of rustic homeliness and a suggestion of simple comfort that was very eye-pleasing and peace-bestowing. Here and there we observed a door opened with an old-fashioned latch, instead of the less characteristic modern handle. Slindon stands high upon the wooded hills, and is blessed with bracing airs sometimes, when the wind is in the south, scented with the salty flavour of the sea ; all around is spread out a glorious country, abounding in interesting rambles, scrambles, and drives. My surprise is that Slindon has not been turned into a health resort. Let us hope it never will be. Perhaps I had better say no more about Slindon, lest any poor praise of mine might help to bring about the change I dread.

On leaving Slindon we drove alongside of Slindon Park, famous for its beeches. The Elizabethan house here has taken the place of a much older one, in which Stephen Langton, that high-souled Archbishop of Magna Charta renown, died. Then the Church held aloft the flag of freedom.

> Seven times the bells have tolled
> For the centuries grey and old,
> Since the stoled and mitred band
> Cursed the tyrants of their land,
> Since the priesthood, like a tower,
> Stood between the poor and power ;
> And the wronged and trodden down
> Blest the abbot's shaven crown.
>
> . . . . .
>
> Now too oft the priesthood wait
> At the threshold of the state,
> Waiting for the beck and nod
> Of its power as law of God.
>
> . . . . .
>
> Tell me not this needs must be,
> God's true priest is always free—

> Free the needed truth to speak,
> Right the wrong, and raise the weak ;
> Not to fawn on wealth and state,
> Leaving Lazarus at the gate—
> Not to peddle creeds like wares,
> Not to mutter hireling prayers.

From Slindon gradually we descended to the long, low, level plain that here lies between the Downs and the sea. It was a land of deep-green meadows and well-cultivated fields. The country had no marked features, nor any point of special interest that we noticed till we came within four miles or so of Chichester, when, glancing northward, we chanced to observe, half buried in trees, and only a short distance from our road, some apparently ecclesiastical ruins surrounding an ancient church, which showed its former, if not present, importance by the flying buttresses to its clerestory, an arrangement I do not remember ever having seen before in a simple country church, and which gave it quite the look of a small abbey. These ruins took us wholly by surprise, as we had no idea that there was anything of the kind in the locality, so we called a halt in order to consult our map, and found the spot marked thereon as Boxgrove Priory. It may prove how shamefully ignorant I am of the places of interest in our own country, but I am fain to confess that until then I had no knowledge whatever that there was such a ruined priory in England, set, too, in such a picturesque spot. Those monks of old—jolly or austere, from whichever point of view we look upon them—had a rare eye for scenery !

Entering the village of Boxgrove (a name that surely explains its origin), one of the first cottages we came to had a notice over its doorway, " The keys of the church kept here." So we tapped at the door and inquired for them, whereupon a pleasant-faced woman came forth and offered to go with us over the building. Maybe she did not like to trust the keys to utter strangers; anyhow, with us she went. To judge from the slight ruins that remain, Boxgrove Priory must have covered a considerable extent of ground in the days of its prosperity. At some distance north of the church stands the ancient Refectory, now, alas! roofless and ivy-grown, with grass in place of pavement. Approaching the church, we noticed at the northwest end a cluster of curious old Norman arches standing all alone. These are small and low, much ravaged by exposure to the weather, and more graceful in design and more delicate in adornment than Norman work generally is. They are gems in their way. On the bases of the buttresses of the church are some curious incised circles, with lines radiating from their circumference to their centres, like the spokes of a wheel. We could make nothing of these, and our guide, in reply to our query about them, simply remarked she had never noticed them before; indeed, our guide appeared to know nothing about the place but that it was very old, a fact that we did not need any information about. " Perhaps it's as old as your grandfather?" we suggested. She thought it might be, but did not seem very sure; in fact, she did not seem very certain whether she ever had a grandfather or not. It was a manifest case of guiding the guide!

The interior of the church is of great interest. The transepts have a quaint arrangement of galleries enclosed within carved oak screens. These were probably intended for the lay worshippers, and prove that the medieval builders did erect galleries, though some authorities have declared "such abominations" were unknown before the Reformation (which they are pleased to term the "Deformation") and are the greatest glory of the Churchwardens' era. But the chief object of interest here is the beautiful and elaborate canopied tomb of Thomas, Lord de la Warr. This is in the Renaissance style, and is covered with curious sculpturing and carved coats of arms, gilded and coloured. There is some resemblance between this tomb and the one of the nineteenth Earl of Arundel in the Fitzalan Chapel we had seen that morning.

A pleasant drive along a level road now took us into Chichester. On the way we caught a glimpse of Goodwood House peeping out of the woods at the foot of the Downs, then by degrees houses on either side of the way took the place of the pleasant green fields and shady trees, and we found ourselves, as a notice on an obelisk informed us, within "the boundary of the City of Chichester," the dusty country roads giving place to muddy streets, owing to over-abundant watering. Soon after this we drove under the archway of the old-fashioned "Dolphin Inn," where we found a hearty welcome, most comfortable quarters, excellent fare, combined with reasonable charges (as we discovered when we paid our bill the next morning), and what more could the most devoted inn-lover desire, or a tired, dust-stained traveller expect?

CHAPTER XII

An old prophecy fulfilled—Chichester market cross—An old-world village—Traditions—The legend of the bells of Bosham—An historic church—Old words and expressions—An English Holland—The invention of ox-tail' soup—Sea and land—Porchester Castle—Fareham—Church towers—Titchfield Place gateway—Bursledon bridge—Southampton—Ferries old and new.

OUR cool and comfortable room at Chichester faced the venerable cathedral, a dream in architecture, surrounded by trees, over whose foliage the mass of the hoary pile rose dim and gray in the fading light. The chiming of the bells from the time-scarred and weather-stained campanile floated down to us on the still evening air in a mellow, musical harmony, contrasting greatly with the clanging and clashing of most modern church bell-ringing, that only adds to the wear and tear of life by its tedious din, and arouses so much unchristian-like feeling amongst compulsory listeners, besides being so hurtful to the suffering invalid. In crowded cities it would be a mercy could some of the church bells be rung a little less noisily, or not at all! Perhaps it is too much to expect that they should be soft and sweet in tone and ear-delighting.

Chichester is the only English cathedral that

now possesses a campanile (Salisbury had one that the last century improved away). It was presumably built to save the central tower from the strain caused by the constant bell-ringing. Possibly this tower showed signs of weakness at the time, as it did in the following century. On 21st February 1861 it fell, or, to be accurate, it subsided bodily and perpendicularly through the roof, thus literally fulfilling the old proverb :—

> If Chichester Church steeple fall,
> In England there's no king at all.

Nor was there, for a queen was reigning then.

Besides the cathedral, our window looked upon another relic of the never-returning past, a less famous structure, but one scarcely less beautiful—to wit, the ancient Market Cross, an octagonal building full of gracefulness, richly decorated on all sides with carved and fretted panels, niches, and pinnacles, and all that goes to make the glory of Gothic work that sings its spirit in stone. The central shaft, uprising from the base, is supported at the top by flying buttresses ; the decorative finial that doubtless crowned the whole has apparently been displaced in favour of a bell turret surmounted by a weather-vane. The turret contains the bells of a clock that was presented to Chichester and placed in the cross by one Dame Elizabeth Farringdon, "For an hourly memento of her goodwill to the City," as an old inscription quaintly puts it.

This old cross gives a special character to the thoroughfare (or thoroughfares, for it is placed at the junction of four cross streets) in which it stands.

It is a charming bit of medieval work, and interesting as showing what could be accomplished by Gothic architects when useful or commercial purposes were studied, and not purely religious requirements, with all their binding traditions.

As to the interior of the cathedral, I must leave that for the hand-books to deal with, merely venturing to mention one feature wherein Chichester is unique amongst English cathedrals, namely, that it possesses four aisles, two on each side of the centre nave.

Next morning we resumed our pleasant pilgrimage early, as was our wont. The country we passed through at first was flat and uninteresting. At Fishbourne, however, where a creek of brackish water comes inland as far almost as the road, it improved a little. There we noticed a tumble-down old mill standing solitary and deserted by the reedy margin of the creek, and this lonely mill gave quite a charm and a character to the otherwise desolate prospect, so little goes to make a picture. It was "a bit" that would have delighted the eye of a Dutch artist. Then after many windings through narrow lanes we reached the old-world fishing village of Bosham, that stands pleasantly on an estuary of the Channel.

Bosham is one of the most primitive and picturesque places imaginable. I think after famed Clovelly (I am not sure even that I am correct in making this saving clause) that it is the quaintest spot in England, a spot well worth a thousand miles of driving to see. It is historic too, and simply abounds with legendary lore. This peaceful little harbour was the Portsmouth of the Romans during their occupation of Britain. King Canute had a palace here, and here is the supposed site of his rebuking his courtiers when they placed his chair by the incoming tide, a childish legend that hardhearted authorities declare to be apocryphal, as also the story that is told as to how the manor of Bosham, formerly the property of the Church, came into possession of the powerful Earl Godwin. Tradition has it that Earl Godwin went with an armed band of his followers ostensibly to pay court to Æthelnoth, Archbishop of Canterbury, and with well-assumed humility addressed the Primate, "*Da mihi Boseam.*" The Archbishop, understanding that he asked for a kiss of peace (*basium*), said he would give it him, whereupon the crafty Earl turned to his followers to witness that he had been given the manor of Boscam, and forthwith set forth to take possession of it.

Then there is the legend of the "Bells of Bosham," that bears a certain resemblance to the legend of the "Bells of Bottreaux" in Cornwall. According to the tradition relating to Bosham, the Danes—one version has it the Norsemen, but this is a trifling detail—sailed up the creek and stole the bells of the church, which they carried off with them as trophies, but as the pirates were sailing away in triumph a storm suddenly arose, and the galley with the bells was swamped, and sank with its spoils to the bottom of the sea. In truth of which legend any one who stands at Itchenor Point,

BOSHAM, LOW TIDE

just across the water, may to-day hear the sunken bells repeating the peal from Bosham church. The fact is, there exists a very fine echo at this point that gives back the sounds of the Bosham bells one after the other.

It was from Bosham that Harold set forth on his ill-fated visit to William, Duke of Normandy. The first scene in the Bayeux tapestry—that most eventful history woven in wool—represents Harold, hawk in hand and hounds running before him, riding with his knights towards Bosham, the church being conventionally pictured as a Saxon building with roof of shingles, but without a tower. A few years ago I saw an excellent copy of this most interesting tapestry in the South Kensington Museum, and it may possibly be there now.

On entering Bosham, it at once impressed us with an indescribable feeling of old-world tranquillity, a feeling that was enhanced as we leisurely explored it. It was all so quaint and dreamily quiet, so utterly unlike any other place we knew or had heard of, it seemed as though by some strange magic the hand of time had been turned back and we had been transposed into another century. Our first view of the land-locked creek we shall not readily forget, it was so strange-looking. The quiet sheet of water—the tide was up at the time—seemed to be a veritable ships' cemetery, for there all sorts and conditions of worn-out vessels were anchored when they could float; some were water-logged, some were sunk to the bottom, and merely showed their black green ribs above; most were mastless, and all were more or less decayed or useless. When the tide ebbed, all these were left stranded on the mud.

Walking round by the shore, we discovered that if this were the last resting-place of many an old sea craft, here also some were born, for right amongst the low-roofed cottages, and even amongst the trees, we observed new craft being built, one or two with their sterns facing the water, ready to be launched. Yet for all this Bosham looked the sleepiest and most uncommercial place imaginable; the small ships, schooners, and trawlers seemed to grow rather than be built, for there was a strange absence of all noise or bustle. "What an odd place!" we both exclaimed,—"delightfully, picturesquely odd." There is enough picture-making material here to last any ordinary artist a lifetime. We exhausted all the two dozen plates in our camera very soon, and wanted more.

As we made our way along the shore we passed a most picturesque old watermill, its gray-green wheel droning as it turned lazily round, as though in no hurry. This mill suggested a scene in an opera, with its great gables and stream running down to the sea. Then we came to a sort of jetty built of wood, all dark and ancient. From this spot another view of Bosham was revealed to us, for it faces the creek on two sides, showing its ancient Saxon church (much altered and restored, alas!). The tower of this is now crowned by a Sussex shingle spire. The sea winds have sadly ravaged the stone walls of the old church, but have also given them a rare texture; they have weakened yet beautified them. There is no sculptor so cunning as the salt sea wind.

Here we managed to secure a boat to explore the creek and get still different views of the quaint old place. The boat was big and heavy, slow to move along, but it was steady and absolutely safe, good for sketching purposes and for exercising the muscles. I suggested to the owner that possibly it was built in the days of Noah. He replied he "shouldn't wonder if it were," then he added that if I liked to buy it for a curiosity he would sell it to me at a fair price. I rather fancy that burly mariner was not so simple as he looked. We spent a pleasant time on the water "outward bound," and we secured a few hasty sketches; but never shall I forget the return journey against the tide in that ancient tub. However, we managed to struggle back again, and handed the burly mariner his boat; he hoped we had enjoyed ourselves. We merely remarked that we thought it would be a good boat to hire by the hour when the tide was going out. He may not have seen the point, for he made no reply.

Our water expedition over, we went in search of the keys of the church, built, according to tradition, by King Canute. Knocking at the door of a cottage, where we were told the clerk lived, a woman came forth key in hand and volunteered to go with us. The church, standing on an open bit of ground surrounded by elms, makes a pretty picture. Entering the building, the first thing to which our attention was drawn was the floor, which at the restoration had been lowered two feet, and exposed once more the bases of the pillars, for ages covered up. These bases greatly interested us on account of their antiquity, and because, in my humble opinion, they are undoubtedly ancient Roman; there is an indescribable something about them that speaks their origin. On the site of the present church the Romans had a basilica, and very probably the bases of the pillars belonged to it.

Next we were conducted to the spot, at the south side of the chancel arch, where tradition asserts the daughter of Canute was buried; this is marked on the floor by a yellow tile with a raven thereon (Canute's badge). The woman told us that during the restorations in 1865 search was made at this point, and a few feet below the surface a small coffin of Purbeck marble was discovered. Her husband was employed on the work and helped to lift the stone lid, which was nearly a foot thick. On raising this there was revealed in the coffin a mass of dust and a child's crumbling skeleton. After this discovery an artist—she had forgotten his name—painted and presented the tile we saw, to mark the spot.

It is strange that after eight centuries, fraught with important changes, the tradition as to the exact place of burial of the Saxon king's daughter should exist; stranger still that a coffin containing the remains of a child should have been unearthed on the very spot. This perhaps should make one feel a little more respectful to tradition, though the mere fact of a child's skeleton being found there is not of itself conclusive proof of the truth of the tradition. One point that raises a serious doubt as to this in my mind is the fact that in the chancel may be seen the broken stone effigy of a little girl with a lion at her feet, which effigy was originally placed over the site marked by the tile with a raven on it. Now this effigy is apparently thirteenth-century work—certainly not earlier. The explanation of this curious circumstance by learned antiquaries, who hold to the Canute legend, is that at that period some one caused this effigy to be placed in Bosham church to mark the spot where Canute's child was interred. This explanation, however, appears to me rather unhappy and far-fetched, and I feel that there can be no reasonable doubt that the period of the effigy represents approximately the date of the death of the child buried beneath it. Still one does not like to spoil pretty traditions, so I will say no more.

The tower and chancel arch are, I feel sure, Saxon. On the interior wall of the tower we noticed a window with a triangular head—that is, it had two stones placed at the top angle-fashion in place of an arch; this, as well as a small square opening alongside, are undoubtedly Saxon. On the south wall near the door, and under a stone canopy, is the recessed tomb of Herbert de Bosham, secretary to Thomas à Becket, a native of the place. Close to this some steps descend into a remarkable groined Early English crypt, in old days, sad to relate, much used by smugglers as a safe store-house for their cargoes, for who would dream of searching a church for contraband goods? The parson, rumour has it, was not wholly unaware of the proceedings.

On leaving the church our guide pointed out an old tombstone with a ship on the sea carved on the top. Both this and the inscription below were difficult to make out on account of the mosses that had spread over the stone. We were told that this recorded the death of some men at sea who were killed by a horse. This rather puzzled us until we discovered that hawser was intended. It appeared that this tomb was much esteemed by the population, and used to be scrubbed clean once a year, but that the scrubbing had been neglected of late. Then close to the churchyard an ancient moat, still full of water, was pointed out to us as being the very moat that surrounded the palace of King Harold.

As we were bestowing our tip on parting, the woman exclaimed, "I've a book at home with short tidings about the place, maybe you would like to see it." We were glad of the expression "short tidings"—it was perfectly fresh to us. Even in these School Board days old-fashioned terms and words prevail in country places; already we had made note of the following since we had set out: Emmets, for ants; runagate, for a worthless tramp; direction posts, for sign-posts; trug, for basket; tempest, for thunderstorm; drafting, for drawing; and others.

Our road on from Bosham until we came in

sight of Portsmouth was wholly void of any scenic attractions; indeed, the "scenery" consisted mainly of a succession of poor straggling villages, with short stretches of flat country, watered by stagnant streams, between. The villages were noticeable chiefly on account of the number of public-houses they contained; about every third house appeared to be one, and the traffic on the highway struck us as consisting mostly of brewers' drays laden with barrels containing the "necessary" for the said public-houses. It was an excellent country to travel through by rail!

Still, if not beautiful, the drive was in a way interesting. We are not of those "who can travel from Dan to Beersheba and cry, 'Tis all barren." Inlets of the sea came near to our road now and again, and past the low-lying meadows we caught frequent peeps of moving sails and stationary masts of anchored craft; the landscape was not wanting in character, it distantly reminded us of the Fen district. The villages too had an indefinable marine flavour, that made one pardon their utter want of picturesqueness, for there is a certain feeling of poetry in all that pertains to the sea, that highway of the world that brings you in touch with the furthermost corners of the globe.

At Emsworth a narrow arm of the sea comes right up through the very centre of the town, and this we crossed by a bridge. Looking to the left the combination of red-tiled, irregular-roofed houses, the green leafy elms behind, the gray water creeping slowly up the creek, with the shipping upon it, formed a very quaint and Dutch-like prospect. Certainly had we been suddenly set down there, without knowing what country we were in, we should hardly have guessed it to be England. The variety of English scenery is truly surprising, even the variety obtainable during one day's drive!

A little farther on we noticed, also to our left, the ruined keep of Warblington Castle, a very picturesque feature in the landscape, and the only picturesque one we had seen since leaving quaint, old-world Bosham. Perhaps it may have been the contrast of the places we passed through, with the beauties of Bosham, that made them seem somewhat commonplace. Havant succeeded Emsworth, with the usual strip of semi-country between, and there we pulled up at the "Bear," and baited our horses and refreshed ourselves. On a table on the landing of our inn stood an excellent model of an old-fashioned three-decker, made of bone, the waitress told us, by the French prisoners confined at Porchester Castle during the Napoleonic wars. It was at that time, and at that castle, by the way, that these same prisoners invented ox-tail soup. It appears that ox tails were given to the Frenchmen as being of but little value, but they managed to convert the despised tails into a delicious soup, so much so, that when the officer appointed to inspect the food at the prison tasted it, he demanded angrily how it was such luxuries were provided for them.

On from Havant our road maintained much

the same character as the first part of the stage, only that perhaps there were rather more green fields than houses on the way. To our left we had a fine view over Langston Harbour, with its sluggish, winding waterways and dreary stretches of mud flats. Then Portsmouth became dimly visible ahead, half hidden as it was by its own smoke, above which, in the clearer air, the masts of several huge men-of-war were visible. To our right was the long line of the Downs, with the massive Portsdown forts ranged at intervals along the top. The sudden transition from the placid, peaceful country to this land bristling with fortifications was almost startling, to say nothing of the iron-clads at anchor in the bay.

Passing through Cosham, and crossing at the same time the old London and Portsmouth coach road, we came to another salt-water creek running far inland, the mimic waves of which washed our very wheels as we drove along. Soon afterwards the gray weather-beaten keep of Porchester Castle came into sight, an interesting ruin showing both Roman and Norman work. From the top of the keep is a comprehensive view of Portsmouth Harbour, the ships therein, and the town. Porchester Castle would be a most delightful spot were it not for the presence of noisy excursionists and picnic parties from Portsmouth, that effectually prevent all romancing there or quiet enjoyment of the place.

After Porchester the scenery began gradually to improve, and almost became pretty on approaching Fareham, driving into which we were greeted by a small lake bounded by trees on one side, and by pleasant residences on the other, each set within its own walled garden. Fareham promised well, but the place, after all, proved disappointing. Its outskirts are pretty enough, but the town itself, consisting of one "long-drawn-out," clean, but dreary main street, is uninteresting to a degree. An arm of the sea finds its way up here too, and the little inland harbour it provides is the chief feature in the place. The church is a very fine example of late eighteenth or early nineteenth-century Churchwardens' style in brick, but, for all, the tower is not unpleasing—seen a little way off. The top of this is shaped, and upon it is placed a clock in a square structure; above this is a cupola bell-tower, and the whole is crowned by a gilt weather-vane. These are all needs simply supplied, without any attempt at decoration, or a suspicion even of trying for effect, yet effect of a kind is there. I must confess a slight feeling of sympathy for this bit of work that so simply and plainly expresses its purpose and does nothing more. Ruskin, no mean authority on the subject, declares it to be a *sine qua non* of true architecture, "that every part of a structure should have its recognised function." To that extent, then, this portion of the tower is true art, though there is far higher and better art most certainly; moreover, it is a change from the stereotyped forms of church towers and steeples that prevail throughout the land. Perhaps tradition has taken too tight a hold upon the ecclesiastical architect to allow him much originality in his designs, welcome though such originality would be. Church towers are prominent features in the landscape, and a little variety in their form would not only add to their charm and give them a pleasing individuality, but would materially add to the interest of a view; just as the quaint and unique tower of Sompting church in Sussex (which we shall see on our return) gives a special character to the prospect of which it forms a part, and to the village also.

From Fareham we drove to Southampton, a very easy day's stage of about twelve rather hilly miles. It was a charming country we passed through, delightfully varied by hill and dale, by wood and water. Soon to our left, looking down through the trees, we caught a glimpse of Southampton Water, with the wooded banks opposite, that gave it the appearance of a great lake, though a large ocean steamer spoilt the illusion by intruding on the scene. In another mile or so we came to the charmingly quaint and sleepy old town of Titchfield, snugly ensconced in a sheltered valley. A short way up this valley we caught sight of some very picturesque ruins in the shape of a group of ivy-clad towers and turrets just peeping above the trees. Leaving the dog-cart, we set forth on foot in order to obtain a closer view of the ruins, called, we were informed by a native, Titchfield Place Gateway. We wondered much how it was that the name had not got abbreviated into something more concise; countrymen do not generally fail in the respect of cutting down names—oftentimes, indeed, to an irreducible minimum. This gateway formed a portion of the entrance to Titchfield Place, erst the lordly seat of the Earls of Southampton. We approached the spot through a glade of oaks, and found the structure, externally at any rate, in a fair state of preservation and exceedingly picturesque, just ruinous enough to appeal to one's sympathies, but not too ruinous.

The gateway consists of a central entrance, having an octagonal and embattled tower on each flank, with low walls extending therefrom on either side, each ending in another and smaller octagonal tower. The broken outline of the building caused by these towers of different heights is very effective, and its picturesqueness is accentuated by the graceful masses of draping ivy that now adorn its walls. It is a most charming spot. There are no guides nor notice-boards about, so we presumed that we were well out of the tourists' beat. Returning we watched an angler patiently whipping the stream that runs down the valley and turns a pretty old mill on the way. We asked the same angler what luck he had. His reply was somewhat enigmatical: " Lots of luck, but no fish." As we bade him good day we expressed a wish that he might fill his creel before evening. I verily believe he thought we spoke satirically, for he made no response to our good wishes, and really we only intended to be civil.

Titchfield church, at which we glanced before leaving, is an ancient, picturesque, and interesting structure, a happy and harmonious conglomeration of many styles. Without there are steps to the belfry by the side of the tower, and within a grand altar-tomb, dated 1551, to the first and second Earls of Southampton ; this has square obelisks tapering to the top at each corner. One Earl is shown in full armour, finely decorated, his head resting on a folded mattress instead of the usual helmet, and a curious way of fastening the breast-plate is shown.

We had a mount out of Titchfield followed by a long stretch of level road that led us along at a considerable elevation. We should have had glorious views from here, but thick woods on either hand robbed us of them. Then we had a long and steepish descent to Bursledon Bridge, where we crossed the wide tidal river, the Hamble, on a picturesque old wooden bridge. Bursledon is an exceedingly pretty spot, hemmed in by wooded hills from the progressive modern world and all its ugliness. It was full of brightness and movement that morning. The river, gleaming with light as it flowed on, was enlivened by sundry white-winged yachts and floating fishing craft; these, with the waving woods around, combined to give an inspiriting feeling of freshness and life to the scene.

As we approached the bridge we found that there was a toll-house there, and that our way was barred by a gate; we could scarcely believe our eyes, it was so long since we had seen such a thing on a highroad; the existence of toll-gates had indeed quite slipped from our memory. Here we had to pay 1s., and were further asked if we required a return ticket. It appeared there was no saving in taking a return ticket, but we were told that "it avoids the necessity of pulling up on recrossing, and I always ask the quality the question." We felt flattered in being included amongst "the quality."

On from Bursledon our road was all up and down, with level intervals between. At a spot marked by a sign-post "To Southampton by the Floating Bridge" (why not ferry?) we turned to the left as it directed, deserting the old main road with its long detour to the same destination. As we proceeded, down in the valley far below we caught a peep of the gray ruins of Netley Abbey, drowned in foliage, and of the sea beyond. The ruins are situated in a spot of great natural beauty, though its ancient peace and quiet is being ruthlessly broken by the invasion of the modern builder, to whom no beauty is sacred. Wherever there stands a ruined abbey there one may look for lovely scenery, if no disturbing hand has been at work to despoil Nature of her rightful dower.

We had a long run downhill through shady woods, at the foot of which was the "floating bridge," and across the blue water the towers, buildings, and shipping of Southampton came into sight, all bathed in soft sunshine. The floating bridge is convenient rather than picturesque, otherwise this view of Southampton would appeal to a painter, or the ugly contrivance might be discreetly ignored in the making of a picture. How different this modern ferry from the primitive and picturesque one at Burpham!

CHAPTER XIII

An old-fashioned inn — The money value of a view — The river Test — The New Forest — Stoney Cross — The Rufus Stone — Possible origin of an old saying — The valley of the Hampshire Avon — Ringwood — Anglers' inns — Wimborne and its minster — Old customs — The curfew — A curious tomb — A library of chained books — Sign-posts — Poole Harbour — A peculiar inn sign.

AT Southampton we stayed at a regular old-fashioned inn, with old-fashioned ways, and an old-fashioned waiter to match, and of course we had a four-poster in our bedroom to make the thing complete. Some people, the waiter informed us, regretted that the inn did not move with the times, others liked it as it was—we were quite satisfied. Yet strangely inconsistent seemed the fact that here, of all places, we lost our individuality in a number, whilst hitherto on the road, without exception, all our bills had been made out in our name. I resent being turned into a mere numeral, which I am apt to forget. I positively dislike being asked at table of a huge company hotel by a waiter what "number" I am, nor do I specially delight in a boy coming up to me in the salon thereof demanding if I am sixty-eight!

From Southampton we drove to the New Forest.

Leaving the town, the quaint old High Street, with its interesting Bar Gate and picturesque houses, gradually gave way to the commonplace modern suburb without any interest or charm whatever; and I must say the Southampton suburbs seem to me unduly prolonged. Villas succeeded villas in tiresome monotony—worse still, they stood in long array between us and the lovely Southampton Water, preventing any view of the same excepting tantalising peeps of it, sadly limited in extent, that we got now and again between the buildings. These only served to show how much of beauty we missed. When at last we did obtain an uninterrupted prospect looking right down the water we were well rewarded. Unfortunately, the speculative builder has learnt the value of a view, and frequently places his "desirable villa" in a position not only to obtain it, but, alas! so that it is hidden from, or ruined to, the road traveller.

At the little village of Totton, the first on the way, we crossed the clear-flowing and troutful Test—grown into quite a wide river there—by two stone bridges, one old and gray, the other comparatively modern. The view from this spot looking up the valley is very charming. From the reedy river-side to the gently-sloping hills stretch forth level luxuriant meadows of a rich, restful green. Here and there in these we noticed the meek-eyed cattle were standing lazily about looking half asleep, just slowly and methodically whisking their tails now and then to keep the flies off—a very picture of dreamy contentment. The dominant note of the prospect was perfect tranquillity—a tranquillity that infused itself somehow into us, and caused us to loiter there indulging in the general slothfulness; it is a good thing to be slothful sometimes in this eager world. A very active man was about taking a short holiday, and, meeting his doctor, he asked him where he would best spend it. "In bed," replied the doctor!

It was some time before we got into the real forest, but at Cadnam, a small hamlet, we found ourselves at last there. All around nothing was visible but wild woods and winding sandy roads, with patches of blue and white sky above; but for those roads we might have imagined it to be the "forest primeval." Here we made a sketch of a picturesque thatched and whitewashed inn, called the "John Barleycorn." On one cottage of the hamlet was a notice that read, "Surgery: Attendance Monday and Friday at 11 o'clock," and we could only trust that the Cadnamites manage to fall ill, when they do, on one of those stipulated days. We asked a man who chanced to pass by then, how he managed with his family (we took it for granted that he had a family) if any of them wanted the doctor on the wrong day. His reply was slightly confused, though we grasped its intention: "Bless you, sir," said he, "we never wants no doctor, we don't." Enviable man! Happy family!

From Cadnam we had a long, rough, and tiring pull all uphill. The road was loose and sandy, the day was hot; moreover, the forest trees on either hand prevented any air coming to us. It was a blessed relief to get at last on to the high, open ground, where, for a space, low-growing gorse, heather, brambles, and bracken flourished in place of tall trees. Our prospect, recently so sadly limited to the length and width of our road, bound in by thick woods, now suddenly expanded to miles upon miles in every direction. This bit of open heath, known as Stoney Cross Hill, is perhaps the highest ground in the forest, which encompasses it on all sides. Here we entered upon quite another climate, for the air was sweet, delightfully fresh, and invigorating; indeed, it seemed almost cool after our warm muggy drive in the sheltered valley.

We were greatly rejoiced to find an inn at this ideal spot, standing all alone in restful solitude, with a pleasant garden, and—important detail to us— having stabling attached. We found the inn (which proclaimed itself by an old-fashioned sign-board as " The Compton Arms ") most charmingly situated and scrupulously clean, the landlord obliging, and the ostler one of the right sort. In virtue of which facts—though it was only mid-day and we had intended to have slept at Ringwood, some miles farther on, that night—we suddenly changed our minds. The scenery around was far too beautiful to be simply passed through; besides, the air was delicious, scented with the dry woods, soft and soothing, balmy though bracing; it was a pleasure simply to breathe it. The views, glance which way we would, were glorious and far-reaching; and then there was the garden to moon about in, should we be in a lazy mood : little wonder at our decision. I love a really fine view, and here we had it to perfection.

After having done justice to an excellent repast, served in a cool flower-scented coffee-room, whose windows looked right over the forest and on to the green garden, we set forth on foot in search of the Rufus Stone, which, we learnt, was situated in a hollow a little way below our inn. Before actually starting, however, we loitered on the high ground in order to leisurely admire the all-round views of the leafy sea that was spread out before us, above which Stoney Cross Hill rose like some great island. Look which way we would there was presented to our gaze a vast ocean of woods: hills and valleys of foliage, growing from green close at hand to a deep blue in the far-away horizon—just as though it had been swept with pure ultramarine. Nature is lavish in her colours when in the mood—miles of ultramarine are nothing to her! How space-expressing was the prospect! how unique for England all this vast wilderness of woods extending on all hands as far as the eye can range! To the south we looked over this sea of greenery to the Isle of Wight, and just glimpsed the Solent Water; to the north the view faded away in the far distance into a mystery of blue nothingness, where the earth seemed to melt into the sky, and to the west and east were woods again.

The Rufus Stone we found to be, to use an expression that sounds like an Irish bull, an iron one, with inscriptions thereon repeating the oft-told story of the King's death by a glancing arrow, a story that has caused much controversy as to its authenticity amongst scholars. It has even been doubted whether Sir Walter Tyrrel was in the forest at all on that eventful day, and some authorities will assert that the accident was no accident at all; however, into this controversy I do not care to enter; by accident or design the King was shot, and the Church did not regret the fact.

Near to the Rufus Stone is some of the most beautiful scenery in the forest, and finding our way into a secluded glade, we lay down on the soft sward and indulged in a little day-dreaming—

> Annihilating all that's made
> To a green thought in a green shade.

From time to time we noticed curious sounds that we could not well account for, till at last we discovered these were caused by the branches of the trees rubbing against one another, which may explain the mystery of certain forest fires, as the continued friction in very dry weather would, it seems to me, not improbably cause fire.

Looking over some odd volumes that found a place in the coffee-room of our inn, we extracted the following from an old guide-book. "The descendants of Purkis, the charcoal-burner who carried the body of the king to Winchester in his cart, enjoyed for centuries the right to the taking of all such wood as they could gather by hook or crook, dead branches and what could be broken, but not cut by the axe." It at once struck us on reading this whether it originated the term "by hook or crook." Hanging up on the wall of our inn we also noticed a map of the New Forest, dated 1849, "showing portions enclosed for the growth of Navy timber." This was, of course, in the age of the "wooden walls of Old England."

We were struck by the profound stillness that prevailed at Stoney Cross after nightfall; through our open bedroom windows not a sound came to us, not even a distant murmur of any kind; the silence seemed almost unnatural. We never felt before how companionable sound was—quite as companionable, in a way, as a fire in a room.

Our road out of Stoney Cross took us for some miles through a very wild part of the forest. The country was hilly too, and that with the warm day made progress slow; though on the high ground we did not feel the heat oppressive, still in the valleys it was rather stifling. Our horses were annoyed, too, by the famous (or infamous) forest fly. What the mosquito is to an Englishman on the Gold Coast much the same is the forest fly to the horse. At last we came to the end of the forest, and a wild, open upland, bleak and barren, succeeded it, looking more like a Scotch landscape than a Hampshire one. Here the forest fly suddenly ceased from troubling. It struck us as a curious coincidence that we should leave both forest and fly behind together, but we did.

Driving on, we had extensive views over a rolling country to the left, and in front a fine prospect of the lovely Avon valley, with its winding river and richly-wooded hills. Now a long descent brought us to the clean and neat little town of Ringwood, where we called our mid-day halt. The charm of Ringwood is its river. The Avon here is wide and shallow; it spreads itself out and makes a great show. The river, too, forms a double sort of highway, for we noticed boats upon it, and two carts with drivers proceeding along its bed, the water not being quite as high as the axles. The river is manifestly an important local thoroughfare; we had never observed one used as a road before.

Ringwood as a town is not remarkable for its picturesqueness nor for its ugliness, but its immediate surroundings are very beautiful; a ramble by the Avon side revealed countless pictures, and brought back to our remembrance many an old friend hung on the Academy walls. It was on a wild heath near here that the unfortunate Duke of Monmouth was captured after the rout at Sedgemoor in 1685, when he was brought into Ringwood and kept a prisoner at the "White Hart," whence he was taken on to London.

We started for Wimborne late in the afternoon, promising ourselves a cool and pleasant evening drive, for the day was warm and the weather was fine, and if we were benighted what would it matter? We crossed the Avon by two long bridges, and on the other side of the river we espied a picturesque inn by the water's side called the "Fish." It was a homely little inn, with a thatched roof, such as you see in Devonshire, toned into a delightful harmony of greens and silvery grays, and I have no doubt is a favourite resort of anglers, for both the lordly salmon and speckled trout abound

THE VALLEY OF THE HAMPSHIRE AVON, NEAR RINGWOOD

here; besides, the title of the inn suggested its patrons. Then we pictured to ourselves, perhaps too ideally, the "jolly" evenings that brothers of the "gentle craft" may have passed in that cosy-looking hostel, discussing over a post-prandial pipe their day's sport, or want of sport, and comparing notes thereon, telling their tales—wonderful tales that so delight—the tellers. There is always such a friendly feeling of fellowship amongst anglers, such manifest goodwill and kindliness, as far as I have ever seen or heard, that I often feel irresistibly drawn to become one of the fraternity, just for the sake of their charming, rest-giving company, that, like the quiet gurgling of the rivers they love, soothes the world-weary soul with an untold calm. From time to time, when driving about rural England, chance has taken me to one of these old-fashioned, angler-haunted inns, and the pleasant evenings spent therein have ever been a delightful memory to me. The talk is truly much of fish and fishing, but most anglers, I have found, are ardent nature lovers too, and mingle with their talk charming descriptions of scenery that it is a positive delight to listen to, so fresh, bright, and full of feeling are they just because they come spontaneously and from the heart. I love to simply sit and let their word-pictures drift to me amongst the soothing hum of the conversation. Said a happy angler one day as we were chatting together, "I'm a fisherman because it gives me an excuse to be out all day amidst beautiful scenery, and if, unlike a painter, I cannot bring back home with me any lasting results of my outing, at least I add to the pictures in my mind's gallery."

Then we drove uphill out of the Avon valley and along a perfectly and painfully straight road for miles, with dark woods of pine and Scotch fir on either side. The road reminded us strongly of some American ones because of its business-like look of going straight from one place to another. The resemblance to America was further enhanced by several shanties of wood we passed by. About three miles before Wimborne the scenery quite changed its character: the poor sandy soil and pine trees gave way to rich green meadows and leafy elms, and the wooden shanties to cottages whose walls were of mud. I cannot say that I admire a mud wall, but that may be prejudice; still, mud hardly seems a suitable or pleasant material to build with, if to build with mud be the right expression. However, one of the cottars said the hovels—I mean houses— were comfortable enough to live in, and he never bothered his head as to how they looked outside. The Dorset labourer appears to be a very contented being. Now contentment is a great blessing, but not in all cases an unalloyed one—it oftentimes is a preventive to progress. Had we all been content to travel by coach, the railway might never have been invented, and had we been satisfied with the slow speed of other days, the telegraph might not now have been flashing messages all over the world.

The glory of Wimborne is its minster, a building replete with interest. We paid a visit to it early next morning, expecting to spend perhaps half an hour there, yet somehow the whole morning slipped away inspecting the ancient fane, and then we found it all too short.

We were fortunate to find a verger or clerk to conduct us over the building who manifestly took a great pride in the same and all pertaining thereto, and who declared he was never weary of showing people "over *our* minster." We liked the word "our." He was a model guide, courteous and helpful in showing us all we wanted to see, patient in allowing us time to make notes and rough sketches, besides aiding us to decipher some ancient inscriptions. First he pointed out the font of Purbeck marble that had been in use there for seven hundred long years. Then next in order came one of the curiosities of the building, an ancient clock, constructed in 1320 by Peter Lightfoot, a monk of Glastonbury Abbey. This rare old clock, which stands within the tower, shows the sun and stars revolving round the earth, as the Church then declared they did, and proclaimed those who maintained otherwise as heretics, thus proving to future generations the fallibility of her infallibility:—

> Falsehoods which we spurn to-day
> Were the truths of long ago.

This clock also shows the moon changing from new to full all in due season. The sun as it revolves round the earth in the centre marks the hours, which, with the quarters, are struck by a military figure on two bells; the figure, carved in wood and painted, stands outside the tower, "there being no external clock face to the minster, as there never was one in medieval churches." They would appear to pride themselves here on their genuine medievalism — nineteenth-century medievalism is surely an anachronism? The clerk told us that all the ancient customs were religiously kept up. He rang the curfew at eight every night, the Angelus daily, matins at ten minutes past six in summer and ten minutes past seven in winter all the year through; he walked round the church twice during every service, wand in hand, to wake up sleepers. " Do you ever wake up any sleepers when you go round?" we inquired. The clerk looked meaningly at us: "I never see any," he said, a remark that might be interpreted in two different senses. Sometimes in this world it is convenient not to see!

Even the ancient custom is maintained of covering three or four monastic benches with white linen eucharistic cloths; these are placed in front of the Communion table during the celebration, and take the place of a rail.

The lectern is a good example of ancient brass-work. Engraved upon this are the initials "A. W.," a coat of arms, and the date 1623 below, the initials and coat of arms being presumably those of the donor. We understood the clerk to say that the name for which the initials stand had been forgotten, or there was some uncertainty in the matter, when it was accidentally discovered in a most unexpected way. It appeared that one day he was showing a gentleman with four friends over the church, and one of the party, upon examining the lectern, suddenly exclaimed,

"Why, that's our family crest!" and became quite excited when he further noticed the letters " A. W." above, further exclaiming, "Why, those are my initials too—my name's Wayte." Then he pulled out his watch, which had a coat of arms engraved on the case, and showed the engraving to the clerk, pointing out to him that it was exactly the same as the one on the lectern!

Then we were shown, on the south side of the choir, the fine altar-tomb, with effigy of John de Beaufort, Duke of Somerset, erected in the fifteenth century. Above this is suspended, on a bracket, an ancient helmet found buried in the nave "like so much rubbish" during some restorations. This was found to weigh $14\frac{1}{2}$ lbs., and was placed above the Duke's tomb, as it was presumed to have originally belonged to it.

Near here is a small brass with the following curious inscription and spelling. From this it would appear that the said William Smith was "viker" (surely a unique way of spelling vicar) of Sturminster after his decease :—

> Here lieth William Smith, Bachelor of Divinitie, and
> Sometime Schoolmaster & Fellowe of Eton Colledge
> And nowe viker of Sturminster Marshall & Preacher
> Of Wimborne, who died the 15 of Septembr. A.D. 1587.

On the floor of the chancel is a small brass let into a slab of Purbeck marble, that is stated to mark the last resting-place of Ethelred, King of the West Saxons. The brass is well engraved, and represents the King in his robes with crown and sceptre; it is medieval work, and may have replaced an earlier memorial. The inscription runs thus :—

> In hoc loco quiescit corpus sti Ethelredi Regis West Saxonum, Martyris, qui Anno Dom., 873, 23 Die Aprilis, Per manus Dacorum Paganorum occubuit.

Another tomb in the south aisle is truly a curiosity. This consists of an actual coffin in black marble containing the body of Anthony Etriche. This coffin is let into a niche constructed in the wall, and stands half above and half below the floor; it is covered with coats of arms, all coloured and gilt, with the name of the enclosed dead and the date of his death upon it, thus forming a complete monument. This Anthony Etriche was the magistrate who committed the Duke of Monmouth to prison after his capture. According to the clerk there is a tradition connected with this tomb, which he related to us in this wise. It appears that Anthony Etriche, who was a man of importance in his day, had a quarrel with the Wimborne people, and swore that he would not be buried in their church or churchyard, either over or under ground, and I trust that the Wimborne inhabitants of the period were duly impressed and grieved at this resolution. However, in course of time he repented taking this hasty oath, and desired, after all, to be buried in the church, so he obtained permission of the authorities to make the niche in the wall and place his coffin therein ready to receive his body at death. This peculiar arrangement was come to so that he should be buried neither in the church nor out of it, neither above ground nor below it, according to his oath. So there he lies in his coffin placed in the thickness of the wall of the church, neither within nor without the sacred building, neither quite above ground nor yet below it. The excellent condition of the coffin and the freshness of the heraldic devices, etc., thereon is accounted for by the fact that this said Anthony Etriche left by his will a certain sum of money to be expended annually in keeping his coffin in good and decorative repair. This sum, we further learnt, is to this day regularly paid by the rector of St. James' Church, Poole, out of his tithes from a farm devised by the said will.

There is much else of interest in this grand old minster, and many noticeable architectural features, such as the unique form of the east window, the quaint Norman cylindrical staircase that projects from the north transept, the remains of Norman altars, the groined vestry, and St. Mary's Chapel, now the crypt, but space will only permit my calling attention to one other object out of many that were pointed out to us. This is nothing more nor less than the actual relic chest (the clerk is still my authority) of St. Cuthberga, "the oldest article in the building"; indeed, it was old when the present building was new! It is formed out of the solid trunk of a big oak tree, roughly square hewn, a small portion being hollowed out of the centre to form the receptacle. This was found buried in the ground presumably by the Norman builders. It is now black with age and as hard as iron.

From the church we were conducted up a medieval turret staircase to the ancient Wimborne library, situated above the groined vestry or sacristy. This library was established here in the seventeenth century. All the books are chained to rods, and many are rare. The books were provided for the use of the people of Wimborne without charge, and thus was formed the first free library in England. This old chamber, therefore, with its oak-ribbed ceiling, and great shelves bearing the ponderous chained tomes, has an historic interest as well as an antiquarian one. The said tomes, by the way, appeared to us to provide somewhat heavy literature, that would scarcely suit the tastes of the present-day users of free libraries! There were two hundred and forty volumes in it originally, and every one of these is there now, which speaks well for the honesty of the Wimborne people, albeit the books were bulky, and secured by chains, so as not to be readily stolen. Books were prized in those early days. Had such a thing been possible, I wonder what a medieval Mudie's would have been like!

Amongst the many valuable volumes, the clerk pointed out to us a bound MS. in vellum, so well done that we even imagined it to be print at first sight; this is dated 1343, and is further noticeable as proving the early employment of Arabic numerals.

Then we were shown several other more or less interesting works, and amongst these Sir Walter Raleigh's *History of the World*. It was pointed out to us that this book had a hole burnt through a number of its pages, and thereby hangs a story. It appears, tradition being true, that Matthew Prior, the poet, when reading here surreptitiously one night, let a smouldering spark from a candle he had smuggled in, fall upon the open book whilst he was asleep, and, to his horror, when he awoke he discovered a hole burnt through half the pages. He then filled up the holes as well as he could by pasting paper over them, on which he inserted the missing words from memory—and an excellent memory he must have had. Anyhow there are the damaged places neatly filled in "to prove the story is true." It may be strictly so, but if this be proof, how easy a thing proof is. You may argue beautifully in a circle thus: The Druids built Stonehenge, and there Stonehenge stands to prove the Druids built it!

We had spent so much time, delightfully and profitably spent though, in exploring the ancient minster, that it was again late in the afternoon before we managed to resume our journey, and so we were only able to make a short stage as far as Wareham.

Just out of Wimborne we crossed the Stour by an old stone bridge, from the other side of which, looking back, we had a fine view of the town clustering round the gray towers of its old minster, with the river meandering in the foreground through emerald meadows; this view would make a capital subject for a picture. Indeed, round about Wimborne I fancy an artist might find plenty of fresh materials and suggestions for pictures; some of the aspects of the country, especially in the direction of Wareham, struck us as being particularly picturesque and paintable, not to say full of originality, if I may use the expression.

We had at first a long level stretch of road, with the river on one side and a railway on the other to keep us company as far as Corfe Mullen, a primitive village with a picturesque ivy-clad church, having a flag-staff on its tower in place of a steeple. Here we turned to the left, as directed by the sign-post. There always are sign-posts in villages where you can readily ask your way, but by some strange law of the supply being in the wrong place, they are but too frequently absent at cross roads in wild and remote country districts where there is not a house in sight, and seldom a creature of any kind about.

Presently we found ourselves in a lovely wooded country, made further beautiful by sloping meadows and silvery streams *à la* Devonshire. After a time this green and restful country gave place to a wild, sullen moorland, that rose here and there into sand-hills, bare in outline save in one or two stray places, where some stunted, wind-blown Scotch firs struggled for existence, and whose dark, gaunt forms served but to accentuate the general dreariness. I never remember a more sudden or wholly unexpected transition from the rich and lovely to the barren and austere ; just one bend in the road did it !

Over this wild waste, rough, stony tracks wound in and out, apparently leading nowhere, and looking much like superannuated water-courses, and at times our road appeared as though it might degenerate into something of the kind. This wild region, we observed, was marked as Lychett Heath on our map. Barren and desolate it was, yet not wholly unbeautiful, for its colouring was exceedingly rich and changeful, not to say extravagant, for staid England, infinitely more so than that of a pure pastoral land chiefly compounded of sober greens. The low sand-hills were a burning orange in the setting sun, their warm tints being emphasised by the blue-gray shadows of their ravines and the dark, gloomy green of the Scotch firs; then patches of purple heath, clumps of golden gorse, and straggling sprays of blossoming broom, with here and there the silvery sparkle of wind-rippled water, made gay this waste. Indeed, I am not quite sure whether it were not the most beautiful in colour of any portion of our journey; if we could only have divested our mind of the known fact that it was a barren waste, we might have considered it lovely. Associations have a great deal to do with our estimates of the beauty of scenery. As we drove on we noticed some dead Scotch firs that had failed in their hard struggle for life, their bark stripped off, and their bare trunks and contorted branches bleached white with the weather; they gave the landscape a weird, Salvator Rosa-like aspect.

We crossed a bleak hill here, from the top of which we had a glorious and extensive prospect, again utterly different in character from what had preceded it. High on the horizon ahead was an array of rounded hills, with just the suggestion of a peak-like form here and there; at their feet was spread out what looked like a grand lake, with "promontory, creek, and bay," and woods around its indented shore. This puzzled us, as we knew that there was no such lake in this part of England, yet the view distantly suggested Windermere. Could it be a mirage? Our map, however, solved the mystery: we were looking over Poole Harbour, a land-girt inlet of the sea, some six miles long by four broad, and the purple hills in the distance were those of the Purbeck range. It was a lovely vision of hill and dale, of rock, and wood, and winding water, all the more impressive and charming because it came upon us wholly unexpectedly. Poole Harbour does not sound a very suitable or poetic name for such a large and romantic sheet of water—romantic, at least, as seen from our point of view, with the long range of the undulating hills in the background.

Then as we descended we gradually lost the view, and in time found ourselves in the pretty village of Lychett Minster. Here we noticed a small wayside inn with the curious sign of "St. Peter's Finger." Though we made inquiries, we were unable to discover the origin of this quaint title. One native of whom we asked at once responded, " I can tell yer why it's called St. Peter's Finger; it's just like this: it were always called so, you see." But that was exactly what we did not, and the information so readily imparted did not help us at all.

Then our road led us through thick, dark, gloomy pine woods, oppressive almost in their gloom. The fences on either side of the way were earth walls built of slabs of turf. Altogether the country had anything but a cheerful appearance, and the gathering gloom added to the dreariness of the prospect;

it even sufficed to tone down our healthy, exuberant spirits, and to cause us to drive on in silence, and we were not sorry when our stage came to an end and we found ourselves in the ancient and decayed town of Wareham, where at the old Red Lion hostel we found accommodation and welcome letters from home.

CHAPTER XIV

Wareham—A town within its ancient Roman walls—A deserted Saxon church—The Isle of Purbeck—Corfe Castle—A quaint village—Picturesque houses—Swanage—Old customs—A professional invalid—Pure air!—Durlston Head—The world in stone—A grand cliff walk—Tilly Whim caves—"Wesley's Cottage."

WAREHAM struck us as being a charming old-world town, sleepy and utterly unprogressive, if not actually retrogressive, pregnant with interest for the antiquary or archæologist, and full of quaint bits that so delight the eye of an artist. Like Bosham, its importance is a matter of the past, but its picturesqueness is a thing of the present.

I am not going to dive into the history of Wareham, suffice to say it was an ancient British stronghold taken by Vespasian, who thereupon converted it into a fortified town or camp and surrounded it by walls. The present grass-grown earthworks, that enclose the town in the shape of a quadrangle, are formed over the walls of the Romans. The town has shrunk rather than grown since those early days, and in parts gardens now take the place of houses. Wareham is, I believe, the only English town still contained within its ancient Roman walls. Round the broad top of this grass-grown causeway one may walk and admire the country without and the time-mellowed buildings within.

As we entered Wareham we passed by the side of the little old Saxon church of St. Martin's, curiously built right on the wall, and standing well above the roadway. This church, reputed to have been first erected early in the eighth century, though manifestly much altered and restored since then, still shows in the nave—lofty in proportion to its size—sufficient evidence of its Saxon origin. This ancient fane is now deserted, desolate, and going to gradual decay; it is small for a modern place of worship, and therefore may probably escape further restoration, especially as the diminished population of Wareham can hardly need more accommodation than is at present provided. Such an interesting relic of the never-returning past should be preserved with loving care and maintained unaltered; to repair it is a necessity, to restore it further than this would be worse than a blunder—it would be an archæological crime! Its very stones are histories, they have weathered the storms and stress of centuries, they are time-worn and time-stained into countless hues. The aged pile is quaintly individual, and possesses an indescribably pathetic charm; it is a spot for a peace-seeking pilgrim to journey to, and, when in a dreamy mood, to allow the gathered glamour of its storied past and picturesquely poetic aspect to be instilled into him, for here both heart and eye are satisfied. It mutely appeals to be simply preserved, not to be restored backwards or forwards, for its history in stone is done, nothing now can be added to or taken away from it without hurt.

Within, the ancient church looks sadly forlorn. Nothing, indeed, remains there but the bare walls and ancient font; pulpit and pews (or seats) are gone, the floor is deep in sand. Better this at any rate than modern tiles. In early Saxon churches, it may be remembered, the floors were simply covered with rushes in the summer and straw in the winter time, so that the clean dry sand was not so much out of harmony with the fabric as a pavement of any kind would be, and it has the virtue of making the footsteps noiseless. On either side of the round chancel arch are two openings. One of these we took to be a squint, the other to be a passage to give access to the pulpit. Some of the windows are built up with brick, thus causing a mystic gloom within, a solemn half-light that well suits this shrine of ancient devotion, whose hoary walls seem verily to enclose an aroma of antiquity. Yet this dim, forsaken interior impressed us more than any grand cathedral in the utmost glory of its Gothic splendour has ever done : this poor, simple fane seems to come so close to the heart, to express the greatness of humility, the power that lies in lowliness, and all that made the early Church so beloved before she became rich, arrogant, and then persecuting, employing such Christian-like agents as the torture chamber and the stake, till men were wont to sigh for the wider charity and greater liberty of pagan Rome.

We both sketched and photographed the interesting old church without any one coming to look over

ST. MARTIN'S CHURCH, WAREHAM

us, or standing of set purpose right in front of the camera so as "to be took" and utterly spoil the picture, which unusual experience may prove how courteously behaved are the Wareham folk, or else how little curious. Several people passed by whilst we were at work with the pencil and camera, but no one, from politeness or other causes, seemed to heed us—not even the boys. Remarking upon the fact to an intelligent-looking native afterwards, he replied, with a broad grin worthy of Leech or Keene, " Lor' bless you, sir, 'twould take a sight more nor drawing nor photographing to rouse the Wareham people, they're so solid"—we presumed he meant stolid. However, we preferred to consider them polite. It is always so much pleasanter to look on the good side of human nature—and sometimes the good side is the true one!

Being at Wareham, we determined to drive across the Isle of Purbeck—a curious misnomer, for it is no island at all—to Swanage, as we had never been to that spot nor to Corfe Castle ruins, that lie on the road thither. Just out of Wareham we crossed the sluggish river Frome, on an old, gray, five-arched bridge; from this bridge is a fine view of the town, with the stream winding round its southern walls. Then followed a long, low, level stretch of land where once flowed the sea, a sea over which ships sailed right up to ancient Wareham; now it has retired and left the Dorset port, like Rye and Pevensey, a mile or more inland. After traversing the site of the former sea we passed through the dull and dreary village of Stowborough. My wife would have it that its proper name was Slowborough, and that the "t" for "l" was manifestly the map engraver's blunder. After this we came upon the wild stretch of open country known as Creech Heath. Heather, gorse, and a wiry sort of grass seemed about all the vegetation that flourished there. On either hand the gorse, in full flower and fragrance, spread around us like a golden sea, and scented the air with its peculiar perfume—a golden sea bounded in the near distance by the purple Purbeck hills, that rose mistily and majestically before us in the hazy summer atmosphere. What a country this Isle of Purbeck is for colour, with its gorse-spread commons, wine-stained heaths, purple hills, that fade away into soft, blue, dreamy distances, and gleams of sapphire and sparkling seas. It may have been due in some measure to the almost perfect day, but such a feast of rich and varied colour I never remember having beheld anywhere before : the glories of Italy and Turner's poetic visions of many-hued landscapes seemed to pale before it. Should any landscape artist find that he is getting his pictures too gray or dull, I would seriously advise him to hie hither with his canvases and pigments, and try to paint up to the brilliant colour and joyousness of the Purbeck hills and dales and the gleaming summer seas that wash the rock-bound coast around.

In front of us rose Creech Barrow, a conical peak strongly marked in outline from all around, and not unlike in form the cone of some volcano; then on a rounded height in a deep gap between the long range of hills the gray ruined towers and broken walls of Corfe Castle came into view, the ruin being the only dark spot in the bright sunlit landscape, which was suffused with light. Why did the ruin stand out so sombre and gloomy, when all around was so gay and fair, rejoicing in the cheerful unshadowed sunshine? Was it in mourning for the past, for the dark deeds done within its battered walls? The approach to Corfe Castle by the Wareham road is impressive; you drive round the base of the steep conical hill on which it stands. The rent and rugged keep above towers on its isolated height, so that you have actually to crane your neck to look up at it. Were it to give way it would come crashing right down on the road below, as some massive portions of the masonry have already done when the fortress was destroyed by order of Parliament, and still remain, half buried by the force of the descent, in the grass across the way. It is a stiff climb up to the keep, but the views therefrom on to the hills and over the wild country around well repay the mount, even when taken on a hot and tiring day. The history of the castle is long, tragic, and heroic. It ended its career in the usual manner of most English castles being held for King Charles I. and duly taken by the Parliamentarians. Now it is one of the most picturesque ruins in the country by virtue of its fortunate position and happily-disposed arrangement of broken walls and ruined towers. Without knowing it, the stern Puritans were often picture-makers; time and they have converted a frowning fortress into a rugged romance! They destroyed better than they imagined!

But the village of Corfe itself is as interesting and as worthy of consideration as the castle—more so indeed to us; there are many ruined castles in England, but not another village quite like Corfe: it is as full of character and as unique in its way as more famous Clovelly. Till lately Corfe has been out of the beaten tourist track, but now the railway has found it out, and who knows how long it will retain its primitive picturesqueness? Fortunately there are no large cities or towns near that breed the noisy tripper, for when he invades a spot there is a truce to all romancing, and the luxury of a little harmless day-dreaming becomes an impossibility.

The village of Corfe charmed us. In the first place it was delightfully clean. Its stone-built houses have a substantial look of solid comfort that pleases the eye; they, too, have roofs of stone slabs, all toned down, more or less, into a restful harmony of silvery grays, varied by green moss and enlivened by golden lichen. Ivy, moss, and lichen are the three great beautifiers of our buildings. Strip lovely Tintern or any other ruined abbey, castle, or ancient manor of these three inconsidered things, and where would be their charm? Now the railway has come to this ancient village, the new houses, should any be built, may be of brick, and they surely will be roofed with cheap slates of chilly blue hue. A traveller of half a century hence looking down upon Corfe from the castle height

will need no one to tell him what houses have
been built since the railway came there; he will
be able to tell from their slated roofs, as a friend
of mine once did in a Yorkshire town, to the
astonishment of a native thereof, who was puzzled
to divine how a perfect stranger could point out
exactly every new building that had been erected
there since the coming of the iron way.

Though built of stone, Corfe is not a hard-
featured place, like many of the north country
towns; the softer climate may have something to
do with the difference, but not all, I think. Some
of the Corfe houses are quaint, and therefore interesting; they are individual, and attract attention
to themselves; you cannot well pass them unheeded
by, notably one that stands facing the little square,
and looks upon the gray steps that erst supported
the old market cross. This cross probably came
to grief when the castle was "slighted." There
is also another very interesting great gabled house
on the Swanage road that makes a very pleasing
picture with its mullioned windows and low wall-
enclosed courtyard, entered by a pillared gateway
from the road. This courtyard, the paved way
across which was adorned by flowers in tubs when
we were there, keeps the house private and pleasantly retired from the village street, besides adding
to its quiet dignity. Those old builders knew
what they were about. Then there are two homely
and picturesque inns, one, the "Greyhound," bearing
the date 1733 on its front. Both these inns have
a projecting gabled story, beneath which is the

doorway, well sheltered from the weather, as an inn doorway should be, and just below the castle is a gray old droning watermill. Almost every corner of the village forms a ready-made picture, with the hills around for a background, that give the prospect a snug, enclosed appearance.

On from Corfe to Swanage our drive was a dream of loveliness. The railway extends as far as the latter place, but hitherto it has done but little to damage the primitive picturesqueness of the country. Ever and again, as we journeyed on, we had charming visions of green woods, sloping velvety meadows, gleams of silvery waters, and purple hills, with old-time homes and scattered farmsteads dotted irregularly about. Passing the village of Herston, and an ideal and ancient stone-built modest mansion a little way beyond, we soon found ourselves driving down the long hill into sunny Swanage, with right ahead of us the brilliantly blue and sun-sparkled sea rolling in before a brisk breeze, its white-capped and crested waves breaking on the curved shore in mimic fury.

Swanage welcomed us with a smile. It impressed us as being a most delightful seaside resort, with a light, pure air, a splendid sea, and provided with grand coast or lovely inland scenery for the fortunate sojourner therein to explore : the sublime or the beautiful, just as the mood of man or woman may desire. The visitor to Swanage is not confined to seascapes or sand-hills in the rear ; within a moderate walk or easy drive there are lovely landscapes to look upon, as green and treeful as though they were set right in the heart of some Midland shire. At Swanage you have the double charm of the seaside and the country-side, the marine and the rural in happy proximity; the sea, too, there is interesting. You look across it, not to the usual long, unmeaning, horizontal line, but on to stately cliffs crowned by rounded downs, with, to the right, a far-away peep of the Needles, and the Isle of Wight beyond looming up, a tender mass of pearly gray that melts into the sky.

We found a very comfortable hotel at Swanage, and after a rest and refreshment there, we set forth on foot to explore Durlston Head, with its grand cliff scenery and the famous quarries near by, where the renowned Purbeck marble comes from, so much employed of old in the shafts, pillars, and monuments of our cathedrals and churches. The Purbeck quarriers are a race apart, with their ancient and peculiar rights and customs, all firmly maintained from the distant times of the Edwards down to this day. No one but a descendant of a quarryman, or a man who has married a quarryman's daughter, is permitted to work in the Purbeck quarries. The men are all enrolled in a sort of trades' guild, known as the Court of the Free Marblers; any outsider, however introduced, is termed a foreigner, and quickly given to understand he is not wanted, and had better depart peacefully. Some outsiders have not taken the hint, and have afterwards regretted it. So much at least we gathered from a communicative stranger with whom we got into a long conversation whilst smoking a farewell pipe on the sea front a little later on; for Swanage appears to be a friendly sort of place, where people—English people—are not afraid to speak civilly one to another even though they be strangers. I once asked a refined and much-travelled American gentleman what impressed him most in England. Replied he, "The beauty of the rural scenery and the innocent snobbishness of the people: they seem afraid to speak to one another without a formal introduction." Still there are exceptions to every rule, and now and then one comes across a stray Englishman as genial and talkative as any American. We have met many such on our road travels, but very few indeed when journeying by rail. Yet how charming and delightful in conversation an Englishman can be when he throws off his armour-clad reserve and is simply natural.

Swanage happily has not yet quite developed into a fashionable watering-place, for it still retains much of its pleasing and sociable primitiveness. Now the stranger we fell into conversation with interested us: his friendly, jovial manner was a novel experience. He at any rate was not reserved. After a time he ventured to ask us where we came from, to which we replied that we were on a driving tour and had started from Eastbourne. "Ah!" exclaimed he, "I know Eastbourne. It blows 365 days in the year there. Here it blows 300. Now perhaps you would like to know what I am." We mildly hinted that we should. "Well, I'm a professional invalid—that is, I make a business of being an invalid; it does me good." The man was an enigma; his talk was puzzling; we could not exactly comprehend what a professional invalid was. Would he explain? "Why, certainly," replied he. "I had been overworked. The doctor prescribed perfect rest for three months, and said if I did not get it at once I should get it in the cemetery in less than the three months. I chose to take it at once and not to wait for the cemetery. I was positively forbidden to do work of any kind, but being an active-minded man, I found time hanging heavily on my hands, so I became a professional invalid to save myself from *ennui*, and went the round of the different watering-places and started trying all the cures. It gave me an interest in life. I think I know all the faults and all the virtues of every English spa." "Well, what is the special virtue of this place?" we asked. "The purity of the air," he at once replied. "You can take a freshly-caught herring and place it on a stick upon Durlston Head and it will simply dry up. The experiment has been tried often with the same result, but elsewhere a herring will putrefy if so treated. You just try one on Beachy Head. So the air here is proved to be almost free from microbes."

But I am rather previous. This conversation took place after our return from Durlston Head, and should by correct chronological order have been recorded after that climb. Let me hark back to where I was before starting on this over-long digression. Leaving our excellent hotel, we at once proceeded to the Head, the summit of which we found to consist of a wild rock-strewn moorland.

Here, on a ledge of the cliff below a huge restaurant that is an eye-sore in the grand prospect all around, is a curiosity in the shape of a huge stone globe some ten feet in diameter, representing the earth, with its continents, islands, mountains, rivers, and seas all carved on the surface in slight relief or the reverse. It gives an excellent idea of our planet, but its proper place would seem to be in some museum, and not facing the wild waste of tumbling waters that dwarfs it, large though it be, into insignificance. Around this globe are stone seats set at different angles, and marked accordingly: East, North, North-West, and so forth. Also two large stones set up on end, with the following inscription on the top of each :—

> Persons anxious to write
> their names will please do
> so on this stone.

A precaution, we presume, to save the globe from being disfigured. We observed that the two upright stones were well covered with names. The idea seems an excellent one, and might with advantage be used elsewhere. The stones would, of course, require frequent renewal!

From the globe we had a truly glorious walk along the rough top of the rocky cliffs high above the tumbling and foaming sea. The walk is protected by a stone wall on the outer edge of the crags, or else it would be dangerous ; now it is both grand and safe, and forms one of the finest and wildest marine rambles in the kingdom. It was a truly enchanting stroll we had that day along that breezy height, with the deep, dark indigo blue sea far beneath us breaking into the masses of yeast-like foam amongst the jagged rocks, or else rolling with a dull and frequent boom into the wave-worn caverns far below. We looked right down also on the white glancing wings of the circling gulls whirling about in mid air, their weird and plaintive cries being plainly heard above the prolonged thunder-tones of the ocean's roar. It is not often that one can watch the flight of a bird thus from above.

At one spot we observed a large stone inserted into the wall, on which the following apt verse was inscribed :—

> An iron coast and angry waves,
> You seem to hear them rise and fall
> And roar, rock-thwarted, in their bellowing caves
> Beneath the windy wall.

Presently the rugged cliff road ended at the mouth of a descending and dark subterranean passage or tunnel, cut out of the solid rock ; this led us down to a most romantic spot, a wide ledge right on the steep side of the weather-beaten crags, from which a number of dark, gloomy caverns opened, known locally as the Tilly Whim Caves. There is nothing here to be seen but the caverns, the wild crags above and below, and the unquiet sea. Standing alone in this solitary spot, with nothing visible but rock, and sea, and sky, one might almost fancy oneself at the end of the world :—

> . . . in a waste place, where no one comes,
> Nor hath come, since the making of the world.

We lingered long on this romantic ledge. It was very soothing and peace-bestowing after the crush of crowded cities to feel, if only for a brief time, thoroughly out of the world, and we gave ourselves up to the illusion of remoteness that the spot produced in our minds. Sky, and sea, and rock are the same to the sight as they were ages long ago, and from our mid-cliff standpoint this was all we saw. There was nothing to tell the eye in what century we were living; neither ship nor sail was visible on the tossing waters, only a long uneven streak of heaving white showed where the hurrying waves fretted and fumed in hurtless fury along the foot of the dark gray crags. Even the shrill cry of the wandering gull that mingled with the sounds of the surging seas uprising from below seemed but to emphasise the loneliness of the spot—at least it seemed lonely enough to us when we were there. One almost selfishly wishes that so charming and romantic a spot were not so near Swanage—now that the railway has come thither.

Returning the way we came by the zigzag cliff walk, we had a grand ocean panorama nearly all the way before us, with fine views over Swanage as we descended into that most charming of seaside resorts, though, alas! there are signs that Swanage has been bitten with the improvement—save the mark—mania. Any alteration in Swanage now must be for the worse in a picturesque point of view; rows of commonplace lodging-houses of the ordinary watering-place type would play havoc with its ancient beauty. At any rate let us hope, for the sake of the amateur artists who, amongst other company, may come to Swanage in the future, that the dear old gabled watermill, close by the church, with its green moss-grown wheel, gray old walls, lichen-laden stone roof, and clear flowing stream, may be left for many years to gladden their eyes. The old mill looks as though it simply existed now for the sake of the water-colour painter. A stone label on the end gable bears this legend :—

Ben Barlow
of
Southamton
Fecit 1754.

On glancing at its dusky interior we noticed that the creaking wheels that conveyed the motive power from one point to another were of wood, and their teeth also, a curious survival in this present iron age, and showing what primitive arrangements prevailed in these parts as late as the eighteenth century, and showing also how delightfully unprogressive Swanage has been content to remain. Even to-day the ancient mill still bravely works on and slowly grinds its corn.

As we ascended the hill up which old Swanage climbs inland from the sea on our return and evening drive to Wareham, we passed, in a hollow to the left of our road, a picturesque creeper-covered cottage of one story, with dormer windows in the lowly roof. We had not noticed this pretty old cottage on entering Swanage, and our attention was now especially attracted to it by the following inscription thereon :—

John Wesley's
Cottage
August 13th,
1787.

On inquiring, we learnt that John Wesley slept two nights there during a visit he made to the Isle of Purbeck on purpose to preach to the quarrymen. The rest of our journey was a repetition of our morning drive, only taken the reverse way, and it was curious to note how fresh and unfamiliar the landscape looked simply from the different views thus obtained of it. To get the full benefit of the beauty of the country when driving, one needs almost to have eyes both back and front ; the only alternative is to take frequent looks round so that nothing may be missed. We discovered some charming and quite unexpected scenic gems this way, the more especially later on when journeying up the lovely and little-known Cerne Valley.

CHAPTER XV

Curious inscriptions—An amusing blunder—"The Bloody Bank"—Hills and heather—A haunted manor—Wool Bridge—Bindon Abbey—Winfrith—Roadside acquaintances—A primitive interior—The story of a pew—Maiden Castle—Dorchester—An evening ramble.

BEFORE starting in the morning from Wareham we indulged in just one more stroll round the quaint, sleepy old town, and during our ramble we came upon the curious Church of St. Mary's, that we had previously missed, it being hidden away in an odd corner from the public gaze. Not content with possessing a rare old Saxon fane, Wareham must needs have a second church of almost equal interest within her ancient walls. The door of the building chanced to be open, and, marvellous to relate, the clerk was inside ; he must have divined, though why I cannot profess to say, that we had come that morning to see and not to pray, for he at once offered his services to show us over the church. Accepting the inevitable, we placed ourselves meekly in his hands to be "personally conducted." The average clerk appears to distrust any stranger who is so singular-minded as to desire to inspect a church quietly alone, and perhaps in some instances there are reasons for his distrust, for I have heard of two cases in which churches have been robbed of their brasses by strangers, one of whom, perhaps the better to disarm any possible suspicion, was dressed as a clergyman!

The font was the first thing pointed out to us. This is a quaint and rare specimen of Anglo-Norman metal casting and chasing; it is of lead, and hexagonal in shape, having figures around it of the twelve apostles in relief. Near to this a large massive stone coffin is preserved, with a recess cut for the head and rounded angles outside. This is supposed to have contained the body of King Edward the Martyr, and " there is nothing to show that it did not," which kind of negative proof does not greatly commend itself to my precise mind. Presumably the coffin belonged to some important personage, for the labour of quarrying and chiselling out such a huge block of stone must have been considerable, and as King Edward was buried in this church after his murder at Corfe Castle, it may possibly be his; but possibilities are not facts. Then at the south-east corner of the church we were conducted down some steps to King Edward's Chapel, which has a groined roof, and appears to be now used as a robing-room for the clergy and choir-boys; so is its ancient glory dimmed. This chapel is said to be built on the site of an Anglo-Saxon stone one, which in turn succeeded one of wood or wattle, and here the body of the martyred king lay till it was removed to be enshrined at Shaftesbury. It is possible that then, presuming the stone coffin referred to belonged to him, the remains were removed from the heavy and rude stone receptacle into a lighter one for the convenience of transit.

Strangely placed over King Edward's Chapel is another small one, to which access is gained by an Early English door constructed in the south wall of the chancel. This little chapel is provided with an altar and an east window.

Built in the east wall of the north aisle is a curious and crumbling stone sculpture of the Crucifixion, with an inscription in very puzzling letters below. Before the restoration in 1842, we were told, this sculpture was inserted in the outside wall of the church and over the north porch. The inscription is supposed to relate to a bishop of the fifth century, and has been read as " Catug consecravit Deo." We, however, could make nothing of the lettering even after being made aware of how it ought to read; it appeared to us that with a little imagination it might be construed into almost anything. Inside the south porch several more ancient inscribed stones were pointed out to us, built into the wall; these, the clerk remarked, had been too much even for the learned authorities who had deciphered the "Catug" legend. Outside the church is a portion of the old priory house, that, with its time-toned walls and crumbling gateway, makes a very pleasing picture.

Apropos of deciphering inscribed stones, a gentleman related to me an amusing experience which came under his notice. It appears that upon a certain occasion he joined an Archæological Society's excursion, and that one of the members, during the expedition, discovered a curiously-carved stone in the wall of a farm-building. On the top of this stone was a rudely-cut mark, that one of the learned lights of the party pronounced to be a crude representation of a bishop's crosier, and the lettering below to be certainly Anglo-Saxon, and expressed his opinion that the stone was an important "find," as he had little doubt but that it was a portion of a memorial to an early bishop. Just then the farmer appeared on the scene, and in reply to inquiries as to whether he knew anything about the stone, replied, to the chagrin of the learned light, but to the amusement of the others, that it was carved by a shepherd of his father's a long time ago, when he was a mere boy; he believed that the shepherd had done it just to amuse himself, and that the design on the top was intended to portray his crook; the rude letters below were intended to spell the shepherd's name. Which only shows that it is not wise to jump too readily to the conclusion that any old-looking carved or inscribed stone that does not easily explain its meaning, or is not at once decipherable, is on that account a veritable antique. On a former journey I was innocently deceived by a pseudo-Druidical circle, formed by some huge and weather-stained boulders being set up Stonehenge fashion on a wild common near Bramdean in Hants, only in this case the undesirable joke of setting up those stones to puzzle future generations of travellers must have been an expensive one.

We left Wareham by the west gate, now merely a gap in the grass-grown earth-works, or rather walls. Near to this is a spot locally called "The Bloody Bank," where a number of unfortunate men were executed by order of the infamous Judge Jeffreys for taking part in Monmouth's rebellion, the Judge excusing his severity by stating that "treason must be stamped out of the land." He might have remembered Sir John Harrington's epigram :—

> Treason doth never prosper. What's the reason?
> Why, if it prosper, none dare call it treason.

Our road was level at first, with wide grassy margins on either side of the way, and glorious views to the south of the Purbeck hills, that melted on the horizon into a wonderful gray-purple tint. The charm of the rare colouring of these hills was a delightful and continued surprise to us. After a time our road opened out into a rugged gorse-spread common dotted with a few ragged Scotch firs. Here was colour again : the bright yellow of the gorse all aglow in the summer sunshine, its brilliancy set off by comparison with the dark, gloomy green of the firs.

As we drove gently on we had a fine view to our left over a well-watered valley, in the centre of which stood the pretty village of East Stoke—pretty from our distant point of view at any rate. The village was situated close by the side of a winding river, which was spanned by a gray old bridge; then passing by some thoroughly Dorsetshire cottages of mud walls and thatched roofs, we came to a wild and extensive heath, on which nothing but stunted heather seemed to grow. The sun just then was "baking hot," for on some days the sun can shine in England in a manner worthy of India, but no shelter of any kind could we obtain. However, we might have been worse off had we been caught in a thunderstorm in such a bleak and inhospitable region. The road was in our favour, and far ahead, in the direction we were travelling, we caught a welcome glimpse of a green and tree-shaded country, with a river winding through it.

We were not sorry to part company from the parched and heated uplands. It was refreshing once more to come to a lowland country of cool, silvery streams, fresh meadows, leafy hedgerows, and wide-spreading elms, with all their wealth of shady foliage. Driving on, we reached the banks of the slow-gliding river Frome, a charming and clear little river that flows through a lovely country. Just before crossing the river on a past-century bridge we espied the gray gables and chimney-stacks of an ancient home. The sight of this at once caused us to pull up and get out our sketch-book and camera. Wandering up to the old house, we knocked at the door and begged permission to photograph it, half out of politeness and half with the hope that somehow, by so doing, we might be able to obtain a peep inside, for the place had an indescribable look that suggested to us a quaint and interesting interior. We were somewhat of impostors, I must confess, for before we begged permission we had already "snapped" just one or two views of the building with our camera. Certainly a *good* hand camera— it need not be a detective—is a great addition to the tourist's kit.

The servant who answered the door said she would ask her master, who at that very moment chanced to come on the scene, and at once most courteously granted us the permission we sought. " You're very welcome," said he, "to photograph the old place from wherever you like ; just go round about where you please," and we did, and openly obtained some very pleasing results, the master of the house going with us, and manifestly taking great interest in the proceedings. During our conversation with him we learnt that the old house was known as Wool Manor, the village of Wool being across the river, and that the bridge was also called Wool Bridge. The manor-house was now doing duty in its old age as a farmstead, and our host, who was the tenant thereof, had been farming there for thirteen years ; moreover, strange to say, he did not complain of the bad times. As we were wandering about he pointed out to us an ancient building, now used as a barn, which he said was formerly a chapel belonging to the house, and it bore signs of having served some such purpose. " Certain portions of the place," he said, "were erected as early as 1300. It is a strange old house inside, and there are some wonderful old pictures there too." Our curiosity was raised, but our hopes of an invitation to follow to view the interior were suddenly damped by his further remarking, "If you're passing by another day I should be very pleased to show you over the inside ; it's a funny old place, that it be. But to-day is washing day, and the place is a bit upset in consequence, and the missus wouldn't like it if I took any one over, and that's a fact." We were terribly disappointed, and wished the washing day in the middle of next week ; so did the farmer, as it was not much in his line, but we could not see any way of propitiating "the missus." There was nothing for it but to depart resignedly.

Before leaving, the farmer called our attention to the fine old porch, and showed us a curious fastening to the massive door there, remarking, "You won't often see the likes of this." It was a solid beam of oak that slid into the thick wall alongside, and when pulled out, held the door fast in the same way that an iron bolt would on a smaller scale. Over the doorway is a date carved in stone. This we naturally took to be the year in which the house was built, but we were informed that this stone had belonged to an exterior building pulled down some time back, and that the landlord had it put where we saw it for ornament, which is another proof of what pitfalls beset the unwary archæologist who trusts overmuch to what the eye sees, for this weather-worn date-stone might have deceived the very elect. After this, with many thanks for his kindness, we bade our worthy host good day, not forgetting also to wish him a prosperous harvest, for good wishes cost little and please much.

Then we crossed the bridge and made a sketch of the ancient home from the farther side of the river. Whilst we were doing this the farmer came up and greeted us once more, exclaiming that he had forgotten to tell us the house was haunted, and he

HAUNTED! WOOL BRIDGE MANOR-HOUSE.

thought we might like to know it; he had indeed
heard one gentleman say that he would not sleep
a night in it for any money. This was interesting,
not to say exciting, news. It is not every day one
comes upon a haunted house inhabited. This
was a matter for inquiry; we felt anxious to obtain
all particulars about the ghost. Had the farmer or
any one of his family seen it? did it disturb them?
what was it like? and so forth. Came the reply,
" Lor' bless you, sir, I don't let the ghost worry me.
I'm not a nervous man. He never did any of us any
harm. Now, do I look like a nervous man?" and
we felt bound to confess that in our estimation he
hardly did. But we were not getting the precise
information we desired, so we had to bring the
farmer to the point. " What was the ghost like?"
explaining, as an excuse for our curiosity, that we
had never yet seen a real ghost, only imitation ones,
and we wanted to know what the genuine article
was like. " Well, sir," he responded, " our ghost "—
we were struck by the expression, it seemed to give
a sort of private ownership to the spirit or goblin, or
whatever it was—" our ghost consists of a coach and
four, with a ghostly coachman and all complete, but no
passengers, and it drives right out of the top window
there, at midnight generally ; but he's very irregular
in his movements, and he goes so mortal fast that I
can never see him myself, but folks around all
swears as how they do. It never bothers us indoors, it's the rats as make it lively at nights. I've
no complaint to make against the ghost." " Well,
but," said we, " how can a coach and four get

through that small window—there's not nearly room enough?" The farmer was equal to the occasion. "That's not my affair," replied he, "now, is it? That's purely the ghost's business," and we felt that the farmer had the best of us.

About half a mile to the east of Wool Bridge are the slight remains of Bindon Abbey, one of the oldest foundations in England, it dating from 1172. The ruins are charmingly situated in a leafy wood. It is, in truth, a pleasant spot, made musical by the songs of birds and the gurgling of wandering streams. The bases of several pillars of the nave are left, but nothing of any height or importance; still the ground plan of the building can be clearly traced. However, it is more for the sake of the quiet beauty of the spot that visitors would go there than for the interest of the ruins.

In a mile or two from Bindon's "ruined fane" we reached the pretty little village of Winfrith. Here the "Red Lion," a modest roadside inn with stabling, tempted us to call a halt, for the day was hot, and we felt a trifle hungry and very thirsty. There was a wide stream curiously running round the inn between it and the road, and there was a shallow ford over this to the door by which those who drove had to approach; a wooden foot-bridge provided access for pedestrians. This stream, ford, and bridge gave the long, low, two-storied hostel quite a quaint appearance; it had, too, the charm of novelty. Here we were shown into a clean, cool, low-ceilinged parlour, and a simple repast of bread and cheese, with butter and a fresh, crisp salad, was quickly set before us, and served on a spotless cloth; nor must I forget the clear, nut-brown, frothing ale that to our thirsty palates seemed a drink fit for the gods, and infinitely to be preferred to the finest champagne fair France could produce.

We had a chat with the landlady, who appeared to be a very busy body, for the thirsty travellers on the road seemed many and poor, but for all she had a smile. In the little bar we observed a notice hung up conveying this intelligence :—

> Our Credit Department
> Is closed for Repairs.

Queried one patron, "When will it be open again, missus?" The answer was to the point, "When folk don't want credit," and then a good-natured titter went round the room. It does not take much to amuse English country people, and I think it a good sign when people are easily amused. It is the upper classes who are so difficult to arouse into any enthusiasm or laughter; they are trained in a school of reserve; poor folk do not bother their heads about precedence, formality, or being introduced, or belonging to a certain set—they are companionable at once. Whilst we were there enjoying our simple repast, a touring cyclist arrived and sought rest and refreshment at our inn—a quiet-spoken gentleman. He was shown into another parlour to have his meal, and it was only outside the inn, whilst smoking a pipe, that we were able to make friends with him. I must say I like when I am travelling to exchange views with those I meet on the way, from the peer that chance has brought me in contact with on rare occasions at country inns, to the peasant and ploughboy always at command.

Our road on to Dorchester was a delightful one ; the country was interesting and the scenery beautiful. To our left there rose a long range of low, undulating, grassy hills, a golden green in the sun and a cool gray green in the shade, a range of hills that reminded us distantly of the South Downs, only more varied in form and colour, though not so grand in mass. The first place we passed by was Warmwell, with a quaint old manor-house. The heat of the sultry summer afternoon caused us to make a feeble joke as to the inappropriate name of the village during the hot weather. The next village was all stone-built, and had a somewhat austere look. The churchyard there, we observed, was raised well above the level of the roadway, presumably by long-continued interments. We noticed an ancient holy-water stoop outside the west door of the church, and that was all of interest we could discover.

Now the country became undulating and the scenery pleasantly varied ; great rocks peeped up in places through the soil, and meadows, that gave a feeling of the sterner north country. A mile or two farther on, at the bottom of a dip in the road, we reached another small and primitive hamlet with the long name of Winterbourne Came. The ancient church here, approached by a footpath across a field, was picturesque-looking with its ivy-grown tower, and in its peaceful God's acre we saw the stump and steps of an old churchyard cross. The interior of the building was primitive to a degree, simple and unadorned enough, indeed, to have delighted the heart of a Cromwellian Puritan. The roof was of flat plaster, and there stood the old-fashioned pews of our forefathers in the nave. Along the walls by the side of these were rows of plain wooden pegs for the congregation to hang their hats and coats or cloaks on; the floor was of rough stone slabs, worn uneven by the tread of long-departed generations of worshippers. Yet there was something about that poor and primitive fane that appealed to us. I think it must have been the utter absence of all pretence, it was so genuinely, unblushingly innocent of any architectural effect—as plain, in truth, as any barn. After all, there is a certain charm and virtue in utter simplicity; it may be ugly, but it is honest. A window plainly glazed, through which one can see the blue sky, moving clouds, and green leaves, is far less offensive to the art-loving eye than a pretentious traceried one, filled with poor stained glass of wretched design and crude colouring. I have even the bad taste to prefer—greatly prefer—a simple stone slab floor to one of garish tiles, that always suggests the entrance passage of a modern villa to me; and I prefer almost anything to the usual stock selections of bright Birmingham brass ecclesiastical fittings that follow one everywhere throughout the land from cathedral to chapel. Glare and glitter, crude colouring, and an over-abundance of decoration that does not decorate are best left for the public-house.

Writing of old-fashioned, high-backed pews calls to remembrance the following authentic circumstance.

Many years ago a country clergyman obtained the needful authority to have all the high-backed pews in his church cut down, which was duly done, one member of the congregation alone objecting, and he was so annoyed at having his old seclusion intruded upon that he actually had the floor of his pew lowered, and descended into it by steps!

Approaching Dorchester, we caught sight, to our left, of the dark mass of Maiden Castle rising conspicuously from a bare down. This ancient and vast British earth-work, covering over a hundred acres, with its steep and successive ramparts, is an amazing product for the time, and would, I imagine, be reckoned an important achievement in the present day. Bearing in mind the amount of labour and time, even with steam and modern appliances, that would be required to move and embank all this earth, and remembering also the engineering feat accomplished in transporting and erecting the mighty monoliths of Stonehenge in their upright position, besides the raising and securing the huge horizontal imposts above, one cannot but wonder whether the ancient Briton were such a complete savage as he is generally regarded. Maiden Castle and Stonehenge at least prove that he was fully capable of carrying forward engineering works of considerable magnitude—works that have lasted long enough to have outlived their history.

Entering Dorchester, we learnt by a street name-board that we were driving along the " Icen Way," and another notice-board on an open grass space at the top of the way informed us that this was "Gallows Hill." Here it was that after Judge Jeffreys' "Bloody Assize" a number of unfortunate prisoners who received sentence of death were executed. Wherever you go in England you come upon historic ground, but seldom so hatefully stained as when one follows the footsteps of this infamous judge. So cursed was his memory here that for long years afterwards the worst expression a man in a quarrel could employ against his opponent was "May the bloody judge get hold of you."

At Dorchester we found comfortable quarters and excellent stabling at the "King's Arms," an old coaching house duly mentioned in our *Paterson's Roads*, and if our worthy pre-railway forefathers fared as well as we did there, they had little to complain of; an old-fashioned coaching inn that maintains its past traditions is a delight to the modern wayfarer, and brings to mind good old Dr. Johnson's much-quoted saying that "there is nothing which has yet been contrived by man, by which so much happiness is produced as by a good tavern or inn." By the way, I wonder much what that famous Englishman would have thought of a modern gigantic company-managed hotel, with its stony-eyed stately manager in place of the jovial landlord of old, its German waiters (how the worthy doctor would have adored them), its general glare and feeling of unrest, where you can obtain almost everything but a home away from home.

In the evening we took a stroll through the green meadows that stretch along by the side of the Frome, which river, a mere brook here, flows between the town and the country and marks the boundary line of the two. A very pleasant stroll it was, the cool, clear, rippling water and the grateful gray-green gloom of the overhanging trees being very inviting and refreshful after the sultry heat and sunny glare of the day ; then as the gloaming slowly crept over the landscape we returned townward and sought the ease and comfort of our inn. During the evening we consulted our map as to our next day's course, and eventually determined to drive up the Cerne Valley, and so over the hills at its head to find our way to Sherborne.

CHAPTER XVI

A Dorsetshire poet—Uncertain weather—The restorer in his glory—A ghastly sight—A lovely valley—Godmanstone—The art of seeing—Cerne Abbas—Old legends—Cerne Abbey gateway—The Cerne Giant—A deserted mill—A grand mausoleum—Long Burton—A picture for a pilgrim.

EARLY in the morning we took our usual tiny tour of inspection before starting on our day's expedition. Dorchester charmed us by its clean, bright appearance and its pleasing look of quiet and contented prosperity, to say nothing of the civility of its inhabitants as far as we came in contact with them. In the churchyard of St. Peter's, just above our hotel, we noticed a bronze statue, set on a pedestal, of a man with an open book in his hand; the pose of the figure was natural and easy, graceful and pleasing. The sculptor had manifestly not striven for effect, and therefore was effective. There is a wonderful power and charm in restraint, that so few artists seem to realise; they fail too often by telling us all they know and leaving nothing to the imagination. On the pedestal below the statue we read as follows:—

WILLIAM BARNES
1801-1886.
Zoo now I hope his kindly feace
Is gone to vind a better pleace,
But still wi' vo'k a-left behind
He'll always be a-kept in mind.

There are, and have been, so many notable people in the world, whose numbers ever increase, that it is almost impossible to keep them all in memory, and I had inwardly to confess to myself my inability to call to mind the name of William Barnes from amongst those collected together in the ever-lengthening roll of fame, so I sought information of an intelligent passer-by. "Not know who Willie Barnes was!" he exclaimed in tones that suggested to us a suspicion of reproach, "why, I thought everybody knew him. He was a great Dorset poet, and wrote his poems in the good old Dorset dialect, like the notice there. What Burns is to Scotland, Barnes is to Dorset." We thanked the stranger for his information, and returning to our inn, ordered the horses to be "put to," and were soon on the road again.

The weather had been very fine ever since we started on our wanderings, but as we left Dorchester dark ominous-looking clouds were gathering on the horizon which foreboded a thunderstorm, a not unlikely thing to happen after the heat of the previous day. So threatening did the weather appear, that had we not actually started, I do not think that we should have ventured forth, but having once started we both agreed that it would never do to turn back. However, as we drove on the clouds cleared off in that wonderful manner they sometimes do in England, and all was sunshine and serenity by the time we reached Charminster, the first village on our way. I like the English climate for its very faults; it is interesting because so fickle and uncertain, and a storm makes the sunshine that follows so much more enjoyable, besides freshening up the landscape. I verily believe our day's pleasure was vastly enhanced because of the early vision of those storm-suggesting clouds: they made us appreciate the fine weather we had all the more.

As we passed through Charminster our road led us close by the church, and here what a sight met our astonished gaze: the churchyard was turned into a veritable builder's yard; the body of the poor old church was completely gutted, it being windowless, floorless, and doorless; we were relieved to find it was not roofless too. Masons were busily at work within and without; stones were being chiselled and mortar was being mixed in the erst quiet God's acre. The flat tombstones, we noticed, came in handy for the workmen.

We had come upon the restorer in the supreme height of his glory. Remarked one workman to me as I glanced over the wall, in reply to my astonished or grieved look, I suppose, "We're restoring of her; she'll look like new when we've finished," and we saw no reason to doubt the statement! "But will she be as good as when she was new?" we ventured to query. The reply was prompt if not convincing, "Why, to be sure she will; we're making a thorough good job of it." The modern British workman *versus* the masterly and trained medieval craftsman; and oh! ye gods, the confidence of the former. Well, all I can say is I heartily wish that the medieval mason had built the house I live in.

After this I should have driven on, but a sudden

impulse—one of those things that come without reasoning—impelled me to cross over and take a glance inside the poor old fane. Just approaching the doorway we came full upon the rector, or curate, I am not sure which, chatting with the foreman of the works, or it might have been the arch-restorer himself. The clergyman was most courteous, and kindly gave us permission to look round, besides giving us full particulars of the proceedings. It appeared, according to our authority, that before the restoration the church was in a very bad way; it had a plastered ceiling, whitewashed walls—the plaster and whitewash on the walls being nearly half an inch thick—old wooden pews, a wooden floor, and other abominations; now the building was being restored as far as possible to its pristine condition. When the floor was taken up, we learnt that the vaults below were found to be in a shocking condition, some half full of water, in which the rotting coffins lay, and "the stench was horrible." The vaults were all filled up with solid concrete, and one could not but wonder how it was that no epidemic had broken out amongst the congregation sitting there confined Sunday after Sunday over such a mass of corruption. The church being in a low situation, and the water getting into the vaults, of course made bad matters worse; but there are doubtless many other old country churches in a similar plight to-day. It was a gruesome revelation to us, and the detailed particulars of the sight displayed when the floor was removed and the vaults exposed to view with their ghastly contents haunted us for many a long day afterwards. One burly old farmer, we were told, nearly fell into a vault beneath his pew, as there was only an old rotten plank floor between him and it! We were not sorry to change the subject. During the alterations we understood that much Perpendicular work had been revealed, especially some pillars supporting the tower, to which our attention was called, but these had been so tooled and pointed up that they looked as though they had been only just erected; all the ancient uneven surface had been scraped away and made smooth and precise, with an utterly uninteresting mechanical result of a kind the modern builder loves, because he cannot do otherwise; it is the limit of his art *when he builds as well as he can*, and that he seldom does, because he has no real pride in his work. It is comparatively easy to be simply precise; it calls for no thought, for the workman is turned into a machine of flesh and blood, and it suggests nothing in return. *Ex nihilo nihil fit.* Here and there in the tower the letter "T" is carved in a curious scroll fashion—possibly the initial of the founder, or it may be that of Sir Thomas Trenchard, who gave largely to the building at a later period.

As we drove slowly up the narrow Cerne Valley from Charminster, with the gently-sloping, tree-clad hills rising up on either side of us, and the crystal river Cerne gliding, gurgling, and plashing down through leafy overhanging woods, and past the greenest of green meadows, now turning a slothful old gray stone mill in a leisurely way, as though haste were a thing unknown in this peace-haunted valley, now loitering along in a lazy mood, undisturbed by so much as a ripple, we thought this little-travelled glen one of surpassing loveliness ; but the subtle charm of the scenery defies analysis and beggars mere written description. The nearest word that I can coin to at all convey the impression of our soothing surroundings is peace-bestowing.

All things seemed to us so tranquil and mellow as we journeyed on : the old-world villages, time-toned farmsteads, and low-roofed cottages appeared to vie with each other as to which could be most picturesque and eye-pleasing ; such buildings smack of the soil ; they seem as much a natural growth as the grass or the trees around ; they are the very poetry of civilisation. Nowhere had modern progress placed an ugly blot on the fair landscape ; we seemed to have discovered a veritable Arcadia. The Cerne Valley has the "gift of beauty," but so far the gift has not been a fatal one ; it has not attracted the railway nor the tripper ; it lies happily apart from the tourist track. Here we felt far removed from the fevered hurry and rush of the steam-driven world ; here for a time we could " contain our souls in peace"; we had left the fussing and fuming locomotive out of sight and sound for at least one whole day ; even the ubiquitous telegraph lines did not follow us!

It is well both for body and soul to escape now and again into such a rest-giving spot as this, to give oneself up entirely to the pervading serenity of the quiet scenery with its soothing calm. Hither the monks of old came in search of seclusion, and found it, and they were no bad judges of a suitable resting-place for souls weary of the burdensome world, and here in the heart of the lovely vale they built themselves a lordly abbey, though perhaps a more humble building would have been better in keeping with their profession and their faith.

Following the gentle windings of the river, our road wound in and out with many a graceful curve, each fresh bend in the way revealing to us some new beauty; so we drove on and on, ever kept in a delightful state of expectancy, each prospect as it opened out seeming fairer than the one before ; our stage that day was nothing but a succession of pictures. The next village we passed through was Godmanstone. Its old gabled cottages, with their weather-toned roofs all green and gray and gold, its small and ancient church, whose hoary walls told of pious builders dead and gone to dust ages long ago, formed a very pleasing picture of rural felicity. Here the river for a moment winds away from its sylvan solitude, and widening out a space, forms a tiny bay by the roadside that does duty for the village pond; a stilly bit of backwater, with scarce the sign of a current thereon, in which the cotters' ducks were swimming and diving in blissful contentment.

It might have been the sunshiny day, it might have been its lovely position bosomed in the wooded hills, it might have been our happy, healthy frame of mind that beheld beauty everywhere that morning, but whatever the cause, we thought Godmanstone one of the most charming and retired hamlets we had come upon for many a day. In truth, it seemed to us an ideal spot hidden from the vulgar gaze and crowd in an ideal valley, so naturally and unpretentiously picturesque was it, yet so delightfully unconscious of its primitive picturesqueness. Perhaps it might so be that were we ever here again we should see things differently, for, after all, the poetry of a scene lies greatly in the eyes and momentary mood of the beholder ; we see mainly what we look for ; so two artists' pictures of the same place painted at the same time differ from one another, because they saw what was before them differently. Sentiment, too, has a very great deal to do with our ideas and ideals of beauty. I was told by an American citizen that a countryman of his, an artist, had been away in Switzerland painting in company with a famous English art critic and author, and whilst the art critic sat down with delight to draw in full and faithful detail an old tumble-down chalet, whose bent roof and uneven wooden walls were full of subtle curves and wonderful hues, mixed with soft gray shadows, the American artist was content to sit idly by, discontentedly doing nothing. After a while, observing that the thoughtful American was not working, the critic exclaimed, "Why don't you paint that lovely old chalet, it's as beautiful as a dream in colour and form ?" The American's answer was curious. "Well," said he, " I just guess I can't paint *that*. I don't see the beauty in it you do. The roof suggests wet coming in ; the walls suggest draughts and chills and misery for its inhabitants ; the whole place suggests painful poverty to me. I can't paint it. I don't see any beauty in the decay that causes human suffering."

Another day, as I have said, should chance bring us here, instead of the cheerful sunshine filtering down through fleecy clouds, the sky might be louring and of a leaden gray ; a sullen, steely east wind might be blowing ; the wooded hills might be blotted from sight by misty rain ; our mood might be wholly different, and under the changed conditions Godmanstone might fail to find any charm in our eyes.

As we drove on, the valley increased in beauty, and reminded us somewhat of that of Llanthony in Wales, wherein also the monks had built themselves an abbey. No artist ever had a finer eye for scenery than those knowing monks of old, I trow ! It would be interesting if we could obtain a faithful and unprejudiced insight into the inner life of an early monastery, to know the real monk, not the poetic creation of his friend, nor the black picture of his relentless enemy.

We reached Cerne Abbas about mid-day, and found it a quaint and very interesting little town. Here we obtained comfortable accommodation at an old stone-built hostel rejoicing in the not very appropriate title, considering its age, of the " New Inn." We entered this by an old-fashioned archway in the centre, above which still runs the ancient legend " Posting House," and a real, live posting house it is, for if you have to travel from or to Cerne

Abbas, go by road you must. It was a clean, two-storied, long, low building that ancient hostelry, and we were shown into a cool and cosy parlour much to our liking on that warm summer noon. Here we were close upon the ruins of Cerne Abbey, but there was not an engraving, nor even a photograph of it hanging up in our inn, which shows how happily infrequent is the genus tourist in these parts. For at all sight-worthy places that the tripper haunts I have ever noticed that the local inns and shops about abound in photographs. At Cerne we could not even purchase a photograph at all. This mattered not to us one jot, for we could take our own, but it did prove what an unsophisticated place Cerne is, and that it may long remain so is my hearty wish. I have made a mental note to hie me to that unpretending little inn some day armed with a goodly stock of colours and sketching materials, not forgetful of the camera, and to spend a delightful holiday sketching amongst the ancient quiet of the woods, and hills, and streams around.

Our old copy of *Paterson's Roads*, that, besides showing us the way, did duty as a sufficient guidebook, has the following note on Cerne Abbas:—

A small town, consisting of four or five indifferently-built streets, is situated in a pleasant valley, surrounded by steep hills and watered by the river Cerne, from which it derives its name. The place is, however, only remarkable for the remains of its abbey, which, though not extensive, are highly interesting, and consist principally of the gate-house, or chief entrance, a large, square, stately, embattled tower of three stories, in tolerable preservation. There is also a large and magnificent stone barn, supported by buttresses, standing at a short distance from the

A PRE-RAILWAY GUIDE

gateway, that still receives the produce of the Abbey farm. . . . An immense chalk hill, terminated by a mountainous prominence, rises hence, on the declivity of which may be traced a gigantic figure, cut in the chalk in the manner of the famous white horse in Berkshire; it represents a man holding a club in his right hand, and extending the other. The figure is 180 feet high, and proportionably made.

I quote this to show the style of guide-book description that our road-travelling ancestors were provided with. It will be noted that the account is concise; the reader is not worried with a long, wordy history of the origin and rise and fall of the abbey; it gives you in a short space all that is absolutely needful to know; it simply suggests what is best worth seeing, and then leaves the traveller to make his own discoveries in detail. I even think that some modern guide-book compilers might take a hint from almost forgotten *Paterson*.

After having rested and refreshed ourselves at our inn, we sallied forth in search of the ruins. On our way we passed the ancient village church, a cathedral in miniature, with a very fine Perpendicular tower. On this tower is a niche, with a canopy over enshrining a carved stone statue of the Virgin Mary with the Child in her arms. The face of the Virgin has either been wilfully damaged or much weather-worn; we should imagine the latter, as any one who would damage the head might so easily have damaged, in part or in whole, the rest of the figure. It is strange that this "superstitious image" should have escaped the vigilant eye and fury of the Puritans. Possibly Cerne Abbas being so out of the world may account for this bit of "Popish" carving being preserved.

The exceedingly picturesque old ivy-grown gateway, with the remains of a fine tithe-barn and some unimportant ruins, are all that now exist of one of the most stately abbeys in England. The site of the abbey, surrounded by woods and encircled by hills, is most bewitching; a fairer site on which to raise a fane of solitary prayer could hardly be imagined or desired. Close by where the abbey stood rises a crystal stream of the purest water. According to tradition this marks the spot where Saint Austin struck his staff into the ground, from whence issued

> The fairest well stream
> That runneth on earth.

There are, however, many similar traditions elsewhere of other saints with their staves, and springs flowing from the land where the latter touched; sometimes by way of variety the staff itself took root, flourished, and grew into a tree, as in the medieval legend of St. Joseph of Arimathæa at Glastonbury. That saint, approaching Glastonbury on foot, and being tired, sat himself down on a hill overlooking the spot, at the same time sticking his staff into the ground—the hill since then going by the name of Weary-all-Hill—the staff being a common hawthorn; the dry, dead stick thenceforth became living, grew and blossomed every winter on Christmas Day, so it is said, until the stern Puritans came and grubbed it up. Whatever the virtues of the miraculous tree, it could not save itself, any more than the relics of the saint could.

CERNE ABBEY GATEWAY

> Not great Arthur's tomb, nor holy Joseph's grave,
> From sacrilege had power their sacred bones to save.

Cerne Abbey gateway, with its embattled top and two oriel windows, one above the other, ornamented by bands of carved stone panels bearing time-decayed coats of arms and heraldic devices, with its wide Gothic doorway below giving admission to a groined chamber of fan tracery, makes a very pleasing and pretty picture, backed, as it is, by deep green woods and rounded hills. It is a simple poem sung in stone. Access to the rooms above and to the top of the building is gained by a spiral staircase; the ancient chambers, however, are bare and desolate except for their broken stone fire-places and a few ancient tiles on the floor; the dust of ages and countless cobwebs have found an undisturbed resting-place therein; possibly the spiders are descendants of the old monastic spiders. The changed times have not depressed or dispossessed them, for there they were, looking plump and prosperous enough!

Some portions of what we took to be the prior's guest hall, that includes a fine traceried window, are incorporated with some farm-buildings, as is also the grand and spacious tithe-barn, forming together a picturesque and time-stained group that would have delighted the eye of Samuel Prout. Indeed they suggested Prout to us. It is manifest, from the ample size of the barn, that if the monks were assured of their souls' salvation, to their own satisfaction at least, they were by no means neglectful of this world's good things. Happy beings, to make sure of heaven and the best of earth! By the way, "As big as a tithe-barn" is a significant Dorsetshire proverb. A popular proverb, like a popular song, is a powerful factor in history, and shows the drift of public feeling. It is said that the Marseillaise upset kingdoms, and cost Germany nearly a million of lives. As Andrew Fletcher once remarked, "If a man were permitted to make the ballads, he need not care who made the laws of a nation."

Returning to our old-fashioned inn, we discovered the landlord busily employed painting a mail-cart, that does postal duty here, a brilliant vermilion, and whilst he painted we indulged in quite a long and interesting chat with him about the old times and the new at Cerne Abbas. "We call it a town," said he, "but it will soon become a village, as more people leave it each year than are born in it, and there's nothing to induce strangers to come here; we're so out of the world." Well, truly Cerne is a spot for a peace-seeking pilgrim, not for a person in search of a fortune or fame, or perhaps even a living, unless he be a happy landscape artist.

As we proceeded on our way up the lonely, lovely valley, on the steep slopes of the Downs to our right we caught sight of the Cerne Giant, a huge figure cut out of the side of the chalk hill, represented as holding a club in one hand, whilst simply extending the other. The origin, age, and purpose of this are unknown. There is another somewhat similar figure cut on the South Downs just above the ruins of Wilmington Priory, only instead of a club the Sussex giant has apparently a simple staff held in each outstretched hand, though some ancient drawings of this make the two staves respectively a rake and a scythe, or some instrument of a like nature.

Whether two such figures, each being cut in chalk above a monastery, point to their being the work of the monks, I cannot say, but knowing what we do of the monks, were these figures of heathen origin, I think there is little doubt but that they would have been carefully obliterated. Certainly the monks would not have preserved them as they seem to have done, otherwise such easily-erased figures would scarcely have remained visible to the present day. There may have been others lost to us through later neglect.

As we ascended to the head of the valley, with the river sparkling through the trees below us on our left, an inviting by-road dipped down between overhanging woods to a disused old watermill; th ; looked so temptingly picturesque that we could not resist stopping to make a sketch of it. Here the river, narrowed to a rippling stream, was spanned by an ancient foot-bridge, the road crossing it by a shallow ford. The roughly-built old mill, deserted and given over to decay inside and out, its dark green moss-grown wheel motionless and tumbling to pieces, with the clustering trees around, the old-fashioned ford and primitive foot-bridge altogether formed a most charming ready-made picture, its beauty being for the moment emphasised by a stray gleam of golden sunshine that rested on the gray gable of the forsaken building and on the babbling stream below. Abandoned abbey and forlorn mill are decayed, useless, and vanishing, but the bright laughing stream flows on, seemingly as young and fresh as ever; though I dislike moralising, still I must confess that it touches a chord of thoughtful sadness to find how man's works disappear in time, unless constantly upheld, whilst Nature, all uncared for, is ever young and vigorous; the one so mutable, the other so immutable.

Now as we gradually ascended the valley, the woods grew less luxuriant, the bare hills told more prominently forth, the air grew fresher and keener, and the scenery less beautiful but more bold. The mind, however, loves change, and after the sylvan sweetness of the sheltered valley, with its zephyr-like airs, the more open and, if I may be allowed the expression, the more masculine features of the higher landscape, with its tonic and bracing atmosphere, were very welcome.

At last we ceased our climbing, and, reaching the head of the valley, went down on the other side by a long and steep descent marked on our map Revels Hill. Here before us was spread out a vast level stretch of wooded country, that faded away in the north into the blue and shapely hills of Somerset. As we descended, the climate gradually changed again, the bracing airs of the hills gave place to the balmy ones of the lowlands, and great oaks and flourishing elms by the roadside and in the fields showed plainly not only the change of climate, but the change of soil.

. A long stretch of level road now brought us to Holnest, where, in a large and sparsely-filled churchyard, stands a tiny church, completely dwarfed by a huge mausoleum set right in front of it. This mausoleum is a massive structure with a rounded roof, and if it belongs to any style of architecture at all, may perhaps be called Lombardic. Inquiring of a passing labourer if he knew who was entombed in this splendid sepulchre, we learnt that " It be Squire Drax as was; he lies in it on a shelf overground; he bain't buried in the earth like us poor common folk. Why, he's got a far better home dead nor we have living, and he can't enjoy it either. It don't seem to me quite fair, nohow, as how a dead man should have a better dwelling nor a live 'un. It were a great mistake as I was born poor, and I be that mortal thirsty, and I cannot afford the price of a glass of ale, and maybe you won't believe me, but water don't suit I." We duly sympathised with him, and the sum of twopence changed hands, which he gave us his word should be spent in a glass of beer. He need not have done this, we had no doubt whatever as to how our money would be invested. It is a strange thing, but I have travelled right across America from the Atlantic to the Pacific without ever being asked to "stand a drink," but I do not think I have as much as driven across an English county without at least some one urgently desiring to "drink my health."

The poor old church looked quite insignificant beside the magnificent mausoleum. I wonder if any other country church is thus dwarfed and out-done in glory by a tomb in its own grave-yard? Of old, when the mighty and favoured of the land were interred within the house of God, their monuments, though often large and ostentatious enough, had the virtue of being of necessity smaller than the building that enclosed them.

Then passing through woods that bounded our road and limited our vision, the country once more opened out, and we reached the little village of Long Burton, which possesses a few rather quaint stone-built houses, some having thatched roofs that appeared a little out of keeping with the solid stonework below. We glanced inside the church here, as it was close to the road. On the north wall by the porch we noticed the following inscriptions below a royal coat of arms :—

> Feare thou the Lord and King and
> Meddle not with them that are given to change.
>
> PROVERBS xxiv. 4.
>
> 1662.
> C. R.
>
> Cvrse not the King—noe not in thy Thought.
>
> ECCLES. x.

Considering the date and the facts of history just then in vivid remembrance, these inscriptions tell their own tale.

In a corner of the church, or it might have been a private chapel, we discovered two fine coloured and gilt altar-tombs. One of these was to the memory of Sir Henry Winston, and of "the Lady Dionise his wyfe" and of "his sonne Lievtenant of the Bril," whatever that might be. An inscription below informs one that

Eleanor, one of their daughters, now wyfe of Leweston Fitz-James, beinge dyned to repayre and erect these Remembrances in the Church of Standick, where they lie bvried, hath transferred them thence, and placed them here, where part of their posteritie is now by the mercifull Providence of the Almightie planted.

P. E.

Shortly after this the country dropped, as it were, right down in front of us, and we looked over a sheltered valley with a slow-gliding river and a rushing railway winding through it. Far below us the sleepy town of Sherborne lay, gathered round its ancient abbey church, and backed by distant woods of greeny gray, above which rose across the quiet valley a wilderness of gloomy hills. The sun was getting low, and its last rays rested lovingly and long upon the hoary fane and upon some of the higher buildings of the old town, making many a window glow with its golden light and more than one restless weather-cock glint again; the rest of the town was lost in a dreamy indistinctness of blue shade. The warm tints of the sunlit towers, gables, roofs, and windows, contrasting forcibly with the cool blue shadows, formed a wonderfully effective prospect— a prospect that delighted the heart of a certain pilgrim, even though a nineteenth-century one, who made his pilgrimage luxuriously on wheels, and not painfully on foot with *unboiled* peas in his shoes or sandals, as, according to tradition, certain pilgrims of old did, and, moreover, proclaimed to the world the fact. Wherein lies the religion or virtue in suffering needless pain or discomfort that can do no one any possible good? However, each century has its own special views, and on the whole I am not sure that I should care to change the present age, with all its faults, for any one that has passed, even had I the choosing of it, notwithstanding that Mr. Barlow proclaims this to be

> The saddest century since the news went round
> That death was sceptreless and Christ was crowned.

CHAPTER XVII

Sherborne—House names—Bell inscriptions—An ancient abbey conduit—Sherborne Castle—A wild and hilly drive—Bruton—A church with two towers—King Alfred's Tower—A monastic pigeon-house—Somerset hills and scenery—Frome—Bishop Ken's curious tomb—An easy stage—Westbury White Horse—A charming village—Trowbridge.

AT Sherborne we found a most comfortable hotel with excellent stabling; besides, to make our happiness complete, a very delightful, shady garden to wander in—a garden that looked on to wooded hills and not on to houses, as most town gardens do. If only all hotels were so provided, how pleasant would be the lot of the traveller! It is refreshing after a long and perchance dusty journey, when the heat and glare of the summer day are over, to moon about the garden of your inn in the cool and restful gloaming and to smoke a peaceful post-prandial pipe whilst discussing the incidents of the day's drive and making fresh plans for the pleasures of the morrow.

Sherborne, which we inspected next morning, proved to be a charming little town, clean, neat, well-built, and with a pretty country around, glimpses of which could be had from almost every street. Here for a time we escaped from the tyranny of cheap brick, as the houses of Sherborne are constructed of stone—and stone of a rich and pleasant colour too. Some of the buildings possess both picturesque and interesting exteriors, and are full of the charm that comes of individuality. One tiny house, we observed as we passed by, bore the quaint title of "The Nutshell." Elsewhere on our journey we observed a pretty creeper-clad cottage named "The Nest," and in the neighbourhood of the sea "The Anchorage" and "The Cabin" told of the homes of the retired mariner. "What's in a name?" Well, some names are suggestive of cosiness and comfort.

There is a subtle charm and quality in the varying grain and tints of chiselled stone that makes mere machine-made and moulded bricks appear very monotonous and characterless. Bricks are all of one shape and size, whilst stone-work varies and shows the marks of the mason's tools; the surface of one is of no interest, the surface of the other is full of it.

We first made our way to the abbey church, which unfortunately is spoilt externally by its stumpy tower; the building sadly wants a central focus for the eye, and has none. Here we noticed the gargoyles were reserved for their original purpose, and not, as generally is the case, retained as simple ornaments, their functions being superseded by modern rainwater pipes. A medieval cathedral must have been a curious sight in heavy rain with all the gargoyles throwing the water from off the roof in a succession of miniature cascades! The interior of the thoroughly-restored church is impressive on account of its truly magnificent stone groined roof, with its rich and beautiful fan tracery and stately rows of Perpendicular pillars. Wandering round the building in the old processional path that runs behind the high altar, our eyes were arrested by a brass let into the floor and thus inscribed :—

> Near this Spot were Interred
> The Mortal Remains of
> Ethelbald and of Ethelbert his Brother
> Each of whom in his turn succeeded to the
> Throne of Ethelwoulf their father king of the
> West Saxons and were succeeded in the kingdom
> By their youngest brother Alfred the Great.

Cardinal Wolsey presented to the abbey church its tenor bell, which was cast in Tournay; this is inscribed :—

> By Wolsey's gift I measure time for all,
> To mirth, to grief, to church I serve to call.

There is also another famous bell here, known as the "Fire Bell." The legend on this runs :—

> Lord quench this furious flame,
> Arise, run, help, put out the same.

Which reads to us more like an order than a prayer.

Perhaps the most picturesque architectural "bit" in Sherborne, amongst a number of picturesque and charming architectural memorials of the past, is the old abbey conduit, a fine example of fourteenth-century work. This has an open arcade round it, enclosing a space sheltered by a groined stone roof with fan tracery like the church. In general appearance it resembles the usual medieval market cross, and stands in a recessed corner well off from the road, so that luckily it is not likely to be improved away some fine morning on account of the presumed exigencies of traffic needing the widening of the thoroughfare. How many priceless architectural and historical relics that might well have been spared have been lost to us on this precious pretext and the cuckoo-like cry of progress! The ancient conduit gives the charm of special character to the street in which it stands.

Rambling round the pleasant outskirts of the town, we presently found ourselves in close proximity to the ruins of Sherborne Castle, which consist chiefly of an ivy-clad and crumbling keep standing on a wooded rocky knoll that rises directly from the river. As a ruin the castle is a picturesque object, but the remains are too slight to be of much architectural value; in fact, it appeals more to the artist than the archæologist.

We had decided over-night that we would drive from Sherborne to Frome, twenty-four hilly miles as it proved. We were aware of the distance, but were not quite prepared for the hilliness of the country. Our road gradually rose out of the town, and continued to rise for some distance till it brought us to a spot high up in the world where nothing but grass seemed to grow. We were in a desolate country; great bare hills, green, and gray, and blue in the far away, circled all around us. As far as the eye could reach, hills succeeded hills in bewildering confusion, with lonesome valleys between. The landscape had a forsaken look, the vast grassy slopes around us were void of any life, not even a stray sheep could we see. On this elevated region how buoyant and bracing was the air; sweeping over the vast moorlands unrestrained, it came to us fresh, free, and tonic-laden, as enlivening and as inspiriting as champagne. Even the horses made a show of sniffing it with delight, and in spite of the roughness of the road, the constant collar work it entailed, and the long journey from the start they had already accomplished, they pranced about as lively as though they had only just left their stables. We were impressed with the sense of silence and solitude of the scene: not a wandering bird was visible; we actually felt grateful for the company of the drifting clouds above—they at least had the charm of movement. For a vigorous mind the wild prospect had its delights, though it was desolate enough to have satisfied an anchorite.

At one spot we descended for a little through bare rocks that showed the stony nature of the country. The railways go where the country is most populated in search of traffic, so that only those who travel across country by road can form any idea how wild and desolate are some parts of England now. Small wonder that districts like this, where the soil is so poor, and where minerals do not exist, are deserted, when even rich farming lands scarcely pay to cultivate. The depopulation of rural England is becoming a serious question: the downfall of the mighty Roman Empire was hastened, if not brought about, by the loss of her hardy tillers of the soil, from whom her soldiers were recruited. The sturdy English yeoman seems to have been improved, by unhappy circumstances, out of existence, and the English peasantry are fast following in his wake. A farmer told me that one of the chief difficulties he had to contend with was the scarcity of good labourers who could or would work; all the young men, he said, rush away to the towns, leaving us only the old, the lazy, and the lame. Long ago, when agricultural affairs were not in the present sadly depressed state, Goldsmith gave a note of warning—a warning that is more than ever needed now :—

> Ill fares the land, to hastening ills a prey,
> Where wealth accumulates and men decay.
> Princes and lords may flourish or may fade,
> A breath can make them as a breath has made;
> But a bold peasantry, their country's pride,
> When once destroy'd, can never be supplied.

For miles our road led us along at a considerable elevation, with the silent hills of Somerset for solitary company. Over the long ranges of uplands mighty patches of golden sunlight and vast cloud-shadows swept in constant succession. There were simply two features in the prospect—land and sky; these in time became a trifle monotonous, so that we were not sorry when at last our ambitious road suddenly began to descend down a long and steep hill into the green valley below. So far since we left Sherborne we had not seen a soul; in the valley, at a point where four roads without a signpost converged, we met a woman, of whom we inquired the way, and she did not know it!

On our way down we passed a deep, green glen, in the shelter of which a leafy wood grew and flourished, and very pleasing its fluttering leaves looked after the bare, brown, treeless district we had so recently left behind. Crossing the valley, a gentle rise brought us into a very "land of Goshen," a land of rich luxuriant meads, from which great branching elms arose, and in the meads, sleek-looking cattle stood deep in juicy grass. What a change from the first portion of our road! Then after some more up-and-down-hill work, at the top of an extra stiff ascent we came to a very pretty spot, from whence we looked down upon the little hamlet of Pitcombe right below us, embowered in trees. So steep did the hillside fall here, that it seemed almost as though we might have thrown a stone down the chimney of the cottage of some worthy inhabitant. The name of the village appeared very appropriate, for it is built in a sort of pit within a regular combe, as a combe is understood in Devonshire.

Then in another mile or so we reached the little town of Bruton, charmingly situated in a wooded valley and encircled by hills. A quiet little old-fashioned town is Bruton, that pleased us greatly; it is all so delightfully quaint, old-world, and unspoilt— a town with a special character of its own, and not resembling any other place. The curse of uniformity and the wearisome monotony it creates has not spread hither. Bruton is natural, and does not ape any other flourishing or better-known town at second hand; it is content to be itself. We made our mid-day halt here, and pulled up at the "Wellington," an ancient inn that had a suggestive look of having welcomed and entertained many a tired and dust-stained traveller in the posting and coaching days gone by. The chambers of these ancient inns are something more to me than merely four square walls enclosing so much space. If they could only speak, what romances might they not tell—stories more interesting than any novel. In these conventional times the railway and the huge company-managed hotel have supplanted the road and the restful old inn, and much of the discomfort and all the romance of travel have gone.

At the "Wellington" we found an obliging landlady and a civil ostler. The landlady told us that they did not often have strangers there, they were so out of the world, with nothing particular to see, besides being on the road to nowhere. "We used to get a fair sprinkling of cyclists at one time, but very few find their way here now, the roads are so hilly and rough, and I expect cyclists tell each other about it, and so avoid the district. One cyclist, who arrived here hot and tired one day, remarked on departing, 'Never no more.'" Which was expressive, if not exactly good grammar or quite gracious. I ventured to remark that the scenery looked very fine around, and I thought that might, to some extent, compensate for the badness of the roads, but was met with the rejoinder, "What's the good of beautiful scenery to a cyclist who has been thrown off his machine, or having escaped this, is too fagged to care a straw about the country?" As I did not feel called upon to argue the matter, I kept my peace.

There are several interesting old stone-built houses in Bruton, and some of the ancient inns possess rather good and decorative iron supports to their signs, notably the "Bull Inn." A pleasant little stream runs right through the heart of the town. We were informed that this was the Brue *river*, a pointed accent being placed on the word "river" by the party of whom we asked information. This stream is crossed by two or three old bridges. One of these spans the water by a single arch of rather bold design, joining the opposite houses together in a fashion that gives a sort of Venetian flavour to the view.

Crossing the river, we saw before us the fine church, which is very curious, as it possesses two towers, one strangely placed over the north porch, the other in the usual position at the west end. These two towers give the fabric an odd appearance, but why it should be so over-provided we were unable to make out. The church, which is mostly Perpendicular, has been thoroughly restored within, so it did not detain us long. We noticed the absence of the usual east window, and also that the chancel was in the Classical style, with a plaster roof, sadly out of harmony with the rest of the building.

The vicarage that adjoins the churchyard is a peculiar structure; it is apparently built against the long buttressed wall of the old abbey, the windows facing the other way; some of the buildings in Bruton seem to be a little eccentric. Viewed from the road, at first we took the vicarage to be merely the abbey wall, for Bruton once boasted of a fine monastery, and this is what is left of it. Just beyond here is Creech Hill, a high conical knoll, on which stands a tall, solitary, roofless tower, that strongly reminded us of a border keep; this was a bit of unexpected picturesqueness. From this spot there is a fine view all around. We asked a boy we found there what was the name of the tower, and he replied, "We calls it the Pigeon Tower," but the reason for its being so called he could not give beyond the usual stereotyped reply, "It were allus so called as long as I can remember." As the lad was perhaps twelve years old, this did not further us much. We imagined that possibly it might have served the purpose of a pigeon-house for the prosperous monks, though why built so tall was a puzzle—perhaps for a landmark, perhaps merely for the sake of a picturesque object in the view, for the monks of old studied the picturesque as well as the useful and useless, just as they loved the beautiful whilst rejoicing in the grotesque. I wonder whether those devout and ancient craftsmen (we presume they were devout) really believed in the demons they so cunningly carved in wood and stone; they made them look so grinningly good-natured that one can hardly imagine that they took their own creations seriously. Those monks sang and laughed in sculpture, their angels were sedate and beautiful, and their devils generally had the expression of a jovial joker. If we may judge them by their handiwork, they do not seem to have taken religion very miserably—at least the latter-day monks.

Out of Bruton we had a long and gentle ascent, and gradually as we rose our prospect, confined at first, opened out, till, to our right, a grand and extensive view was presented to us down and along a wide, well-wooded valley. On one of the highest points of the hills that bounded this we noticed a tall tower, showing very plainly against the light sky-line. A farmer looking over a hedge, apparently at the crops, told us, in reply to our question, that it was "Alfred's Tower," and further remarked, "It be built on the spot from where King Alfred set forth to fight the Danes, or the Romans, or some other people— I'm not quite sure which." We suggested the Greeks. "Well, it might be them; I don't know; I don't pay much count about things that happened such a terrible long while ago. You can get to the tower if you likes—it be only five miles off." But the day was getting old, and we did not see our way to make the long detour that a visit to the tower would entail; however, we made a note of the spot, as it looked interesting—this in case we should be in the neighbourhood some other time. We were content to leave some things unseen; besides, so doing allows scope for the imagination. It would be a dull world without a little romancing, and when you have only viewed a place through your field-glasses, you can idealise about it to your heart's content. I actually consider that there is a virtue when travelling for pleasure in purposely avoiding seeing everything. It leads you to form poetic pictures that the stern reality might rob you of. An artist once confided to me that the finest landscape he ever painted was done, not from nature, but from a vivid description of a certain spot in a book over which the writer had thrown the glamour of his pen. The marvellous word-picture inspired the artist, and he painted a dream of scenery. The finest art-work is not a mere transcript or reproduction from nature ; a man may draw mechanically perfectly and yet be no artist. Poetry must be wedded to fact to make a work of art. So from one thing to another our thoughts rambled on. Jogging slowly along a quiet country road is conducive to desultory reflections.

Our road kept on high ground for the rest of the stage until we came near to Frome. It was a grand road too, with wide views on either hand over vast tracts of pleasant country. To the westwards Glastonbury Tor was plainly visible, and northward beyond, the undulating Mendip hills could be traced, gradually receding in the far distance, till all form was lost in a pale blue haze, an apparent blending of land and sky. To the east we looked upon a distant wilderness of wild and barren hills. The outlines of these were very marked and full of character. Judging from our map, we presumed them to belong to Wiltshire and to form the western boundary of Salisbury Plain. Somersetshire is a land of fine prospects, and its hills, though never high enough to be exciting or to call forth wonderful adjectives, have the charm of wooded bases, variety of form, and grace of outline ; moreover, amidst the Somerset hills are hidden away many valleys of rare beauty, some even deserving the too often misapplied term of romantic. A Somerset valley is either lovable for its tender beauty, or charming for its romantic scenery.

Then as we drove on we suddenly found ourselves in the outskirts of Frome, and we were not sorry to arrive at our night's destination after our long and hilly journey; moreover, the bracing air of the breezy uplands had given us healthy appetites, and when a traveller is really hungry a good hotel appeals to him more than the finest scenery. This much I think I may concede, but I cannot go so far as to say "that the finest scenery is improved by a good hotel in the foreground," an opinion expressed by one of our modern novelists, and that has been strangely fathered on to Dr. Johnson, possibly because he was so great an inn-lover; in the same way, I suppose, that Sterne's saying, "God tempers the wind to the shorn lamb," is frequently quoted as Scriptural on account of its sounding so, and possibly if one put the question as to where it may be found, most people would promptly and wrongly answer, the Bible.

A walk round about the town next day proved Frome to be a prosperous-looking, stone-built place, set on the steep side of a hill. It may be a fanciful idea on my part, but I always feel that stone houses and shops give an appearance of solidity and substance to a place, and a general, indefinable air of well-being. You cannot easily build meanly with stone. The general impression that Frome gave us was one, as I have said, of prosperity, and therefore pleasing, yet withal the only building of any real interest we could discover there was the ancient and well-restored Church of St. John the Baptist. If all churches were restored in the conservative spirit that this seems to have been, I should have nothing but good to say of restorers, but for one old church fraught with the antiquity of ages past that is thus lovingly restored, ninety-nine are more or less ruined—often more than less.

This Church of St. John the Baptist at Frome is approached by a *Via Crucis*, a steep ascent of steps, on the rising wall to the left of which are a series of stone sculptures representing the Stations of the Cross. From the top of these we wandered round to the east end of the churchyard to view the grave of the faithful Bishop Ken, "who dared with royal power to cope." Bishop Ken, it may be remembered, was one of the seven bishops committed to the Tower by James II.; he was buried here, according to his desire, "under the east window, just at sunrising." His tomb is a shrine for the Protestant pilgrim to journey to and to ponder over. His grave is curiously covered with iron bars bent into the shape of a coffin, and upon the top of these are laid a mitre and crosier in wrought iron, the whole being partially protected from the weather by a stone canopy supported on pillars. This singular monument is more impressive than any stately altar-tomb, and is described by Lord Houghton as

> A basket-work where bars are bent,
> Iron in place of osier;
> And shapes above that represent
> A mitre and a crosier.

It was the reading of this verse that took us to Frome. Such is the poet's power!

Retracing our steps, in a niche on a buttress on

the north wall of the church we noticed a carved stone figure of the Virgin Mary and Child, carefully glazed from the weather. What would the ancient Puritans have said to this, I wonder, or to the other "superstitious glass pictures and images" within, of which more anon? I do not remember having seen any other external carving protected by glass in this manner. This one, covered thus, had certainly a curious look, which, to my mind, was not wholly satisfactory. It was beyond doubt quaint, but quaintness is not always a virtue, or desirable.

Entering the church, we saw from a glance within what would even more have startled the eye of a stern Puritan. When we had got accustomed to the deep religious gloom and the "twilight saints and dim emblazonings" of the stained glass windows, we discerned a rood loft, with a large carving in oak of the Crucifixion standing aloft on the top thereof, having sculptured figures of the Virgin Mary and St. John on either side. Before the altar—I am given to understand that is the right term nowadays—were seven hanging lamps alight, and there were gorgeously embroidered processional banners on either side of the chancel. It all looked very rich, artistic, and "Catholic," and perhaps pleasing to those who do not see in all these things "the mark of the beast." Still, as a fairly unprejudiced onlooker, one who can equally worship in a cathedral or a barn, I cannot but query if, on the whole, all this imitated medievalism is as profitable, in a religious sense, as it is undeniably picturesque. It gives much offence to many worthy, if possibly bigoted, Christian worshippers; it makes the Church enemies in an age when friends are sorely needed—that is, at least, if I read the times aright. The lesson of the Puritan rising seems to be wholly forgotten. It was a curious thought that came quite unbidden to me, as I stood meditating in that gorgeous fane, but I could not help wondering what St. Paul would say to that ornate House of God, were he to come in the flesh and see it.

One is getting accustomed to such interiors, and notices in the daily papers somewhat similar to the following, which I extracted from the *Standard* of 29th October 1890, seem to call now for no comment. " The dedication festival of the Church of St. Mary the Virgin, Worksop, took place yesterday. . . . Two Bishops took part in it, the Bishop of Argyle and Bishop Smythies of South Africa, each of whom wore his mitre in the procession. The communion table was lighted with candles, incense was used, and the Angelus bell was rung at the consecration of the elements and at the elevation of the Host." The ultra-Protestant must be thankful for the small mercy that the term "communion table" was employed, and not altar.

Here, too, is a picture of the modern church as given by the Rev. Dr. Horton in his thought-begetting work *The Teaching of Jesus*, a description that is so poetical, yet so faithful to fact, that 1 am tempted to quote it. "The Church looms large, a venerable and beautiful building, the growth of many ages, with crumbling images of the saints, and storied windows of far-off and half-forgotten things, intricate, bewildering, subduing, a sum of impressions rich in antique associations, half Christian and half pagan, half worldly and half heavenly. And in some niche or other of the great edifice is Christ, a conventional Christ, in the Virgin's arms it may be, or swung on a colossal crucifix from the chancel roof. . . . Perhaps a preacher, in the midst of much talk about Sacraments, Saints, Fasts, and Feasts of the Church, confession, decoration, contribution, mentions, with a distant reverence and a customary inclination of the head, 'Our blessed Lord!'"

Leaving the dim and religious interior and walking back along the busy streets to our hotel, it verily seemed as though we had suddenly stepped out of the centuries past into the living present; the glamour and gloom of the ancient church with its very real medieval look made even our old coaching inn appear quite modern and gay, which before had seemed old and quiet-toned.

After our horses' hard and long day's work of yesterday we determined that we would only make a short stage on from Frome, and after consulting our map we resolved to drive to Trowbridge, only nine miles away. A gradual ascent took us out of Frome, and we were soon again amongst the green fields and leafy trees. To our right we had a good view of the Westbury White Horse, a gigantic figure cut out on the side of the chalk downs, a little below an ancient earth camp. The position of this White Horse suggests the idea that possibly it may originally have been formed to celebrate King

Alfred's victory over the Danes, the more especially as tradition and some authorities assert that the battle was fought in the vicinity. We saw the White Horse under a peculiar effect that at first glance was almost startling; it was a hot east-windy day with a gray heat-haze hanging over all, and the distant downs were merged in the sky. The White Horse showed vaguely out of this mass of gray as though it were a sign low down in the actual sky. The effect was truly quite weird. As we drove on we had no notion that any downs or White Horse were there, it seemed merely like misty space, so that the unexpected vision that appeared to rise up suddenly before us at a bend in the road naturally excited our momentary wonder till we became aware of the cause of the phenomenon.

In about two miles we found ourselves in the charmingly pretty and architecturally interesting village of Beckington. Some of the old houses here, with their high-pitched, stone-slab roofs, great gables, mullioned windows, ivy-grown fronts, and genuine old English gardens, retired from the road and vulgar gaze by time-toned walls, make delicious pictures. Beckington is one of those unspoilt, old-world spots that are fraught with the rare poetry of a bygone civilisation. It is not a perfectly ideal village—perhaps there is no such thing to be found —but it approaches very near to it.

We had now an excellent and level road with lovely pastoral scenery—two good things combined —and soon we reached another pretty village called Road, that earned, some thirty odd years ago, an unenviable fame as the scene of a terrible tragedy connected with the name of Constance Kent, a tragedy that may still linger in the memory of some people. From here to Trowbridge we had a grand trotting road "as smooth as a billiard table," to use a familiar and exaggerated expression; a road that would surely delight the heart of the cyclist, and for once we took advantage of the propitious circumstance "to make the pace," delighting in the rapid motion, knowing that it was no exertion to the horses. Our short stage soon came to an end, and almost before we were aware of it we found ourselves in Trowbridge, where we pulled up at the "George," a comfortable old-fashioned hotel set in the heart of an uninviting commercial town. I wonder why modern commerce should needs always gather round its centres so much that is grimy and commonplace. It is the haste to make money that is the root of most of the ugliness of the age. I know of some rural industries, where the motive power is by primitive water-wheels, that are essentially picturesque. I have in my mind at the present moment some small country tweed manufactories in Wales where they make excellent cloth and ladies' dress material; the owners, though they produce picturesquely admirable goods, pleasant to look upon and lasting in wear, do not make fortunes, but they lead healthy, happy lives, and, after all, mere money-making is not everything in life.

CHAPTER XVIII

An uninteresting town—A quiet spot—Seend—God's garden—"Shane's Castle"—A hill-climbing canal—The "Bear" at Devizes—The glamour of a name—A curiously-inscribed market cross—"The Island"—A wayside monument—Another white horse—An ancient earth-work—Upavon—Benighted on Salisbury Plain—An oasis in a desert.

WE found absolutely nothing to interest or detain us at Trowbridge, which certainly might be our fault and not that of the place, but so it was; we were therefore not sorry when the morning arrived and we once more renewed our rural wanderings. Much out-of-door country life spoils one for towns, especially manufacturing ones.

When we set out from Trowbridge we planned first to drive to Devizes, and from thence in turn to strike forth in a south-easterly direction and to take our chance of the road, so that on starting we had not the slightest idea where we should sleep that night; such uncertainty gave an added zest to our day's wanderings.

At Trowbridge the ostler volunteered the statement that it was a very hilly stage on to Devizes, but we considered the road to be fairly level, with the exception of one long hill when entering the latter town, and as we journeyed on we kept wondering when the collar-work was coming, till at last we ceased wondering altogether and concluded that the ostler did not know much of the country, or that he might have recently arrived from some part of the eastern counties, where every rise seems to be considered a veritable hill. A gentleman who had paid a visit to Cambridgeshire vouched to me for the following story. Taking an early morning walk with his host through a part of the country "as flat as a pancake," he was told that at a certain point there was a good view of some hill—I have forgotten the name now, but that is a detail of no importance to the story. Coming to the spot, my friend could see no sign of a hill, and made a remark to that effect. "Wait a bit," replied his companion; "when that hay-cart moves on, you'll see it"!

The scenery as we progressed improved with every mile of the way, but beautiful though the country was, it was not of a kind to be readily described; its charms were of the placid, peace-bestowing order, a happy blending of green meadows, tilled fields, woodlands enlivened by the gleam of still water and bounded by low-lying hills of tender blue, and here and there in the spreading landscape stood gray old homes, pleasant-looking farmsteads, and many a lowly cottage dwelling, all so mellow and typical of tranquillity that comes of long abiding. The most soothing scenery is soothing just because it is uneventful, with nothing specially striking about it, nothing for the guide-book compiler "to catch hold of," to use an expressive term. Such scenery calls for no strain on the attention of the traveller, but it lulls him with a dreamy sense of repose—it is the essence of peacefulness. And on account of this fact I feel that a driving tour through rural England is the very perfection of a real and restful holiday. However, we are not all cast in the same mould. There are some people who really find a rest, after the rigid routine of professional work or the dry drudgery of business, in rushing about as fast as rail and steam will carry them, and verily, I believe, they would go faster if they could. But paradoxical as it may appear, I maintain you cannot travel fast and far and see much.

At one point where our road dipped down we had a curious spectacle presented to us. On what appeared to be a straight stretch of grassy upland, well above the highway and the surrounding country, a large sailing barge appeared—at least the sail of it did—moving slowly along; manifestly this was an elevated canal, but at first sight from our point of view it did look strange to see a large barge sailing so much above the level of the surrounding land. This canal ascends the long hill into Devizes, a town that stands high up in the world, by a series of no less than thirty-nine locks; we did not count them all, but we were told that was the number. These locks, one after the other, follow up alongside of the road, or nearly so. But I am progressing too fast—we are not near Devizes yet.

The day was sunny and warm, and at a pretty spot where some leafy overhanging trees cast a welcome shadow upon the road we pulled up for a while to rest and refresh our horses, and to allow them the costless luxury of a handful of freshly-plucked grass. Just opposite this spot a rutty and narrow path led down to an old water-mill, with a tranquil pool in front fed by a clear, flowing stream that turned the big mill-wheel. This stream was crossed by a gray old bridge, and close to the building were an ancient dove-cote and a row of bee-hives ; beyond, a winding lane led past some pretty cottages and up a wooded bank, and then disappeared in a mass of cool greenery. Mill, shimmering and gliding water, old cottages, dove-cote, the deep green meadows around and tree-clad hill behind framing all together, formed a charming picture, and forcibly reminded us of Tennyson's painting in verse :—

> I loved the brimming wave that swam
>   Thro' quiet meadows round the mill,
> The sleepy pool above the dam,
>   The pool beneath it never still.
>
> The meal-sacks on the whiten'd floor,
>   The dark round of the dripping wheel,
> The very air about the door
>   Made misty with the floating meal.

This spot, we were told, was called Seend Head, a retired nook that abounds in alluring subjects for the sketcher from nature.

Driving on, we soon came to another wayside beauty bit, where the same pleasant stream was crossed by another one-arched bridge, with another ancient mill close by, and a gable of a thatched cottage just beyond, peeping above a wealth of foliage, completed the prospect. Our road that day was nothing but a succession of pictures, and our sketch-book and hand camera were called into frequent requisition, the latter so much so indeed, that our day's supply of photographic films was soon exhausted.

A little farther on we noticed the rather quaint Bell Inn that stood close to the side of the way, but a few feet below the level of the road; we presumed that since the house was built the road had been raised here. On a weather-stained and worn sign nailed to the side of the gable of the building we read the date 1698, so that the old inn has outlived many generations of travellers and seen many changes in the mode of travel; its early landlords would have been astonished could they have known that iron and steel horses would pass its door in shape of the slow, lumbersome traction engine and the speedy, lightsome cycle.

A little way beyond this old inn we entered the village of Seend, a charmingly pretty spot, and amongst the delightful homes of past days that line its wide and quiet street one especially attracted our attention. It was a cottage built somewhat in the Tudor style, with a great chimney projecting on one side towards the roadway, and having a sun-dial on the top; there was plenty of character about that pleasant abode. I like a house with character; it makes it at once interesting and individual; and character in building need not be a costly gift, for a cottage may possess it to the fullest degree, and a palace may be utterly without it. It is the misfortune of a mechanical age that it makes for a dead level of uniformity in both people and buildings. What a picturesque feature a sun-dial is on a house! and it is sometimes a useful one too; so is a well-designed weather-vane and a bell-turret; all these are comparatively small items, yet they often give an interest to a structure that otherwise would have no claim to be noticed by the passer-by.

The church at Seend is interesting chiefly from the lovely position it occupies on the crest of a gentle hill, and the glorious view to be had from thence over many-tinted woods in the vale below to the long line of undulating hills beyond; not a roof-tree did we see in the green and extensive panorama. The churchyard is beautifully kept; it is a God's garden rather than a "God's acre," and bears the same relation to the average churchyard that a garden does to a field. In the porch of the church we noticed a collecting-box "For the Churchyard," and it seemed to us a very fit and proper thing that the last resting-place of the beloved dead should be cared for tenderly thus; it is surely somewhat inconsistent that the fabric of a church should be carefully maintained without and adorned within, whilst but too often the churchyard where the sacred dead lie sleeping is neglected and allowed to become the home of rank grasses and crumbling tombstones. One could well spare some of the modern Minton tiles on the floors, the nineteenth-century garish stained-glass windows in the walls, the crudely-carved reredos above the altar, the obtrusive bright brass lectern of stock pattern fresh from Birmingham, that are supposed to adorn and beautify sundry of our country churches, and do with simpler things, if only the solemn graveyard were better cared for. How can an artist feel in a proper frame of mind for worship seated in a church with a staring, badly-designed, defectively-drawn, and hideously-coloured stained-glass window before him to torment his eye and vex his soul? Would he not a thousand times rather see a bit of unspoilt nature through a prettily-leaded light window?

Entering Devizes we passed, at the junction of two roads, a small castellated building that looked much like an old toll gate-house in spite of its crenellated walls and the grandly-sounding title of "Shane's Castle" it bore. We asked an old man why it was so called, and he replied laconically, "'Cause it is, I suppose. I don't know no other reason," and he even appeared astonished that we should ask the question.

At Devizes we rested a while at the sign of the Bear, a famous coaching-house, and one of the best patronised on the road, it having a reputation for good dinners and wines, warm feather-beds, and for a landlord "who read Milton, and whose son recited his poems," a curious mixture, it seems to me; one can hardly fancy a modern hotel being famous for its feather-beds, nor do I think that it would be any attraction for modern travellers to know that the landlord thereof read Milton, and I am afraid that they would consider it rather a bore than a pleasure to have to listen to a youth reciting poems! As we were looking round the hotel our eyes alighted on a portrait engraving hung on the staircase wall and having the following inscribed below :—

Sir Thomas Lawrence's father
Formerly landlord of the Bear hotel.

Thereupon we sought out the landlady, and learnt from her that Mr. Lawrence used to keep the "Bear," and his son, afterwards the famous Sir Thomas Lawrence, as a boy would draw likenesses of his father's guests, much to their amusement and his father's profit—that is, when he was not reciting Milton to them between their games at cards, as tradition asserts. Fancy Milton and gambling! What men our forefathers were!

An original and a valuable painting by Sir Thomas Lawrence used to hang up in the hotel, we were told, but it was stolen one day; nothing seems sacred from the collector, even an ordinary visitors' book in which some famous man has written his name has to be kept under lock and key, lest some one should tear the page out for the sake of the signature. The landlady, observing what interest we took in the place, most kindly showed us over the ancient house. The exterior view of the hotel as seen from the stables had, she informed us, been painted by a well-known artist, and the old hall had also been painted in a picture called "The Masqueraders," which had been exhibited in the Academy. To country people, by the way, the fact of a picture having been exhibited in the Academy proves beyond the question of a doubt that it must be a work of rare merit, and a statement having appeared in print causes it to be accepted as second only in authority to the Bible itself, which shows the glamour of a name and the virtue of print!

Besides its old associations, one of the charms of the hotel to us on that hot day was its delicious coolness. These old buildings, with their thick walls, in which material was not stinted, and their honest construction, do keep out the heat of the mid-summer sun as well as the winter cold. Good, straightforward building, if it costs more money in the first place, pays best in the end, except to the speculative contractor, who builds houses to sell; it costs less to maintain, and it saves considerably on the coal bills in the winter, to say nothing of the comfort and the freedom from draughts and their attendant ills. Speculative building is one of the curses of the age; more disease and suffering is caused by scamped building than the world wots of.

Devizes is a clean, airy, pleasant town, and any one in search of "fresh woods and pastures new" in the way of a holiday outing might do worse than make their headquarters there for a time and explore the very interesting country around. In the centre of the extensive market-place stands a market cross, on one side of which runs a long and curious inscription, a portion of which I give here:—

> The Mayor and Corporation
> Of Devizes avail themselves of the Stability of this Building
> To transmit to Future times the Record of an Awful Event
> Which occurred in this Market Place in the year 1753.

A CURIOUS INSCRIPTION 335

> On Thursday the 25th of January 1753
> Ruth Pierce of Pottern in this County agreed with
> Three other women to buy a Sack of Wheat in the Market
> Each paying her due proportion towards the same.
> One of those women in collecting
> The Several Quotas of Money discovered a Deficiency
> And demanded of Ruth Pierce the sum which was wanting
> To make good the amount: Ruth Pierce protested
> That she had paid her share and said "She wished
> That she might drop down dead if she had not."
> She rashly repeated this awful wish, when to the
> Consternation and Terror of the surrounding Multitude
> She instantly fell down and expired, having the Money
> Concealed in her hand.

We left Devizes early in the afternoon, bound eastward, having determined simply to drive on until we arrived at some inviting wayside hostelry, there to spend the night. Just at the outskirts of the town we observed a triangular built-on plot of ground, bounded by roads and curiously called "The Island." From this point our road gradually rose, and took us alongside of a great barren down; at a certain point here a rough track left the highway and climbed the hill; where the two ways met stood a tall monument with a lion rampant carved in stone on the top; the lion had, however, an iron tongue and tail. We at once called a halt to discover, if possible, the purport of this striking structure, for such wayside erections are rare in England, and when we do come upon one, we always make a point of inspecting it. Carved on the stone is a long inscription, which I give in part as follows:—

> *Qui Coluere Coluntur*
> An. Dom. 1771.

> This Monument
> Was erected to the memory of
> James Long
> Whose publick spirit was remarkably exerted
> In planning, promoting, and compleating
> This New Road
> An. Dom. 1678,
> By which a former tedious and dangerous way
> Over the adjacent hill
> Is avoided
> To the great pleasure and convenience of travellers.
> *In Recto Decus.*

In another mile or so we reached a pretty village with a decayed coaching inn, but this did not look sufficiently inviting to induce us to pull up. From this point, as we approached the borders of the hilly Plain of Salisbury, the landscape gradually assumed a wilder aspect. We had now before us a long, open, treeless stretch of road, with grass-grown banks on either side in place of the familiar hedgerows.

Away to the north across a level extent of country we saw another white horse cut on the steep surface of the chalk downs that bounded the prospect in that direction. It is astonishing how many figures of the kind still exist in England; this is the fourth we had come across on this tour; only now, when nearly everybody travels by train, they are seldom seen, except by the local inhabitants. What this special white horse was called we did not know, so questioned a shepherd, who, with sundry others, was refreshing himself outside a public-house. "It be Alton 'orse," he said, but he could tell us nothing of its history. Then another man of the company put in his word, and in a blunt manner, that would scarcely be considered polite even in Shoreditch society, exclaimed, "It bain't Alton 'orse, it be Crighton 'orse," at least we understood him to say Crighton, but as he could not spell it, I may be wrong in my rendering. Then an altercation sprang up between the two parties as to whether it were Alton or Crighton 'orse. We felt rather inclined to pronounce for Alton, as the champion for Crighton had a beery look in his face, that suggested to us he might not be perfectly sober. The other country folk said nothing, but drank their beer in stolid silence; then the original two who had spoken began to dispute the point so hotly that we deemed it best to depart. Shortly afterwards we consulted our map, and found a place marked Alton corresponding closely with the direction in which the white horse appeared to be, and so, rightly or wrongly, we gave our verdict for Alton.

On the right of our road now rose a massive rounded down, escarped on the top ; another consultation of our map showed this to be Casterley Camp, the most perfect British earth-work there is. In an age when much of the land was a wild tangle of forests, the aborigines of Britain appear to have congregated on the open uplands, and I should imagine that these large camps were really fortified towns, for as simple fortresses they are needlessly large, a fact also that would make them more difficult to defend on account of the number of men required, besides entailing quite unnecessary labour in construction. Furthermore, from examining many of these ancient camps, I should conjecture that the top of the escarpments was provided with a palisade of wood, or some similar additional defence, otherwise the mere earth-works might be rushed, and would scarcely be sufficient to render a camp tenable, especially against a sudden night attack. This is all pure guess-work on my part, but when proof of any kind is impossible, inferences may be allowed.

Just beyond the encamped down, the charming village of Charlton came into view in the valley below, making a very pretty picture with its thatched cottages embowered in trees, from which cottages curling films of blue smoke arose, and its flint-built church standing in an open spot apart by itself. Here by the roadside we remarked a rural inn, and at the porch thereof some much-worn mounting-steps, graphic reminders of the vanished past, when the roads hereabout, and especially across the Plain, were mere bridle-tracks, rough even at that, and farmers and their wives, and, in fact, all travellers southwards, had to journey on horseback or afoot. Primitive and picturesque times those, pleasant to romance about, and to exclaim " How delightful " to oneself—that is, in the bright and sunny summer weather, but not perhaps so suggestive of delights when the cold storms of winter are raging. A little leaven of fact oftentimes takes a good deal of the gilt of romance away.

At the foot of the great bare downs here (downs that were impressive on account of their mass and extent, if not their height), in sheltered hollows, were green wooded nooks, very refreshing to look upon, coming in such sudden and sharp contrast with the bleak hills above, on which neither tree nor shrub was visible. There is a restful sense in harmony that is dreamy and soothing, but to a vigorous mind contrast appeals most. A drop in the road took us into one of these sheltered nooks, where we found the pretty and prosperous-looking village of Rushall, and we felt inclined to rest there at the inn for the night, but the horses appeared so fresh, and the late afternoon, with its lengthening shadows, was so cool and pleasant, that we determined to drive on and tempt fortune further. After travelling so long and so far, this was, perhaps, rather a rash thing to do, as we were now entering upon the lonesome Salisbury Plain, but we felt in a careless, adventurous mood, we were so thoroughly enjoying ourselves: the fresh, cool air was a delight to us, and the wild scenery just suited our present humour, so we felt impelled to be mildly reckless. On, therefore, we went, and, turning southward, ascended into the vast shelterless region of Salisbury Plain. A long stretch of open road brought us to the hamlet of Upavon, a picturesque collection of old cottages gathered round a very ancient time-worn church. Here we met a former friend in the Avon, that we saw last at Ringwood as a wide and spreading river; at this spot in the heart of the hills it is quite in its infancy, a little narrow, humble, chalk stream. At Upavon we baited our hard-worked horses at a primitive inn called the "Antelope." It was not an ideal hostel with bay windows, an ample porch, a pleasant garden, and all that, but the landlord was most civil, and ushered us into a tiny sitting-room, very clean though poorly furnished, but somewhat stuffy for the want of an open window; possibly the landlord considered that he had a superabundance of fresh air here without admitting more than forces its way in unbidden during the blustery weather. However, he provided us with an excellent tea that greatly refreshed us. We might possibly have put up for the night at this remote inn, as the stables were good, and the house, if humble, was clean, but it was not to be. On making inquiries if we could be accommodated, and if we could see a bedroom before finally deciding, the landlord informed us that his wife was ill in bed with "the rheumatics," and he really could not manage to put us up without her. So we inquired of the road ahead, and learnt that about five miles farther on, at East Everley, there was an inn where we might perhaps be accommodated, but there was no other inn on the road, he believed, between Everley and Andover, a good seventeen hilly miles away.

This was not altogether acceptable news. What if the hotel at East Everley were full? There was the rub! What a pleasant predicament we should be in, belated with tired horses in the middle of the inhospitable Salisbury Plain! If we could not get in, perhaps we could get quarters for the horses, my wife argued, and we might at a pinch tramp on the twelve miles to Andover. The prospect did not commend itself to me. I threw out a gentle hint that this was a pleasure trip, and that for two tired souls to tramp twelve weary miles over lonely roads in the night time, even granting that we did not miss our way in the dark, was not exactly my idea of pleasure. Then we both simultaneously remarked what fools we were to have passed by such an apparently comfortable hotel as the one at Rushall, but this did not help us much. There was nothing for it but to push on with what speed we might. The evening was coming on apace; the round, red sun was slowly sinking behind the long line of the downs in the west; soon the gloaming would follow, and then the darkness. Under the circumstances we ordered the horses to be "put to" at once, and drove on. A suggestion that perhaps it would be the wisest and safest course to "hark back" to the despised hotel at Rushall was scouted as promptly as it was made: we had never turned back yet on the road, and we never would! Besides, why should the inn at Everley be full? We knew of no reason why it should. The unsatisfactory point was that the landlord at Upavon did not seem to know much about the inn at Everley. It might, from all the definite information we could gather from him, be a poor public-house; he was evidently anxious, with his wife ill, for us to proceed. Was he making the best of things to induce us to depart?

Already the sun had dipped behind the western hills before we left Upavon, and so we made what haste we could along the deserted road that stretched straight before us, a long white line lengthening out towards the dim, mysterious distance. There was a gloom and grayness coming over the landscape, and the contours of the downs were becoming indistinct.

Then our road began to mount for a mile or more in good earnest till it brought us on to high ground, on to the top of the world, as it were, at least to what was the world to us just then; from this point we looked down upon a wilderness of low, barren hills. Stopping here for a few minutes just to give the horses their breath after the long pull up, we were struck by the sense of solitude and silence, the consciousness of vast space, and the utter loneliness of the spot. There was a feeling of intense desolateness over all, for no sign of man or his handiwork was there, except the hardly-discernible rough road we were on. A cool, brisk breeze had risen as the sun had set, and the clouds above were drifting rapidly, being wind-driven into weird, fantastic forms. It seemed just then as though we had somehow reached

> . . . a solitude profound,
> Hill-girt by Nature from the outer world.

Land and sky were both impressive: all around us looked so sullen, eerie, and forsaken, if not inhuman, that we felt almost as though we might be wanderers in another planet suddenly transplanted there by some unknown magic, or that we were gazing upon a portion of a primeval world and were the first travellers "that ever burst into that silent" land. So much for sentiment.

However, we had no time to spare for fanciful romancing, the darkness was creeping on apace, the stars were beginning to glimmer in the moonless sky, and the golden light in the west was gone.

The practical fact remained that we were benighted on Salisbury Plain! The one thing to be done was to drive on as speedily as circumstances would allow. The air now became so keen and cold that we were glad of all our rugs and overcoats, and, worst of all, our horses began to show signs of fatigue, owing possibly more to the ruggedness of the road than to the distance travelled; for the first time during the journey we had to urge them on, though this was done rather by encouragement of the voice than by the whip. Presently a short, steep drop downhill led us to a spot humanised by a few scattered cottages, and made less melancholy by a pond that gave a dreary gleam of leaden light to the general gloom; then a rise followed, and we found ourselves at last in East Everley, an oasis of green trees in a desert of barren downs, but the trees increased the darkness and the difficulty of driving.

At the end of the woods we dimly discerned a building that we took to be the inn. At that moment we had a suspicion of some one passing by, and we shouted to know if our conjectures were right, and the welcome answer came out of the darkness that it was the "Crown." Strangely enough, not even a solitary gleam of light showed forth from door or window, and we half feared that the house might be empty. However, with the aid of our lamps we found our way to the entrance, only to discover the door locked, so we rang the bell, and after a time the landlady appeared with a candle in her hand, which the wind almost blew out. "Can you put us up for the night?" we asked anxiously. She looked first at us, next at the bright lights of the lamps of the dog-cart, which cast a cheery gleam around, then waited as though considering what to say. Perhaps she was astonished at finding travellers arriving thus late in such an out-of-the-world spot. However, at last she spoke: "I can give you a bed, and stable your horses, but I'm afraid I cannot get you any dinner to-night." Not give us any dinner! Why, I should not have expected such a thing at such an hour at a first-rate London hotel! Ye gods! fancy belated travellers in the middle of Salisbury Plain expecting a dinner at a road-side hostel at that time of night. Did she take us for royalty touring in disguise? We were only too rejoiced to obtain shelter for ourselves and our horses.

There were no guests staying in the house, which fact accounted for there being no lights visible. Soon, however, lamps were lighted in the little hall and in the snug sitting-room into which we were ushered for the time, and what a delightful surprise was ours, I almost think one of the most delightful surprises we had ever experienced on the road, for we found the little sitting-room to be a most charming and cosy chamber, panelled from floor to ceiling, neatly and appropriately furnished—in truth, more like the "snuggery" of some artistic soul or literary genius particular of his surroundings. There was a refinement about the chamber, an artistic fitness that seemed strangely out of keeping with the wild country around. But our surprise did not end here. When we were shown into our bedroom we found it also to be panelled in a similar manner, only the panelling there was painted a creamy white, that gave a clean, fresh, and bright appearance to the apartment. Moreover, it had actually a dressing-room attached. What unlooked-for luxury! We felt almost that we must be dreaming, and that "things were not what they seemed," but no, it was a happy reality.

Long will linger pleasantly in my memory the restful evening we spent in the cosy panelled parlour of that lonely inn, with the soft, shaded light of a swinging lamp shed calmly down on the whitest of cloths, whereon was spread an excellent tea, with a vase of sweet-scented flowers set in the midst to adorn the table. The coming upon this charming inn and its kind-hearted landlady was one of those pleasurable experiences that are the special delights of the road traveller, and it was here that we expected the least, being quite prepared to rough it if we could only obtain shelter of any kind. So happily ended our long and mildly eventful day's wanderings.

CHAPTER XIX

A grand playground—Wild England of to-day—Adventures—Ludgershall Castle—Herring-bone masonry—A decayed town—An interesting market cross—Weyhill—Andover—An old rhyming proverb—The upper Test—Nature's music—Scenery and character—A wooden church—Two old inns—A Roman road—Winchester—A reminder of the plague—The valley of the Itchen—A curious church—Saxon sculpture?

WE were so pleased with our quarters at Everley that we determined to stay over the next day there, at the same time giving our hard-worked horses a well-merited rest. Perhaps to some people the scenery in the vicinity of our hotel might not appear very attractive, but for us it had its own special charms. Round about, the land was open down, and we could wander unimpeded where we would. There is something very delightful in the sensation of freedom, of being able to rove unrestrained for miles in almost any direction; the soft springy turf, too, made the mere fact of walking a pleasure, and the light, tonic air caused us to feel like the British soldier, "fit to go anywhere and do anything," fit to tramp about the whole day long. The buoyant atmosphere was simply life-giving. What a place to brace one up is Everley, and what a lordly playground Salisbury Plain makes! The air coming unrestrained from over the vast uplands, uncontaminated by the smoke of any large town, and distilled in its way over the dry and thymy downs, possesses a rare and peculiar virtue of briskness and softness—it combines in a measure the bracing qualities of Scotland with the balminess of South Devon. What a place for the nerves!

The country round about Everley might well be described by the term rolling; in parts, indeed, it almost deserves the epithet hilly. In this portion of the Plain too, in sheltered hollows, scraggy woods are to be found, and some of the rounded heights are now and again crowned by clumps of wind-blown trees that give them quite a character, and are a special feature in the landscape, and whilst not taking away from the country its wild look, they prevent it from being called desolate or barren.

Early next morning, whilst looking after the welfare of our horses, we discovered the landlord in the stables; so far we had only come in contact with the landlady, and the existence of a landlord came, I hardly know why, as a surprise to us. We learnt from him that the inn had originally been a dower-house, a fact which at once explained the panelled rooms and the well-designed and picturesque interior, an interior that had been as little spoilt as possible in the transition from a private and refined home to a country hostelry.

Since we had started on our tour we had experienced no rain, but that morning there was a goodly supply of suspicious-looking, leaden-tinted clouds louring all round the circling horizon, and now and then we heard a distant rumble of thunder. "Going to have a storm?" we queried of the landlord. "I hope so," said he, "at least I hopes we shall get some rain. We're short of water up here. That's the drawback of the place. We can do with a lot more rain than we gets as a rule. It may turn to wet, but I don't think as how we'll get a thunderstorm; we rarely do. Thunder always follows the water, and we've none up here on the hills. At Upton and down the Avon they gets the thunderstorms often whilst the sun is shining here." We had never heard this theory before of thunderstorms "following the water," but there may be something in it, for certainly the electric fluid when it strikes the earth or a building invariably seeks damp ground.

We spent a delightful and most enjoyable day wandering, fancy led, over the wind-swept uplands, rejoicing for once to be alone with earth and sky, and desiring no other company; enough entertainment for us to watch the Constablesque clouds go drifting by overhead, and to watch the stately sweep of the mighty shadows they cast, raking the curved hills in quick succession. There was an indescribable grandeur in the vast swell of the downs that led the eye away and away till it vanished into a dreamy nothingness of distant blue. How space-expressing was the prospect, conveying a feeling of majesty without ruggedness or severity, the impressiveness of the scenery being mainly due to its revelation of mighty distances!

The roads that cross the Plain here are un-

SALISBURY PLAIN, NEAR EVERLEY

enclosed, and in some cases gradually merge into mere grassy tracks, which in turn lose themselves altogether and land the too trusting traveller— nowhere. We wandered westward into a spacious solitude of breezy uplands encircled by an undulating horizon of indigo-blue hills. Great masses of gray, rounded, drooping clouds charged with aqueous vapours sailed slowly by overhead across a sea of deepest blue, but, strangely, no rain fell. Now and again the clouds just touched the summits of the hills, and for a time half hid their forms; then they appeared to swoop still lower down, and it seemed as though we could almost lift up our hands and touch them, so close to us did they descend. We expected every moment to get a drenching, yet nothing came of it all, but the stormy-looking effects as they swept across the Plain were most striking.

We made rapid sketches of the varying sky scenery, as well as the ever-changing colours of the downs. Now a near hill would be a dark purple-blue in shade, anon it would be a brilliant green as the sunshine burst upon it, turning the gloom into a transient golden glory. A solitary weather-beaten shepherd, driving a few sheep along a lonely, rutty road, was all the life we saw that morning, not even a stray bird enlivened the silent and desolate prospect of land and sky; the only sound we heard was the subdued, hardly audible murmuring of the hurrying wind as it swept over the short grass and startled the stunted gorse. It was a profound solitude, yet—if there can be such a thing—a companionable solitude, a wild nature, but a nature neither austere nor forbidding; there were no frowning precipices, no noisy, rushing torrents, no aspiring mountain peaks to limit the long range of vision, for we could look over most, if not all, of the downs, and rake their valleys below. Our eyes could rove without hindrance over miles and miles of curving greenery that gradually faded away into gray, and then, still farther off, into a mystery of blue where the earth seemed to melt into the sky. It was a grand study of vanishing perspective, the distant downs being dwarfed by space into mere faint lines, and the blueness of the horizon revealing the mighty extent of air—a something almost tangible up here—that we saw through.

So we spent a long, pleasant, and profitable day wandering at will over the smooth-turfed downs, now and again resting to make a sketch by way of change, or simply sitting still on a grassy mound lazily admiring the spreading panorama, or reclining at full length thereon looking up at the great clouds above and studying their ever-changeful forms, for the fine skyscape interested us almost as much as the landscape. We delighted in laziness; it is a splendid tonic for the tired brain, only it is well to be lazy in a bracing atmosphere; the buoyant air will not allow you to remain idle longer than nature needs to recoup herself.

When the next morning came we felt loth to leave our comfortable, not to say luxurious, quarters, but still many miles of pleasant country lay before us and home; it was necessary to proceed, or we should be on the road the whole summer, and circumstances did not permit. Even the longest holiday comes to an end in time, so with this philosophical reasoning we set forth once more on our wanderings, our horses being delightfully fresh after their day's rest. It was an inspiriting morning, for the rain-clouds had all cleared off, and the sky was of a glorious bright blue, dappled with a few wind-woven clouds that foretold fine, if possibly breezy, weather. The sun shone joyously forth in a manner worthy of Italy, and we felt as we drove on in that happy state of optimism that made pessimism seem an unreality ; the world appeared to us a very excellent one that day.

Our road at first led over the wide, open downs that rose and fell around us, ridge succeeding ridge in endless succession. In some parts the grass looked so temptingly smooth that we drove along it, gladly deserting the rough and stony highway for the elastic turf that made driving of itself a delight, so easy and noiseless was our progress ; it seemed unnatural almost to trot along without hearing the sound of the horses' hoofs on the ground, or the crunching of the carriage wheels on the hard or gritty road ; just as at sea, aboard a mail steamer, voyagers get so accustomed to the measured throbbing of the engines that they can sleep right through it, but should, for any reason, the engines be stopped, the unusual silence causes them to awake. So easy was the driving, that we were as comfortable as though seated in an arm-chair ; indeed we might figuratively say that our tour was taken in an arm-chair on wheels!

At one point we reached some way ahead, where another lonely road met ours at right angles, we noticed an old, decrepit, leaning sign-post, and beside this was a man on horseback, standing quite still, for what purpose I cannot say, but there he stood—he and his horse being the only living things visible in all the wild and far-reaching prospect. In the olden days this figure would certainly have suggested a highwayman, and might have caused considerable misgivings on our part; as it was, we merely wondered why he was standing there. We passed him standing on the spot, and the last view of him on our looking back from some way off showed him still there. We bade him good day as we drove by, and he returned the greeting. It was no business of ours what he was doing strangely loitering thus. I must confess that in the days when they flourished, the "gentlemen of the road" would have been a decided drawback to driving tours. True, they might have added a spice of danger to such an expedition, with the possibility of a more or less exciting adventure, but I, for one, am well satisfied to read of these things in books, perfectly content with a peaceful progress. I have experienced some adventures whilst travelling on horseback over "blazed" mountain forest tracks and stopping at lonely ranches in the wild west of America, but I consider such adventures far more delightful to relate "in after-dinner talk across the walnuts and the wine" than to experience in actuality. Better than most of the adventures in this world is the recollection thereof!

As we drove on, the country gradually assumed a less wild aspect: enclosed lands and cultivated fields became visible and increased, till in time tangled hedgerows bordered our road, which had previously been quite fenceless. By degrees the bold down scenery gave place to the softer features of a pastoral and wooded land. Then in a short space we reached the picturesque and interesting village of Ludgershall, once an important town with a strong castle. Of the latter only a fragment remains; this we discovered in an old farmyard, crumbling still further away, a portion of it doing duty as a shed. The ruined keep is constructed chiefly of flints. Originally, judging by the slight portions existing, this was faced with square-hewn stones. We noticed some herring-bone work in the tower; an effective, strong, and enduring way of building with small flat slabs or tiles this, and why it should have so completely gone out of fashion I cannot comprehend, as it lends such pleasing variety to a wall or building, allows the employment of inexpensive material, and has stood the rough test of centuries apparently unhurt. It is a perfectly legitimate way of giving an agreeable diversity to a wall surface. What could be more picturesquely effective in a chalk country than a cottage or a house built of blue-gray flints (the natural building "stone" of the district) varied by bands of red tiles built in herring-bone fashion? Form and colour contrasting, the cool blue-gray of the rounded flints being in juxtaposition with the warm tints of the angular tiles, be they oblong or square. The great fault of the architects of to-day is that they pay scant heed to local material, trusting over-much to the everlasting red brick, because it saves so much trouble. All local flavour and colouring is thus lost, and, architecturally speaking, the land in consequence suffers from a plague of scarlet fever. It is red brick here, red brick there, and red brick almost everywhere. But I am wandering from the castle. The views from the ramparts round the keep, especially looking northwards and westwards towards Salisbury Plain, are very fine.

Some of the old houses in the village look rather interesting, and a large pond in the centre gives it a cheerful look, reflecting as it does the bright blueness of the sky into the midst of time-dimmed surroundings. Near to the pond stands the broken base of what must have been an important market cross. Around this base are some very weatherworn figures, too much effaced to make anything of, at least without more time to study them than we could then devote. The old broken and decayed cross gives quite a character and interest to the village street; it tells of former days and former ways, and points to a past prosperity. I fear that Ludgershall is still decreasing in size, for as we passed through we noticed several cottages being pulled down.

Onward from here the landscape was open and pleasant, with frequent peeps of distant wooded hills. Wide commons, too, gave a sense of space to the country-side, and with nothing further notable we arrived at Weyhill, a village consisting chiefly, judging from our passing glance, of a series of unbeautiful stone booths plastered over with notices of "Refreshments," etc. Weyhill is famous for having the largest yearly fair in England, and seems to exist and prosper, in a fashion, on this one fair, lasting a week, where large numbers of cattle change hands, a vast amount of agricultural produce is sold, and farm hands still congregate for their annual "hiring."

After this, a "give and take" road brought us to Andover, a clean, neat, quiet little market town, boasting of no special picturesqueness or interesting features—at least, if it possessed any we failed to discover them—and with absolutely nothing to attract or detain the average tourist. But its failure to excite us in any way was not without its recompense, for, after a tour of inspection round the town, on returning to our comfortable inn we felt no compulsion or desire to desert the ample projecting bay window of the coffee-room, whence we commanded the market-place and viewed the amusing life thereof (it chanced to be market day). The streets were thronged with farmers and their wives, looking "jolly" and prosperous enough in spite of the proverbial bad times, besides numerous uncatalogued rural folk who moved in and out amongst the crowd.

These market days bring far-apart country dwellers together once a week, and afford an opportunity for a mutual exchange of views—and scandal. It really seemed to us, from what we could gather, that the farmer and his wife come to market nowadays more as an excuse for a mild change and to do a little shopping and a good deal of gossip than for actual business. The whole moving scene, and the many characters thereof that played their parts so unconsciously, were as interesting as any play, more so than many. There were two easy-chairs in that great bay window, and in them we sat the whole afternoon, well entertained. So amused were we, that there we stayed instead of proceeding on our way to Winchester as we had intended; and when the play was over we found it rather late to take the long stage of sixteen miles to that city, so we remained the night at Andover, and as the chance company at our inn that evening proved very entertaining, we did not regret our change of programme.

There is an old rhyming proverb relating to four Hampshire towns, of which Andover is one, that runs as follows :—

> Romsey in the mud,
>   Southampton on the stones,
>   Winchester eats the meat,
>   Andover picks the bones.

This rhyme hardly needs any elucidation, but perhaps it is only fair to remark that though the streets of Romsey used to have an unenviable notoriety for their mud, it is a very clean and bright little town to-day. In the times gone by when Romsey deserved its muddy reputation it used to be a Hampshire saying in speaking of any one who was slovenly or unclean in person that she or he "came from Romsey." Let us trust that the reverse holds good now!

We had a long pull uphill on leaving Andover, as far as a chalk cutting, evidently made to ease the road at the summit of the rise. Looking back from our elevated position, we had a glorious view right over Andover, and over a stretch of wooded country beyond, to the undulating uplands of Salisbury Plain, that bounded the prospect. We tried to trace our road of yesterday, but failed.

The country now assumed a wild and forest-like aspect, and we observed that the district was marked as "Harewood Forest" on our map. Then a long run downhill, with vistas ahead between the trees of a high horizon of deep blue, brought us to Longparish, at least a village of that name was marked there on our map, but as a matter of fact we only saw a public-house and one or two stray cottages; perhaps, in keeping with its name, the hamlet is a long one and not all visible at a glance.

Here we crossed the troutful Test, a wide, silvery stream that flows between reedy banks and past luxuriant pastures. The greenfulness all along the river-side was very refreshing to look upon, doubly so in contrast with the dry and parched landscape all about, for the country for miles around was suffering from a prolonged drought, and the murmuring music of a tumbling weir made liquid melody that was a delight to listen to. Give me nature's music: the soft wind rustling the standing corn, or sur, sur, surring through the forest trees, the gurgling and plashing of some mountain stream, the peaceful babbling of a brook, the tuneful song of free birds, the solacing sound of the distant sea when the summer waves break upon the shore—of such music one never wearies, of other kinds I often do, especially that of a German band!

We pulled up here and wandered down the river and envied a fisherman who, rod in hand, was leisurely strolling along the opposite bank. He looked the very picture of contentment, and was manifestly enjoying the scenery as well as the sport. We were glad to see him, for he made a pleasing figure in our sketch. Unconsciously he stood a while in a picturesque attitude, just where an artist would have placed him for effect; then he began to whip the stream, and we returned to our dog-cart.

It is well to be an angler and to spend the long summer day amongst such cool and restful scenery, and to "take one's ease" at night in some quiet country inn where followers of the "gentle craft" are thoughtfully catered for. Small wonder that the average angler—the old-fashioned angler—is a contemplative being, mild-mannered, and a genial companion, for his hobby takes him into scenes that are eminently spirit-soothing. To a certain extent, I believe that scenery has an effect upon character. I have always found that men and their families who live in secluded mountain valleys, or apart from the world on lonely, desolate moors, are taciturn, austere, not to say morose, whilst dwellers in the fruitful valleys are of a brighter and happier nature. There is something very fascinating as well as soothing in watching the quiet flow of a river, gleaming, glancing, and gurgling round its graceful curves. It is delightful—whether you angle or not—to roam by a river-side, exploring countless backwaters and coming upon unfrequented nooks and corners where cattle descend to drink, and where, perchance, ancient, tree-hidden mills hum drowsily as though business were a slothful affair, and all things seem to live a life of lazy contentment. Nothing appears to be in a hurry by the side of a slow-flowing rural river!

Passing now through a pleasant country without any special features, we reached Bullington Cross, a lonely inn so named, that stood where four roads met. From this spot we descended through a shady tree-lined lane to Sutton Courtney, an exceedingly clean and picturesque village, mostly consisting of thatched cottages; a village that pleased us much. Here we found a wooden church of rather quaint, though modern construction, with timber buttresses in imitation of stone ones, that certainly gave it an original look.

We actually discovered two hostelries in the village within sight of each other, manifestly relics of the coaching days. Both appeared reasonably good for rural inns, and to save ourselves the difficulty of deciding which was the best we simply drove up to the first one, called the "Coach and Horses"; the rival inn over the road was the "Swan." This proclaimed its title by a large white swan, stuffed and enclosed in a glass case, over the entrance, a somewhat novel form of sign. Beyond this was the stable archway, with the date 1767 inscribed over it, and on each side it had iron lamp-brackets *in situ*, though the lamps were gone. Doubtless both these inns had seen better and busier days; they had an indescribable look of having done so, though we latter-day road travellers had no cause to complain of our treatment nor of our moderate bill. How it comes that so remote and small a village should possess two such inns was a problem, but the world is so full of problems that we have long ago given up bothering our heads about such matters, contented to accept facts as we find them.

Sutton Courtney abounds in picturesque bits very delightful to the eye of the sketcher, and very profitable to the amateur photographer. Our ever-growing stock of negatives was considerably increased here, and, besides peeps of sundry old cottages, we took away with us, unwillingly on our part I must confess, the portraits of a number of the juvenile inhabitants—all full-face ones! The younger generation of the rural population is getting versed in the use of the hand camera, and when a portion thereof sees the opportunity, it is determined "to be took in the picture"; so knowledge spreads, and photographic pictures are spoilt.

As we were looking round the inn-yard before proceeding with our journey, a red-faced, watery-eyed stranger came up to us, a shabby-genteel-looking individual, and evidently not a bigoted teetotaller. He was kind enough, in a rather unsteady voice, to express his admiration of the dog-cart, but suggested a few alterations, which he stated would be great improvements. "I sees as how you be a commercial gent," he further remarked. "I can always tell a commercial gent when I sees one." We expressed our surprise that he should be so perspicacious. He did not seem quite to understand us, but smiled knowingly, then getting bolder, continued, "Now what may be your line of travel? I've been wondering ever since you came here." We met this query by another, and said he must tell us what he did first. We thought this would be a poser, and thereupon he would go away and leave us in peace. We made a mistake. "Oh," replied he readily, "my business ain't a very profitable one. I'm the father of a family. It takes me all my time looking after them and the wife." Poor wife, we pitied her. Then fortunately the ostler came on the scene, and the stranger disappeared in the bar, could it possibly be for a drink?

On from Sutton Courtney our road went as straight as a line, with long ups and downs and no regard for gradients. The ancient Romans must have originally planned this road, we exclaimed, and we looked at our map and found it marked "Roman Road." There was something decidedly very businesslike about that road making direct from one point to another without the slightest deviation or turning. The country we passed through was bleak and desolate, a mass of rolling uplands, with scarcely a tree or a cottage to be seen till we came into sight of Winchester. The landscape was somewhat similar in character to that of Salisbury Plain, though it had less distinctive features.

The chief object in our first view of Winchester was the big prison, with its tower set boldly on a hill; not the cathedral, as one might expect; that was hidden in a hollow. It does not lord it over the city as most cathedrals do, fitting emblems of the olden ecclesiastical supremacy.

At Winchester we drove up to the erst famous posting and coaching house, the "George." On approaching this ancient and historic hostelry we noticed boldly inscribed upon it :—

<blockquote>
George Hotel
Established in the XIII Century.
Accommodation for
Driving Parties.
</blockquote>

This was followed by a list of fifteen towns, with the road distances to each from the "George" duly given after them; by which it would appear that driving tours are in vogue in this part of the country, and even that the driving tourist has become of sufficient importance as to be specially catered for, otherwise why this prominent notice? Indeed, we learnt during a chat with the ostler that "quite a number of driving parties puts up here in the summer time. There be three others putting up with me to-night besides yourself. Two of 'em are going to the New Forest. I don't know where the other be a-going to. There's nothing like driving for enjoyment and seeing the country. If I were a gentleman that's how I would like to spend my money." And small blame to you, worthy ostler. May you make a little fortune, or have one left unexpectedly to you, and go a-driving!

Sitting that evening within the old courtyard of the hotel, now roofed over with glass and turned into a lounge, we observed no less than fifteen bicycles resting against the walls. What, I wonder, would the landlords of old have said or thought of such a sight? The waiter told us that the cycles belonged to parties touring and resting there for the night.

We left the cathedral unvisited on this occasion, for we had seen it more than once before, so whilst the light lasted we set out for a stroll round about the city's suburbs, where the tourist seldom finds his way, on the off chance that we might see something of interest—and we did, for on high ground overlooking the city we came upon a gray stone obelisk, on the foot of which was inscribed :—

> This Monument
> Is Erected
> By the Society of Natives
> On the very spot of ground
> To which the Markets were remov'd
> And whose Basis is the very Stone
> On which exchanges were made
> Whilst the City lay under the Scourge
> Of the Destroying Pestilence
> In the Year
> Sixteenhundred Sixty Six.

Early next morning found us once more on the road. After glancing at our map we had planned to drive first along the valley of the Itchen, and so by Alresford to make our way to Petersfield; and after consulting with the ostler we were gratified to learn that this was the only level road out of Winchester.

The valley of the Itchen—from Winchester upwards, that is—surprised us by its gentle beauty; it simply abounded in picturesque bits the whole way. This most charming valley is well worth leisurely exploring afoot; it is very rewarding to the lover of tranquil beauty, to say nothing of the antiquary, for some of the ancient churches and old houses scattered along it are of considerable archæological interest. To both angler and artist it is, I should imagine, almost ideal ground. Winding river of clearest water, many-tinted woods, graceful sloping hills, cool green meadows, with old-world villages dotted here and there, combine to make scenery that truly deserves the term bewitching.

The first hamlet we came to was Headborne Worthy. Here the primitive little church set close to the roadside, with its rude-built flint tower, surmounted by a quaint wooden belfry, interested us; it was such a picturesque and welcome change from the usual type of village church. The ancient edifice is separated from the highway by a running stream of water, which is spanned by a small foot-bridge. We crossed over this in order to discover if by any chance the church door were open, and we had the good fortune not only to find it so, but also the clerk within. The clerk did not appear to consider that there was much to interest any one in the church, excepting that it was very old. However, at the west end we discovered what we imagined to have been a small chapel of Saxon origin. This is divided from the larger though still small church by an undoubted Saxon arch. In this chapel, which is bare to the walls, are the remains of a large sculpture of the Crucifixion, with two haloed saints on either side, presumably intended for the Virgin Mary and St. John. The carving has been chiselled flat with the wall, possibly by the Puritans (it is the fashion to put down all these destructions to them), but the outlines of the figures and cross can still plainly be made out, with the haloes round the three heads. We asked the clerk if he knew anything about this. He replied, " I've heard say as how it's supposed to have been a little Saxon church, and the carving shows the Crucifixion of our Lord, with the two thieves on either side "!

Within the tower of the church the ancient and massive wood-work, black and bent with age, that upholds the belfry is curious; but the idea, to support the bells independently of the external structure, is a sound one, as it saves all the strain on the building itself. On the north wall of the chancel we noticed a quaint little fifteenth-century brass to one " Iohēs Kent," a scholar of the " College de Wynchestre," who is represented, as customary, with his hands folded in the attitude of prayer. On the south wall of the nave, by way of contrast, is a well-executed modern brass to a lady, that bears the date of 1884; but though treated with considerable skill, the modern dress does not lend itself to decorative display, least of all on brasses. What would the medieval craftsman who sculptured the ancient knights in full armour on their altar-tombs, with their dames in ruffles by their side and the faithful dog at their feet, have done with the modern frock-coat and hideous black hat? What indeed? There are some things beyond the power of art to make beautiful!

CHAPTER XX

Itchen Abbas—Alresford—Epitaphs and Burial Boards—A greenland solitude—The fascination of the far away—Rogate—A fine brass to an Agincourt hero—A "leper's window"—Latin or English—A wild heath—Peat-cutting in a southern county—The ruins of Cowdray House—Queen Elizabeth as a sportswoman—"The curse of Cowdray."

As we drove up the lovely Itchen valley, the silvery river, winding in and out of the wooded landscape to our right, kept us welcome company. The next village we came to was Kings Worthy, a neat, clean little place, possessing a picturesque church with an ivy-clad tower. Then followed a pleasant stretch of peaceful pastoral country, with here and there an ancient farmstead, and ever and again a lowly cottage home embowered in foliage, at the end of which stretch we found ourselves at Itchen Abbas, a lovely spot by the river-side. Here we rested some time in order to quietly enjoy the scenery.

At this delightful and dreamy spot the river is crossed by an old stone bridge, gray with years, the many low arches of which double themselves in the glassy surface of the slow-gliding water. On the bank of the stream stood an old mill; this, combined with the bridge, a tumbling weir, and the leafy woods beyond, formed a charming picture, and tempted us to make a sketch of it. It was a wonderfully pretty spot, and after our sketch was finished we still lingered on, lazily listening to the soft wind whispering to the trees overhead, to the falling and plashing of the water over the weir, and to the droning of the great mill-wheel :—

> Such *sounds* have the power to quiet
> The restless pulse of care,

and have a wonderfully soothing effect on the town-tired ear. Rural sounds are as peace-bestowing as rural scenery—one, indeed, is but the complement of the other. Absolute silence, such as one may sometimes experience on the lonely mountain side or on a desolate moorland, is depressing rather than restful, but nature is seldom in such an uncompanionable mood.

Then as we progressed up the narrowing valley, the river became stream-like and even more lovable than before. At Itchen Stoke we passed a fine modern church set on a knoll. The building appeared high in proportion to its width, but what chiefly interested us in it was the introduction of gargoyles really intended for service, and not mere meaningless reproductions of ancient forms without their functions being considered.

Some little way after Itchen Stoke we reached the head of the valley, and came in sight of Alresford, which is approached in this direction by a long avenue of trees by the side of the road. The walk along this would appear to be a favourite promenade of the inhabitants, judging from the number of people we noticed strolling there. Before us a flag was flying on the dark gray church tower of Alresford, that made it look more like some old castle keep than a portion of a place of worship. From our point of view the tower stood well above the roof-trees of the little town, and without much strain upon the imagination we might have fancied ourselves medieval pilgrims approaching a medieval town.

Alresford pleased us much, it looked so neat and clean. Its chief street is wide and sunny, for the houses on either side of the way are happily low, mostly of two stories, so that they cast but little shade. Besides this, to add to its pleasantness, there were trees on the sides of the roadway. I find also that I made a note of the bright windows as we drove in, and the well-kept doorways. Here at the "Swan" we made our mid-day halt, and were shown into a pleasant, low-ceilinged, panelled room, though unfortunately the panel was painted and grained in imitation of wood again, a proceeding that always seems to me the height of absurdity. If a wainscoted chamber must be painted, and darkness is the only possible palliation for this sin, then let the honest paint be proclaimed, and not a paltry sham that deceives no one.

Rambling round about whilst our horses rested, we noticed a public-house with the uncommon sign of "The Peaceful Home." We could only trust that in this case the title was appropriate. Continuing our perambulations we discovered, just outside the town, a large sheet of water, almost deserving the name of lake, and we wandered round its reed-grown banks till we came to a little and very picturesque thatched cottage, which we forthwith sketched; then we strolled back to our inn, and were soon again speeding on our pleasant way.

The country now for a space was not remarkable in any way. At Bishops Sutton, the first village on our road, we called a short halt, as we observed in the churchyard a tombstone roofed over, and we thought, as so much manifest care was taken to protect it from the weather, it might be interesting. However, we merely found on the monument some simple verses recording the death of two infants :—

> These stars of comfort for a moment given
> Just rose on earth, then set to rise in heaven.

Then we turned to another monument, which also recorded the death of three infants, with a curious inscription below, of which I give the first few lines and the last two :—

> Bold Infidelity, turn pale and die,
> Beneath this sod three infants' ashes lie,
> Say: Are they lost or saved?
> If death's by sin, they sinned for they lie here:
> If heaven's by works, in heaven they can't appear.
>
> . . . . . .
>
> They died for Adam's sin,
> They live, for Jesus died.

But why such a startling challenge to Infidelity? This monument is dated 1831. Nowadays it seems that Burial Boards exercise quite a despotic and not always a reasonable or enlightened censorship over tombstone inscriptions. I have it on the authority of a well-known London daily paper that the Burial Board of a certain town not a hundred miles from London "refused to allow a certain verse, which had been selected by a resident, to be inscribed on a memorial in the cemetery to a deceased son, as not up to its standard of tombstone poetry. The lines were:—

> He is not dead,—the child of our affection,—
> But gone unto that school
> Where he no longer needs our poor protection,
> And Christ himself doth rule.

The ratepayer concerned was naturally very indignant," and little wonder! We further learnt from the newspaper account that one of the members of the Board declared that the verse read "like doggerel." Possibly he had never heard of such a poet as Longfellow, who wrote it! It would be interesting to know what is the "standard of tombstone poetry" required by the average Burial Board. We learnt also, on the same authority, that a line of our own Tennyson—

> The finger of God touched them and they slept,

was vetoed by a different Board as irreverent, and I know of other and even more astonishing cases of a similar nature. Truly Burial Boards "dressed in a little brief authority" manage to make themselves supremely ridiculous. That does not matter much certainly, but they give needless pain to others, and this *does* matter.

After Bishops Sutton the scenery improved and soon reached a very high order of woodland beauty. Our route lay along cross-country roads, at least we elected to traverse these in preference to the dusty highway, finding that we should lose no ground, or hardly any, by so doing. Moreover, we reasoned to ourselves that the shady by-ways would be more pleasant to drive on, besides being more likely to lead us into the real heart of rural England—nor were we disappointed in our prognostications.

In a mile or so we left the main road and proceeded up a narrow lane, trusting entirely to our excellent map for our present and future bearings. This lane led us between deep beech woods that reminded us of bits of Buckinghamshire. Then after a while the confined lane opened out into a vast undulating common, or waste upland, whose boundaries we could not see, a greenland solitude dotted over with beech trees, clumps of tangled brambles, and ragged thorns; and across the far-reaching grassy slopes that led down to dark, shady hollows deep in leafy gloom wound narrow footpaths and uneven bridle-tracks that seemed to beg us to stop and explore them; but, alas! it would take more than one lifetime to explore all of rural England! I do not even yet know one county of it thoroughly. Perhaps no man really does! I once had a chat with a guide-book compiler who honestly thought he did, but I soon convinced him to the contrary; he happened not to know as much of it as I did by a great deal! Yet I was less familiar with that special county than with one or two others.

But to return to our journey, and this sequestered part of Hampshire in particular. The wild, open woodland all around charmed us with its tender grace and rich yet restful tints of golden greens softening away into greeny grays. It was all so wild and free, so beautiful without being in any way pretty or petty. The scenery was grand, but lovable; impressive without being stern. From that breezy upland the prospects looking down and all around were simply enchanting. We looked over the surrounding woods on to a blue distance of more woods, that spread away and away to a long range of shapely hills steeped in softest summer sunshine. A dreamy, poetic distance; a mysterious land, remote and vague, where all things seemed possible, the "earthly Paradise" that never is, except in fancy or in the glamour of the far-away! This little corner of England—out of the beaten track of pleasure travel, and out of the sight and sound of the fussy railway as well—is worth exploring; the scenery, though not of the striking nature to lend itself to vivid or sensational description, strongly appeals to all lovers of sylvan quietude.

Leaving this lovely spot with its spacious panoramas of spreading woodlands and circling hills, our road led us on, with many ups and downs, to a point in a valley where four cross roads met; from thence we had a delightful spin into Petersfield, with one sharp and sudden dip down a tree-shaded glen, the road being most of the way in our favour, and the scenery all we could desire. It was late and growing dark when we reached our destination, and cheerful lights were gleaming from many a window and open door of the sleepy old town as we drove along to the "Dolphin," where we found a welcome as well as clean and comfortable quarters for the night, besides entertainment for the mind in the coffee-room by the conversation of a fellow country-lover and explorer, with whom we exchanged notes and ideas till so late an hour that we felt quite dissipated—for the country.

From Petersfield to Petworth through Midhurst was our proposed programme for the day's wanderings. The morning proved fine and sunshiny, with a pleasant breeze to temper the warmth, so that nothing was wanting to complete our enjoyment. All throughout the journey the weather had been kindly disposed towards us, and it appeared as though it were going to be so to the end thereof. There being nothing to delay us in Petersfield, we, as usual, made an early start. It is pleasant to "get away" in the first fulness and freshness of the morning, and to rest oneself and bait the horses in the heat of the noontide; besides, by so doing the whole long summer day is before one, and therefore ample time is secured to linger here and there on the way, as the scenery or fancy may dictate.

We passed at first through a pleasant farming land, a combination of green, hedge-rowed meadows and golden cornfields ripening for the early harvest, great patches of waving yellow in the sunshine and the breeze, varied with bits and wedges of dark woodlands now and then, just to break any monotony. Nature and man have worked together here to make the land an Eden to the eye. The trail of the serpent may be across it truly, but if so, it was not apparent. As we proceeded, the familiar outline of the South Downs became visible in the distance on our right, a soft green in the sunshine and a pearly gray in shade, lengthening out towards the long horizon till lost in a pale blue palpitating haze. What a lovely background and contrast those bare and tender-tinted Downs made to the rich cultivated valley below, aglow with colour, with its seas of golden corn, enriched by the burning scarlet of the spreading poppy, and its gray flint-built farmsteads, with their red-tiled roofs silvered and bronzed with lichen!

Through this lovely country we drove in a delightful day-dream till we came to the pretty and elevated village of Rogate, from which there is a fine view of the Downs. Another pleasant stretch of country brought us to the tree-embowered hamlet of Trotton, set in a shady nook by the side of the little river Rother. Here, close to the road, we observed a gray and ancient church that apparently had happily never known the hand of the restorer nor that of the modern builder. It looked so ancient and hoary that we were tempted to stop on the chance of being able to obtain a glance inside. Somehow we had a sudden intuitive feeling that the church would prove interesting, just one of those impressions that arise one hardly knows how. We fortunately found the door open, which saved us going a-clerk-hunting, and the vicar's wife—at least we gathered from our after conversation with her that she was such—playing the harmonium (for the primitive fane did not possess an organ). On seeing us she most kindly left her practising and volunteered to show us over the building.

Here in the chancel, on either side of the Communion table, are two altar-tombs with ornamental carvings on their bases. They appear to have belonged to personages of considerable importance, but the effigies are gone, and no inscriptions remain to reveal whose memory they were intended to commemorate. Our guide told us that nothing whatever was known about them, nor could anything be gleaned thereof, and even learned archæologists and antiquaries had been consulted in vain ; so hard is it even for the great and mighty to perpetuate their name and fame in this world! Here the inevitable moral should follow, but I refrain ; a twelve-year-old little lady friend of mine informed me one day that she never read tales with morals—they were always so stupid !

In the centre of the chancel we noticed another altar-tomb standing alone in stately dignity. This had a massive slab of Purbeck marble laid on the top, let into which was a large and very fine brass, beautifully executed, and in an excellent state of preservation. We were quite unprepared to find so important a brass in such a remote country church. A legend in Latin informed us that this brass is to the memory of "Thomas Camoys, formerly Lord Camoys, A Baron and Commander for the king and kingdom of England, and a brave Knight of the Garter ; his end he commended to Christ on the twenty-eighth day of March 1419." This Lord Camoys, we afterwards learnt, commanded the left wing of the English army—mainly composed of bowmen—at the battle of Agincourt, and for his bravery on that memorable occasion he was created a Knight of the Garter on St. George's Day following. His wife was the widow of the renowned Hotspur, and she was eulogised by Shakespeare as the "gentle Kate." Mentioning St. George's Day reminds me that our courteous guide informed us that "the church is dedicated to St. George of England." I do not at the moment remember any other church so dedicated.

Now to describe this fine and interesting brass. It bears the figure of Lord Camoys in full plate armour, with the collar of SS. and the Garter on his left leg; his wife is shown by his side, her hand being clasped in his. At the foot of Lord Camoys is the usual faithful dog, and at the foot of his countess is a curious diminutive figure, presumed to be intended to represent her son who died in infancy. The diminutive figure is standing, and gives a very quaint appearance to the brass.

But this most interesting monument (I should imagine one of the finest brasses in the kingdom) did not end our discoveries, for in the floor of the nave, let into a great slab of black marble, we noticed, as we walked by, another large and finely-engraved brass to "Margarite de Camoys," who died in 1310. This wonderful brass (for the period) has nine shields of arms "powdered" over the dress, and there are recesses in the stone showing by their shapes where six other shields have been. This brass is noteworthy not only for its size, the artistic rendering of the figure and dress, and its excellent state of preservation, but as being to a woman, the earliest one of its kind, I believe, in the kingdom. It is interesting, too, as plainly showing the details of the quaint dress of a lady of quality of the time. Much may be learnt both as to dress and the wearing of armour from these ancient brasses; they are histories in metal.

Then the vicar's wife pointed out to us a "leper's window," now built up; the very title seems to-day strange and unfamiliar, and takes us back long centuries into a wholly different civilisation. Then our attention was called to an old tombstone laid flat on the floor with an abbot's crosier sculptured thereon; unfortunately this interesting relic of the olden days was half hidden by the pews. Furthermore, we were shown a brass on the south wall with an inscription in Latin to Thomas Otway, the dramatic poet, who was born here on 3rd March 1651, and who died in 1685. Dr. Johnson said that there was only one language fit for monumental inscriptions, and that was Latin, as it changed not, and could be read by all the educated peoples of the world; still I, for one, in spite of the worthy Doctor's dictum, prefer English that I can read without much trouble. It is curious to note how the language of monumental inscriptions has changed with the changing times; leaving the puzzling Anglo-Saxon out of the question, we have the Norman-French, then the Latin, lastly the simple English.

Leaving the church, our kind guide said we

really ought to see the ancient stone bridge across the Rother, over which the highway still goes; this was built by the Lord Camoys whose splendid brass we had just inspected. In order to obtain a good view of it we were conducted through the garden of the vicarage into a field below, from which the time-grayed, moss-and-lichen-laden structure is well seen, and forms a pretty and interesting picture with the little winding, silvery river flowing beneath and the green woods rising behind.

Remounting the dog-cart, we once more resumed our driving. It was uphill out of Trotton, and soon we entered upon a heathery waste that looked dark and gloomy against the white sunlit sky. Here we noticed peat being cut and stacked to dry, a rare sight in the south of England. By the way, what delightful and healthy fires peat fuel makes! It keeps aglow for hours without attention; it is clean and noiseless to put on the grate or hearth, and instead of sulphurous fumes, it gives off healing and antiseptic vapours. Compressed peat is the ideal fuel for a sick-room. I have been told, indeed, that certain forms of disease have actually been cured solely by the employment of peat in the sleeping-room of patients.

By degrees the heathery waste became dotted with firs, and gradually we descended into a well-wooded country, where the aspect of the scenery was entirely changed. It was a sudden transition from the severe to the sylvan, and from the woods we drove into the clean little town of Midhurst, where we rested for a time to inspect the extensive, picturesque, and interesting ruins of Cowdray House, that lie in the valley about a quarter of a mile off, and are reached by a pleasant footpath across some meadows. Our combined road-book and guide, the ancient and ever-faithful *Paterson*, thus tersely describes this spot (only the Arun should be the Rother) :—" The picturesque ruins of Cowdry House, once the magnificent seat of the noble family of Montague. These ruins stand in a valley near the banks of the Arun, between two hills crowned with woods. Their present state bears evident testimony of the former magnificence and splendour of this justly celebrated mansion."

On arriving at the ruins we found that the present entrance thereto was through a doorway at the foot of a time-rent tower. An old woman, who has charge of the ruins and acts as a guide, lives in the cottage adjoining ; on our approach she greeted us with the remark that "no regular charge for admission is made, but people gives what they like," a very irritating financial arrangement in a small way, as one can never exactly estimate what is a fair fee, and not wishing to be considered mean, probably gives by such an appeal more than the case requires. We, however, estimated that sixpence each would be a reasonable charge, were a charge made, and not being millionaires on tour, nor desiring to be considered such, offered this sum, which proved satisfactory, whereupon the door was opened, and we were made free of the ruins—to explore, sketch, or photograph them at pleasure. We were not even forbidden (as we have been elsewhere) to climb on

THE RUINS OF COWDRAY HOUSE

the walls or towers, but we were told that if we did so it would be at our own risk. This appeared quite fair, only as we had no desire or intention to climb, the injunction did not concern us; but it was a concession to be allowed to break our legs or necks should we so desire. When you can do a thing, naturally you have no wish to do so.

As we entered, the old body followed us and volunteered to act as guide and to "explain all about the ruins; it is so much more interesting when some one who knows them tells you all about everything." Then we asked her if she had many visitors. To our surprise she shook her head, sadly, we thought, saying, "The ruins is my living, but I don't get nearly so many people to come and see them as I used to. I do believe it's all them bicycles; folk used to come here and spend the day in the ruins; now they runs all over the country on them machines and stops nowheres. It's the roads, not the ruins, they admire." Notwithstanding all this, we did notice, as we walked along, two of the said machines lying on the grass outside, and we presumed that the owners thereof were the two youths in knicker costumes we saw within; but perhaps these were the exception to the rule, for truly, as our guide further remarked, "two do not make a crowd." Things differ so from our point of view!

We condoled with the old body, and in our anxiety to comfort her invented a little fiction, the doing of which on moral grounds I candidly confess I cannot defend, but we spoke on the spur of the moment. "You see," we said, "it's been a bad season for ruins lately, they've gone a little out of fashion, but they're coming in again." To this the old body made no remark; perhaps she thought we were romancing, or else she may have considered, rightly enough, that she understood her business better than we did.

Cowdray House is, with the exception of the tower gateways, a roofless ruin, all open to the sky and weather. The walls of its chambers are bare, and its courtyards are green and grass-grown. As we slowly progressed through the dismantled mansion our guide pointed out to us the place where the ample kitchen was; the fine banqueting hall, with its mullioned Tudor windows, in which ivy now takes the place of glass; the chapel aloft, with its floor gone, but with the remains of the altar and sculptures, much weather-worn, "of the apostles" on either side; the spot where the grand staircase ascended, and the chamber wherein Queen Elizabeth had slept; and in its present state we thought that the kitchen appeared as desirable an apartment as any. So does Nature, left alone, work her own will and bring all things down to one equality.

Then we were conducted across the grassy courtyard to the main gateway tower, the arched entrance to which is of groined stone with fan tracery, and in the bosses bears the initials W. S., with an anchor. The initials, we were told, were those of William, Earl of Southampton, upon whose death Cowdray passed by marriage to the Montagues; the anchor was introduced, the Earl being then an Admiral of the Fleet. Over the entrance are the royal arms of Queen Elizabeth carved in stone, probably placed there to commemorate her visit here to Lord Montague in 1591, when she shot four deer in the park from her cross-bow, none of the rest of her court diplomatically shooting more than one. Oh, the gentle art and craft of successful courtiership!

Cowdray is a house with a history that is the delight of antiquaries. The powerful Norman family of Bohun first held it, and retained possession thereof until the reign of Henry VIII. The property, after being in the hands of the Earl of Southampton, passed into that of Sir Anthony Browne, "the king's master of the horse and chief standard-bearer of England," who was afterwards created Lord Montague, and in whose family it remained till 1793, when the house, with its priceless treasures, was destroyed by fire, including the famous "Roll of Battle Abbey," and at the same time the last Lord Montague was drowned abroad, thus fulfilling the "Curse of Cowdray," said to have been uttered by a monk of Battle when a former Lord Montague took possession of the abbey lands, that "by fire and water shall your house and family perish from out of the land."

CHAPTER XXI

Cowdray Park—Petworth—Nineteenth-century ecclesiastical architecture—Bric-à-brac hunting—A novel title—"The Wastes of the Manor"—Happy travellers—The blessing of scandal!—An artist-haunted hostelry—A quaint conceit in inn signs—Stopham Bridge—Washington—Over the Downs—The helmet of "the great Earl of De la Warr."

ABOUT a mile out of Midhurst we crossed the Rother on an old stone bridge. By the side of this was a stone-built mill and a weir, that all combined, with the trees around, to make a pleasing picture. Our road now entered Cowdray Park, a delightful and well-wooded demesne, with great green sweeps of sward gently sloping to the south, and very charming did it look that afternoon with the soft sunlight glinting down the open glades, and tipping the tall waving bracken with a ruddy gold, the bracken itself forming a forest in miniature fit for Fairyland.

The trees here, we noticed, were chiefly beeches, though there was a sprinkling of oaks, mostly growing in the ferny hollows. There was no boundary to the highway, and the park stretched away on either side of it, so that the road looked quite like a private one. It was a delightful drive: the road was smooth and undulating, there was no dust, and the scenery was all that could be desired, so we were sorry when the park, with its restful, green, shady branching trees and cheerful gloom of wooded recesses, ended and we found ourselves once more on the hedge-enclosed country lanes. It is pleasant for a time to get away from fences or boundaries of any kind; it affords such a delightful feeling of spaciousness and freedom to travel through an unenclosed country.

Now our road dipped down through a deep cutting in red sandstone, and a further descent brought us to a spot marked as "Halfway Bridge" on our map. A very pretty spot it was, at the foot of a tree-clad glen, a tiny valley with a wide, winding stream flowing through it, that worked an ancient mill-wheel with much droning and creaking.

Then it was uphill again, and a short drive through an open country brought us to Petworth, where at the "Half Moon"—an ancient inn that has outlived many generations of travellers—we found comfortable quarters and luxurious loose-boxes for our horses.

As there was still an hour or so of daylight left, we set out, sketch-book in hand, for a ramble round the old town, that just escapes being quaint, but is full of picturesque little bits, that appeal, however, more to the artist than the architect. At one part, where the houses suddenly ended and the country began, we found before us a deep and wide valley, over which we had a fine view of the distant wooded uplands, and looked down upon the roof-trees of farmsteads in the vale. I do love these little rural towns ; for one thing, they have no dismal suburbs ; at once where the houses end the country begins—the genuine country, too.

On the crest of the hill, where we stood admiring the pleasant view, we noticed a fine church in the course of construction. This had more of the real medieval feeling about it, save a somewhat too mechanical rendering of the traceried windows, than we had ever found before in a modern building. It even managed to interest us ; as a rule nineteenth-century ecclesiastical architecture produces but costly eye-sores, a mere meaningless piling up of stones—or bricks—and mortar, that profits only the contractor, and certainly never arouses our enthusiasm :—

> In the elder days of Art,
>   Builders wrought with greatest care
> Each minute and unseen part ;
>   For the gods see everywhere.

It has been left for the nineteenth century to reverse this order. It would be hardly profitable to examine the "unseen part" of the speculative contractor's work. He is no sentimentalist : "Sentiment don't pay," as one of these gentlemen once remarked to me. "Sentiment won't pay my butcher's or baker's bill, will it ? I'm not the biggest humbug in the world by a lot. If you want a church or chapel built thoroughly well and honestly, why don't religious people of all others pay a fair price for the work, and not get it done as cheaply as possible ? "

Inquiring of a stranger passing by, we learnt that this was a Roman Catholic church being erected by a gentleman, whose name I have now forgotten, " but where the congregation are to come from," furthermore said he, " I don't know. There are not many Catholics in these parts; they'll just have to make them." This casual, half-joking remark set us seriously a-thinking. What of the twentieth-century religion?

Then returning to our inn we chanced to pass a watchmaker's shop, and we looked in, as our watch had stopped. Here we most unexpectedly discovered quite a small museum of old things; some of these, though not all, were for sale. We purchased an ancient Sussex rushlight holder and a pair of tobacco tongs for a few shillings. We had no idea till then that there was such an article as the last, and we begged to have its use explained to us. It appears that the instrument, which is small, shapely, and neatly made, was formerly employed to lift a live ember from the fire to light the pipe with. The tongs are also provided with an iron stop, the purpose of which was to ram the tobacco down in the pipe. We have never yet returned home from any tour without having bought during the journey some relic of past days, valued both for itself and as a pleasing memento of the expedition. Amongst various other articles we have thus picked up at very moderate prices I may enumerate a perfect "old leather bottel," a fourteenth-century helmet and breastplate, some ancient pikes, all in good condition; a very elaborately carved oak linen chest, black with age; two quaint old brass "lantern" clocks; a very beautiful old English bracket clock in capital order (for which we paid the not exorbitant sum of £4 : 10s.) ; a fine example of a Chippendale corner cupboard for china ; one of those high, bright brass fenders that were our grandmothers' pride ; a dear old spinning-wheel, rather rickety, however, but picturesque to look at, and a charming reminder of the long ago ; a doubtful old master on panel representing the Descent from the Cross, set in a carved and gilt frame. This, we were told, had long been an altar-piece in a Roman Catholic chapel. The picture was protected by a glass door with a lock, and was in a very dusty and cobwebby condition when we espied it stacked amongst a lot of rubbish at the back of a secondhand furniture dealer's shop, so much so that we could make but very little of the painting. I have to confess that we bought it chiefly for the panel at the back ! This was of oak, or chestnut, it was so dark we could not tell which, and was protected from warping by a complete network of oak or chestnut blocks dove-tailed into each other, manifestly with great care, and at the cost of considerable time. We reasoned to ourselves that all these pains would not have been taken except for a valuable painting, and so we speculated. Getting the picture home and cleaned, we found it signed " Francesco Francia," and it was pronounced by a competent judge to be probably genuine, but retouched.

After consulting our map during the evening we decided that we would drive on the morrow to Worthing, crossing over the Downs by Finden.

We selected Worthing, not that the town offered us any attractions in itself, but because the drive there promised to lead us through an interesting country. We were basely making a convenience of Worthing as a place to sleep in!

Out of Petworth it was downhill at first. At the foot of the descent we noticed two gray old stone-built farmhouses and a stone trough for water by the roadside, such as one often sees in the "North Countrie." The dale-like look of the valley, with the picturesque wayside trough and substantial stone farmsteads, recalled to mind Derbyshire.

We now ascended on to high ground, and the country broadened out into a wide and wild common, a bit of unsophisticated nature charming in its ruggedness, a common dotted with stunted gorse and wind-twisted dwarf oaks, between which wound sandy roads. The summer wind blew fresh and keen across this elevated spot. It was mere fancy truly, but somehow high up there we seemed nearer the great white clouds that were driving across the vast expanse of sky overhead. Perhaps the feeling was due to the clearness and rarity of the atmosphere, that apparently so shortens space. I well remember, whilst travelling in California, the exceeding difficulty I had in at all correctly estimating distances in the wonderfully pure air there, the far-away seemed so comparatively near to me; it did not melt away into a blue mystery, as with us, that is so poetical and space-suggesting. I really think that the Dutch and

English atmosphere is the most artistic in the world — it gives the landscape such a mellow idyllic look that it more than compensates for all its other supposed shortcomings.

By the side of the common stood a lonely public-house with the novel sign, to us at any rate, of the "Well-Diggers' Arms." We had seen the Cyclists' Arms, the Blacksmiths' Arms, the Bricklayers' Arms, but we were not aware before that the Well-Diggers had their arms too—and, of all places in the world, to find well-diggers up here in this sandy, sparsely-populated region.

Then as we drove on, our road began to descend once more, and took us, deep in shade, through wild, unenclosed woods, with a thick undergrowth of bracken below. Rabbits ran out into the roadway here and sported about, so tame that they did not hurry to scamper off, as we approached, until the last moment. This charming bit of wild woodland we found by a notice-board—one, alas! of many, for they took away from the rusticity of the spot, and the feeling of freedom it induced, by reminding you that the land was private property, and that you must not do this or that thereon under pains and penalties—we found by a notice-board that this was part of the "Waste of the Manor of Leconfield." The peeps that opened out through the trees, now and again, of the distant country, and of the long line of the blue Downs that faded away into a faint blue mist, were very charming and mutely beckoned us forward. I know nothing so provokingly enticing as a winding English road, each turning luring you on to the next, just to learn what is coming; the whole long day seems too short to see all, and you want to go off in four directions at once!

As we progressed, to our pleasure the country still maintained its wild open character, the wooded waste giving place to a wild stretch of sandy heath, covered in places with dark gloomy pines, that made the immediate landscape look sad and surly, and strangely out of harmony with the golden green of the sun-suffused Downs that loomed up brightly beyond. The pine trees sighed as the wind passed them by—quite a different sound from the cheerful and companionable rustling of the multitudinous leaves of the elm, or oak, or beech in the breeze. But we forgave the pines their gloom in consideration of the delightfully dry and refreshing resinous fragrance that came from them wafted to us; fresh from stuffy towns the sweet and varied country odours are almost more enjoyable than even the changeful scenery. Soon after this we found ourselves in Fittleworth, a charmingly picturesque village set in the midst of gently-sloping hills, with fir-clad heights around, and a country rich in varied beauty stretching away in every direction.

I think Fittleworth must surely be the prettiest spot in Sussex, and that is saying a great deal. It may have been that we were in a mood to be pleased with everything that day, anyhow Fittleworth took our fancy exceedingly, and we used up quite a number of adjectives in expressing our admiration of the place one to another. Happy travellers we to be so pleased and contented; we were on the look-out for beauty and the bright side of life, and we discovered both! Who could help being charmed with Fittleworth, its pretty cottage homes, and dear quaint old church with gay roses growing over its timbered porch in place of the usual dark-green ivy? There was nothing sombre or depressing about that ancient fane, which we noticed was primitively lighted inside with candles; even the churchyard looked quite cheerful; seated round the ancient yew tree there we noticed several natives sunning themselves and chatting—let us hope not scandal! Once to an old gaffer, in a serio-comic way, I ventured to remark upon the sadness of the amount of scandal that prevailed in his village—this was, I may say, after he had poured out a vast quantity of that commodity into my unwilling ear; a cynic might remark it was unwilling simply because I knew nothing of the people or the place, so that the scandal was uninteresting— and the cynic might possibly be right. However, the old gaffer was in nowise disconcerted. "Lor', sir," he replied quite cheerfully, "and 'ow 'ud we get on without it, I'd loike to know? We doan't mean no harm to nobody. I likes my bit o' scandal over my pipe, I do. It 'muses me." Now what can you do with such a man, even if you are a clergyman?

Down in the village—for we descended into it— we found a small country inn, clean and neat-looking outside, but in no way remarkable; within, however, we found a tiny parlour, panelled, and the panels on the walls and at the sides of the windows painted in oil colours with charming landscapes. Then it dawned upon us that this was an artist-haunted inn, and that these panels had been done by some of the artists staying there at various times. So the painters have discovered Fittleworth. Truly it is an ideal spot to come to with easel and colours and to study Nature in her picturesque moods. It is a peaceful, dreamy spot, where

> The fisher drops his patient lines,
> The farmer sows his grain,
> Content to hear the murmuring pines
> Instead of railway-train.

The obliging landlady mentioned to us the names of several well-known artists who had stopped with her. "Why," exclaimed she, "one of them is very kindly painting my sign-board for me now. It's not quite finished, but I think I may show it to you," and she thereupon did. Leading the way into a large and well-lighted chamber, manifestly doing duty as a studio, she pointed out to us the sign-board with a charmingly quaint design thereon, rich in colour and clever in drawing. This represented the swan swimming in a reedy pool with a gold ring round its neck, and a jovial-looking frog (I have never seen such a creature before) afloat in a pewter tankard by its side calmly smoking a long churchwarden pipe, and underneath ran the legend, "Ye Swanne Inne." It was simply a delightful conceit: would that more artists would do likewise. We were told that this was being painted by Caton Woodville. Fittleworth would make capital headquarters for the amateur artist or photographer, for there is plenty of picture-making material round about.

We felt sorry to leave such a charming spot, but it was the same old story, we could not really stop the day at every delightful place we chanced upon, or it would be the winter time before we reached home again. So reluctantly we drove away, and soon afterwards we reached Stopham, where we crossed the Arun on an ancient stone bridge of five arches. The weather-stained bridge and reedy river made such a sweet picture that we stopped to photograph it. Just then a boating party came along drifting down the stream, and backed water so as to be included in the view. We thanked them for their courtesy—fortunately we had secured the photograph before the boat arrived in position! They were a merry party and very obliging; they even offered to pull inshore for us the better to take them, if we liked! We did not like, but simply said we would not trespass upon their good-nature any more, and hurried off to the dog-cart.

Then we proceeded to Pulborough, with the silvery Arun winding through the green, level meadows to our right; the scenery on the way was of the quiet pastoral sort, restful rather than interesting. Pulborough did not appeal to us, so we passed through it, determining to bait our horses farther on, where we found comfortable quarters at a country inn.

At the quaint little village of Washington (a name that reminds one of distant America) we turned to the right and crossed the Downs with a long but gradual climb. I wonder whether the name of Washington has ever attracted any stray American visitors here, as I know for a fact that the name of Broadway — a pretty village in Worcestershire — has. The Sussex Washington is a delightfully primitive and picturesque little hamlet snugly ensconced at the foot of the hills, and some miles from the nearest railway, a bit of real old England set in the midst of the new, the very antithesis of its grand namesake over the Atlantic, that stately city of magnificent distances.

From the topmost point of our road, high on the rounded chalk hills, it was a long run downhill of four or five miles all the way to Broadwater, a spot within a mile of Worthing. *Facilis descensus!* It was delightful driving down : the dog-cart ran along the smooth, winding road of itself, with a gentle gliding motion that almost suggested rest. All that the horses had to do was to keep on their feet! The scenery was pleasant but unexciting. On the way we passed through one or two typical South Down villages with a character all their own.

The only one, however, at which we stopped was Broadwater. Here the church looked interesting, and as we pulled up a moment just to admire it externally, an old body, who had observed our movements, and possibly saw the prospect of a tip, appeared out of a cottage close by, key in hand, and offered to show us over the interior. "It's very old," she said, a fact that hardly needed the telling. However, the woman was so pleasant-spoken that we did not like to disappoint her, so we allowed ourselves to be shown over. A pleasant manner, what a power in the world it is! Emerson declares it to be "the art of all arts," that to the traveller " opens castles and parlours." And Emerson knew!

Within the hoary church of Broadwater, that still shows the handiwork of the hardy Norman masons, we discovered an ancient canopied stone tomb recessed in the north wall of the chancel. This is to the memory of Thomas, Lord De la Warr, who died 1526. It bears a striking resemblance to the elaborate De la Warr monument we saw at Boxgrove Priory, and is noteworthy as showing the skilful mixture of Gothic with the Renaissance. Only with the utmost care and almost perfect judgment can two such opposite styles of architecture be mingled without disaster. This tomb at Broadwater has a flat top, and if ever there were an effigy thereon, it has long ago disappeared. Possibly there never was one, as, judging from the present general appearance and the frequent custom of the time, it is probable that this tomb was designed to be used as an Easter sepulchre.

On the flat top is now placed the ancient helmet of the Earl, secured to the stone slab by an iron chain, but within easy reach of any one who chooses to handle it. Doubtless this was originally suspended on a bracket above, and it is a pity it is not there to-day, out of possible harm's way. Still, be it confessed, we gladly took the opportunity, thus temptingly accorded, to make a careful inspection of this relic of the chivalrous past. The general modelling of the helmet is excellent, but there are one or two curious features about it. On the top of the crown are two holes close to each other. The only purpose that these could have served would be to support the crest, but the crest placed in such a position would prevent the visor being raised. We could only come to the conclusion that the helmet was employed without a crest—as was the custom in the reign of Henry VII., coloured scarves being used in their place—and that these holes were made, after the Earl's decease, in order to fix a crest there purely for funeral purposes.

This helmet also possesses an opening on the right-hand side, manifestly for a larger supply of air than could be obtained through the visor slit; showing an endeavour to remedy the knights' complaints of the stifling heat of the helmets. And little wonder, for with the sun shining on the iron, and the want of any real ventilation, the wearing of a helmet in addition to the rest of the heavy steel armour must have been most trying. I speak from experience, having, to test the matter, donned one of these ancient helmets indoors, with the visor down, and even under those favourable conditions, after about twenty minutes I found the heat insufferable. The opening, in the case of this (Lord De la Warr's) helmet, is protected simply by a piece of steel being bent up in front of it, which would be a sufficient protection against any forward thrust of the lance, but hardly looks quite safe. All other similar helmets, of this or a later period, I have seen, have, for the purpose of better ventilation, been provided with a little steel door, either perforated or solid. This was intended to be kept open till the last moment, when it was supposed to be closed for better protection. It is said that in times gone by this helmet was actually used as a collecting-box, and that the coins were dropped in through the slit in the visor! a fact recorded in rugged verse. The helmet, we are informed, once belonged

> To the great Earl of De la Warr,
> Whose head it saved from many a scar;
> And after being beat and bruised,
> Is for a parish poor-box used.

On the floor of the church we noticed a very fine brass representing a coped priest under a canopy. This is in memory of one John Mapleton, a former rector of the parish, who died "Anno Milleno C quat bis X duodeno," which is a rather complicated way of writing 1432, simple numerals that every one can read at a glance, and that mean the same thing in all languages. There is also another fine though plainer brass to an earlier rector, one John Corby, who died 1415. We also noticed, as we were leaving, a pointed arch with Norman decorations. Outside the church our guide pointed out to us a cross of cut flints worked into the wall. On parting with the old body we remarked, by way of pleasing her, "What a fine old church to worship in!" Again we had a somewhat enigmatical reply: "Ay; that it be, sir. I can't hear a word as the parson says from where I sits"!

CHAPTER XXII

Sompting—A unique church tower—Disappointed cyclists—"The Sussex Pad"—Old Shoreham—Picturesque Lewes—A castle with two keeps—Mystic symbols—Round-towered churches—A Saxon sun-dial—Seaford—Friston Place—The end of the journey.

FROM Worthing we planned to drive to Lewes, skirting fashionable Brighton to the south. As far as Old Shoreham, and for some way beyond, our road led parallel to the sea-shore, but kept about a mile inland. It took us at a gentle elevation along the foot of the Downs, so that whilst we had a pleasant rural country to pass through, we caught at the same time through the trees and over the fields frequent and welcome peeps of the sea sparkling in the morning sunshine. There was a fresh breeze blowing freely from the south, and the air was cool and refreshing with the salt savour of the sea, and the horses sniffed it with apparent enjoyment, and went along as merrily as though they were just starting from their stables on the journey, instead of having nearly completed it, and covered many miles of country day after day over all kinds and conditions of roads, rough and hilly, smooth and level ; but then we had always made it a point to personally see after the welfare of our horses on the way, and we had driven them considerately.

About two miles of pleasant country brought us to the pretty little village of Sompting. Here, walking up a tree-shaded lane, we reached the church, notable for its quaint Saxon tower, of a form unique in England now, though there is said to have been a similar one at Flixton in Suffolk early in the century which was, unfortunately,—I could use a harder term—improved away. This curious tower is well worth attention. It ends in four pointed gables, from which springs a short wooden spire. The form is exceedingly picturesque and full of character, very pleasing also to the eye for its originality. It is to be regretted that church architects have not sometimes copied its chief features—they might have varied the detail—instead of everlastingly working on the old familiar lines. Such a distinctive type of building would give a freshness and a charm to the landscape in which it appeared. Running up the centres of the tower on all four sides are pilaster strips, and some long-and-short work is shown thereon, plainly proving, to me at least, together with the roughness of the masonry, the Saxon origin of this portion of the edifice.

We found the door locked, but as the vicarage was close by, we ventured to ask for, and obtained, the key there. The interior of this ancient fane is almost as interesting as the exterior, and also, I think, shows signs, in places, of Saxon workmanship, though of a less positive nature. On the walls are some crude and curious sculptures. There is, too, a corbel carved with a peculiar round face, a primitive piece of handicraft that caused us to smile whether we would or not, for that face did look so comical. It is quite an original production, and manifestly of a very early period; possibly Norman, though, from certain signs, I am inclined to think it Saxon, preserved from the first building and placed where it now is. This unique church, both within and without, requires, and would well repay, careful study.

As we were about leaving, two men on bicycles came up, hot and dusty. Addressing me, they asked if I would tell them where the Saxon church was. "There it is straight before you," I replied. I was tempted to add, "Can't you see for yourself?" for the church was right in front of them, naturally a prominent object, but I kept the peace. "Call that a Saxon church?" exclaimed the spokesman, "I call it a swindle, and we've ridden twenty dashed miles to see it." We tried to calm him down and to reason with him, but he would have none of it. "Call that a Saxon church?" he retorted, quite indignantly, "why, it's only an ordinary one"! I am not quite sure what he really expected to see, but I deemed it best not to venture on the query, and so departed, leaving the enraged travellers to settle their differences with the church itself.

Then with gentle rises and falls we found ourselves in Lancing, from whence the road gradually descended to the river Adur. Upon reaching the low-lying marshy land we passed a primitive little inn with the singular title of the "Sussex Pad," presumably a name handed down from the pre-coaching days, when this road was a mere bridle-track, and possibly rough at that, and when all travellers thereby had to journey on horseback or on foot, the ancient meaning of "pad" being a slow-going horse, one that carried packs and light merchandise. Doubtless many other houses were so named over the country, but changed their signs to suit the changed times; this remote little inn has, however, happily retained its ancient designation. Such old-day signs are now becoming rare; the "Pack-horse" is almost extinct, and even the "Waggon and Horses" is not to be met with so frequently as of yore.

A little farther on we had a wide view across the flat salt marsh of the blue sea and long succession of white breakers rushing to the shingly shore. At the end of the marsh we crossed the Adur on a long timber bridge. Before driving over this, however, we pulled up in order to make a sketch of the primitive structure, with its planless curves and unsought-for picturesqueness; you do not often come across such a bridge nowadays. On the opposite shore the time-grayed Norman church, with its massive walls and dumpy tower, formed an effective background. The wide river here, with its glancing lines of light translucent greens, running in full flood from the blue Downs to the bluer sea, was full of brightness and life. Below the bridge, and just above the gliding water, a number of sea-gulls were whirling round and round, uttering plaintive, peevish cries, as though they had some special grievance.

Here we had a toll to pay, the second one on the journey, collected by the railway company "for maintaining the bridge," so the toll-collector said. We were now in Old Shoreham, and as we passed close to it and found the door open, just took a glance within the cruciform Norman church; the interior was dark and gloomy, solemn and sombre rather than beautiful. We noticed here that one of the beams across the chancel roof was adorned with the familiar dog-tooth moulding, so frequently to be found in Norman stone-work; but I never remember before having seen wood so ornamented. The reason may be that the Norman wood-work, if they did so carve it, has not lasted like the more durable stone.

From Old Shoreham to Brighton the road was not noticeable for any special features, scenic or otherwise, though one or two of the peeps over towards sleepy Shoreham harbour, with the shipping therein, were interesting in a mild way. From Brighton to Lewes we passed along an uneventful valley in the Downs, and at Lewes we rested the night. A greater contrast in eight miles one could hardly have than from modern, fashionable Brighton to ancient and picturesque Lewes; the two towns hardly seem to belong to the same century!

I think that Lewes is the most picturesque town in the south of England. Truly it is not so quaint as Bosham or Wareham, nor so romantic as Dartmouth, nor so rugged as Ilfracombe and other places I could name ; but for pure homely picturesqueness I feel it deserves the palm. As seen from almost any point on the "daisied Downs" around, or from the meadows below (the eye being licensed to ignore the intruding railway in one or two positions), Lewes makes a most poetic picture, with its time-rent castle keeps perched on the summit of a steep hill that towers above the town and is embosomed in trees, below which the red roofs of the gray flint-built houses are grouped in orderly confusion, or at any rate in artistic irregularity. Unlike most places, there is no one best view of Lewes ; it looks well from all points.

Our first visit was to the castle. Mounting innumerable steps, we reached at last one of the ancient keeps, for Lewes—alone of all English castles—was peculiar in possessing two keeps. Here we found a small but very interesting museum of old-time relics pertaining to Sussex. From the topmost point of this tower looking all round are extensive and eye-delighting prospects ; to the east and west stretch away the curving Downs, growing from green to gray, then vanishing in misty blue on the far-off horizon, their deep, cool, shaded coombes contrasting forcibly with their warm sunny slopes and the brilliant whites of their chalk-quarried sides ; to the north lies the wild Weald of Sussex, extending to Crowborough and the dim fir-fringed hills of Ashdown Forest ; and to the south a vast marshy level lengthens out to the sea beyond Newhaven. Below, you look right down upon a very jumble of red roofs and clustering chimneys, mingled with a

LEWES

mere suggestion of faint blue haze—the very poetry of smoke — that just suffices to soften any hard feature down, and that is all. The views from Lewes Castle keep may rightfully be termed glorious, and are well worth a long journey to see. There is a rare combined quality of grandeur and grace, of stateliness and gentle softness, about the space-expressing prospects that is both pleasing and impressive, and that I have never found elsewhere.

Lewes is a dreamy, clean, picturesque old town of hilly and crooked streets, full of charming bits of ancient architecture, that appeal to the eye of the artist, and are graphic reminders of the storied long ago. I like a place picturesque and clean; you do not always find these go together. One of the old streets we noticed as we walked along bore the romantic title of the "Friar's Walk," a name suggestive of monkish days; this led us to the crumbling ruins of the Priory of St. Pancras, situated down in the low level not far from the river, of course, so that the monks might have their fish-stews and fish "on Fridays when they fasted"—or feasted, as their enemies declared.

Then we went in search of the Jireh Chapel to view the grave of one William Huntington, the reformed coal-heaver and erst famous Calvinistic preacher. We had great trouble in finding this. We asked a policeman (who, as we afterwards discovered, was standing in actual sight of the building) if he could direct us there, and were answered, "I've never heard of no such place." Eventually we found a lad who led us thither—for a penny;

even he appeared ignorant of the place at first, but the promise of a whole penny acted as a wonderful spur to his memory. What will not money do in this world, when such a small sum will attain such a result?

Having found the chapel, the next thing was to procure the key, for the iron gates were carefully locked. This entailed further inquiries, but at last the key was obtained, and we gained admission to both the building and the little graveyard behind, the latter being not unlike the usual London suburban garden. On the front of the chapel—a structure plain enough, externally and internally, to have satisfied the strictest Puritan — we read inscribed :—

Jireh Chapel
erected
by J. Jenkins W. A.
with the
Voluntary Contributions
of the Citizens of Zion
Anno Domi MDCCCV.

We could not fathom, no, not after much deliberation, what W. A. stood for. Could it possibly be meant for M.A., the M having been turned upside down and converted into a W by the illiterate workman? Surely not. So we inquired, and were informed that W.A. stood for "Welsh Ambassador," but this did not help us greatly. "What does 'Welsh Ambassador' mean?" we further queried; but our informant knew no more than the bare fact he had told us, and we were left to form our own conjectures.

In the little garden-like grave-ground behind we discovered one long monument with a sloping top; there were five or six different inscriptions on this; the one to William Huntington runs thus :—

> Here lies the Coalheaver
> Who Departed this life
> July 1, 1813, in the 69th year of his age
> Beloved of his God but Abhorred
> of Men
> The Omniscient Judge at the Grand Assize
> Shall Ratify and Confirm this
> To the Confusion of Many
> Thousands
> For England and its Metropolis shall
> Know that there hath been a
> Prophet among them
> W. H.   S.S.
> Dictated by himself a few days
> previous to his Death.

The mystic letters S.S. we were told stood for Sinner Saved, in place of the sought-after M.A., which Huntington said he had neither learning nor money enough to procure.

Then we retraced our steps up the hilly and picturesque High Street to St. Michael's Church, with its curious round tower of rough-cast flint and shingle spire; the unusual form of the tower—for the south of England at any rate—gives the structure a very odd and ancient look. These quaint architectural bits, that you come upon unawares whilst rambling over the town, give Lewes a special character and charm. The interior of the building is chiefly notable for the mural monument to Sir Nicholas Pelham, with its punning epigram, of which mention has already been made. In old days the clock of St. Michael's that still projects boldly out on an iron bracket into the street, and another clock known as "Old Gabriel," were noted for keeping such incorrect time, that their want of truthfulness in this respect earned for them the irreverent titles of "Ananias and Sapphira"! Even the day when we were there, I regret to say that they both told a different tale as to the hour.

The old "Star Inn" at Lewes, with its fine carved oak staircase, a historic hostelry wherein we rested on a previous journey, has disappeared, or rather changed its uses. This is a pity, as "Ye Starre Inne" bore that sign during Queen Mary's reign, for we have record of "ten heretics" being burnt in front of it in 1557, of whom four were women. We may be grateful that the age of martyrdom is past! Of all inconsistent things in this inconsistent world, the fact of Christians burning and torturing one another is surely the most inconsistent, a sight to make the very angels weep, and scoffers smile with scorn. Truly, it was an age of Catholicism without Christianity, of a Church without charity. I am by no means sure that the Puritans loved ,their enemies as they were bidden to do, and should have done, but at least they did not torture or burn them; the modern ultra-Protestant, even in this century of general whitewashing of doubtful past actions, has not wholly forgotten nor forgiven the burnings, as the following verse from a recent powerful poem proves :—

> None now will buy the heaven thou hast to sell
> At price of prostituted souls, and swell
>   Thy loveless list of lovers. Fire and sword
>   No more are thine : the steel, the wheel, the cord,
> The flames that rose round living limbs, and fell
> In lifeless ash and ember, now no more
>   Approve thee Godlike.

From Lewes our "next progress," to use an old-time expression, was to Newhaven, a pleasant seven-miles' drive along the side of the green, Down-bordered "Level" that stretches southward to the Channel. Certain geologists have it that this was once an arm of the sea; had it remained so, Lewes might to-day be a second Liverpool or a flourishing Southampton, instead of a dreamy old county town.

The country between Lewes and Newhaven has the charm of repose; it is full of character and a quiet beauty, but of a subtle kind, that defies analysis and appeals only to the limited few. On our way we passed through three or four primitive little villages of the pure South Down type, and one not to be met with elsewhere, as far as I have been able to discover. Two of these villages, Southease and Piddinghoe, possess each a quaint little church, having a round tower apiece, the latter church being the more important.

Much good ink has been used in learned disputes on paper as to the reason of the uncommon form of these towers, but the explanation seems simple enough to me. The only building material in the locality is flint, and doubtless in the days of old, when the roads were bad and communications with the outer world difficult, the want of large square stones for "angle-work" compelled the builders to construct their towers circular thus.

Soon now the masts of the shipping in Newhaven harbour came into sight, but the little modern port, apart from its shipping, which is always and everywhere interesting, had small attractions for us, so we passed it by without a halt, bound for Seaford. A short distance beyond Newhaven, on the shore, stands a large and an old deserted tidal mill, built in the last century; this is, or rather was, interesting as a successful example of how the tide could be utilised to drive a mill by a series of undershot wheels, work, of course, never being stopped for want of water. Here we have surely an unlimited source of undeveloped motive power?

After this we made a slight detour of about half a mile inland to Bishopstone, a little world-forsaken hamlet, hidden in a wooded hollow of the treeless Downs. Here on the slopes around we saw the long-horned, sleepy-eyed Sussex oxen slowly dragging along the cumbersome plough of the district, oxen and massive wooden plough looking as though they had just stepped out of some old picture, and brought to mind the England of the long ago. Bishopstone is a primitive, picturesque spot, suggestive of untold rest, or dulness, as the mood of man inclines. Here is a curious old church, much restored — for good or ill — but it still shows signs of rude pre-Norman masonry, and over the south porch is a most interesting Saxon sun-dial carved in stone, having the name of EAD-RIC incised on the top, with a cross preceding the E.

The gnomon is missing, but the hole for it is there. Eadric was probably the name of the builder of the church, or, less likely, perhaps the name of the carver of the dial. It is wonderful to note how well the stone has withstood the weathering of all those long years since it was first placed in position, unless, indeed, it be a medieval copy of a former Saxon dial; but though just possible, this seems hardly probable. Still such things have been, and the excellent preservation of the stone is difficult to account for. The tower of this church is of four stories, each as they rise being about a foot less in width than the one below; around the top, supporting the base of the short spire, are a series of exceedingly quaint corbel heads.

Leaving Bishopstone, we drove to Seaford, where we baited our horses and refreshed ourselves, and afterwards rested a while by the restless sea, contented simply to watch the blue dancing waves, and the fishing-boats with their ruddy tanned sails tossing about thereon. The prospect was so full of joyous movement and brightness, that it instilled a buoyant cheerfulness into us; the air, too, how fresh and invigorating it was! Seaford, having lost its harbour and old prosperity, and having gone into a lethargic sleep for years, is now waking up in earnest, and is striving its best to regain something of its ancient prosperity by becoming a modern wateringplace. It is on the west, and therefore best, side of Beachy Head; its air is bracing without being harsh, and it has the advantage of having some life on the sea, owing to the steam-packets and shipping entering and leaving Newhaven. It has doubtless other attractions, but they did not present themselves to us at the moment.

Two miles westward of Seaford we came to the secluded Cuckmere valley, where we crossed the river of that name, which finds its way through a wide gap in the Downs to the sea. On the farther side of the river we passed close to our road one of those picturesque, rambling old farmsteads that are such a pleasant and familiar feature in the South Down landscape. Then commenced a long pull uphill, and we took the liberty of deserting the rough and flint-strewn road for the smooth surface of the firm turf that Nature has carpeted this favoured district with. As we rose, on looking back to our left we had a charming vision presented to us of the old-world village of West Dean, sheltered in a deep combe, a veritable "Sleepy Hollow." At the top of the long rise we found ourselves in the tiny hamlet of Friston, that appears to consist of a small primitive church, a solitary windmill, and a couple of cottages, with a round pond and a dilapidated signpost. It is a breezy spot, open to all the winds that blow, and the sails of the old windmill were whirling round apace. The miller was watching us from a window in his mill, and shouted to ask if we would like to take a glance inside. " No." " Well, would you care to have a look at the church? I've got the keys, and there are some interesting old monuments within." This second invitation we declined; we had already seen enough churches and to spare, but we said that we would just take a photograph of the mill, and we did; it did not, however, turn out a success, as we afterwards discovered, for we had forgotten to change our plate, and so obtained a composite picture, with the mill right in the middle of Shoreham Bridge, our last exposure! The result was more curious than beautiful!

Looking west from Friston is a wide and comprehensive view of the Downs, and in the valley to our left we espied the red gables of an ancient home peeping out of surrounding trees. We learned that this was Friston Place, in the olden times the residence of the Selwyns (an ancient Sussex family), but now converted into a farmhouse. As we had plenty of time to spare, we wandered down to make a sketch of this picturesque old house, and, whilst so doing, were invited " to have a look over the old place, if we cared to "; we did " care to," and rejoiced in the opportunity that chance had thus unexpectedly thrown in our way.

Within, Friston Place still shows some signs of its former superior estate, but the old house has manifestly been sadly altered for the worse to suit the changed conditions. We entered by what must have been, in the days of its prime, a fine old panelled hall, at one end of which yet remains the minstrels' gallery; by the sides of the large and ample fireplace here—where huge logs of oak and beech used doubtless to blaze forth in cheerful glow— are carved corbels, from which curved beams spring upward, apparently supporting a high-framed timber roof above, as was usual in old mansions of the period; but, alas! as is also usual in later alterations of such old mansions, the top portion of the hall has been converted into sleeping-chambers, and a meaningless flat ceiling of hateful whitewash takes the place of the picturesque open timber roof of old.

In one of the windows of the hall we observed a quaint little sun-dial of stained glass, with a fly painted on it, as though crawling over the glass; a projecting piece of metal (that, if it existed, is missing now) probably threw the needful shadow down to show the time. We made a rough sketch of this curious sun-dial, in order, some day perhaps, to have a similar one reproduced in our own study window. The panelling of the hall is of oak, but this "has been painted over to improve it"! We were told that beneath the paint "the old oak is as black as your hat," in proof of which we were shown a bit of the wainscot where the paint had been scraped off; our hat, or rather cap, happened to be of a light brown, but that is a matter aside; the oak was of a rich, deep, dark chocolate hue.

On the ground floor all else that may have been of archæological interest has been unhappily improved away; besides the hall, the huge rambling old kitchen was the only apartment that at all appealed to us there. Going upstairs, we were shown a panelled bedchamber, possessing a rather nice old carved mantelpiece; it is adorned with a coat of arms and the initials I. S., presumably intended for Iohn Selwyn; this mantel is further "disadorned" —to coin a word for the occasion—by a most ugly modern cast-iron grate that usurps the place of the old-fashioned fire-dogs or andirons.

Then along some rambling passages we were taken to a curious staircase in the centre of the building. This was, however, more like a rickety ladder of blocks of black oak than a staircase proper, and may possibly have formed part of a secret passage. It leads now to a spot under the roof-trees, where we saw the great tie-beams and finely-carved king-post that support the roof. Presumably this was the upper part of the ancient hall. At the end of the wall here, under the eaves of the roof, a narrow space was pointed out to us, looking down which we saw a large chamber reaching through two stories to the ground; but having no floors, and no other known means of access, we had to have a light to see it properly. Whether or not this were a "hiding-hole," I cannot say. It seems, however, unduly large for one, taking up much more space than would be at all needful for such a purpose, and so increasing the risk of detection. Knowing how near Friston Place is to the coast, and knowing also that smuggling was erst a brisk and profitable trade in these parts, I am inclined to imagine that this curiously-walled-in place had some connection with the smugglers of the olden time, a fact that would account for its comparative spaciousness. A rude staircase that may have led to the bottom of it commences near the roof, but now ends abruptly in a wall. Manifestly the geography of the old house has changed much from time to time; its peculiar present planning is suggestive of mysterious doings, of which its innocent-looking exterior conveys no hint.

On leaving Friston Place we could not help noting what a pretty picture the old time-toned house made, with its gray gables and mullioned windows, its little, quaint, wall-girt courtyard having an ancient well at one end, enclosed in an out-building, constructed with an eye to effect, somewhat like a pigeon-house. Within this is a great old wooden wheel, in which a donkey used to be placed to make the wheel revolve, and so draw up the water, a primitive and picturesque proceeding that sufficed for our not over-exacting forefathers—and there is much virtue in primitiveness with contentment!

From Friston it was a sharp descent into East Dean, another peaceful little village set in a sheltered valley that runs straight up from the sea at Birling Gap, where many a cargo has been "run in" by the smugglers of old. Out of East Dean it was stiff collar-work for a mile or more. Then we came on to the top of the Downs, with fine views of the undulating chalk hills around, rising and falling in vast curves, and full of varying but subtle colour. To our right we caught sight of the signal station on Beachy Head, sharply silhouetted against the luminous sky, and now and again we caught glimpses of the distant sea, "that blue end of the world." Then, as the shadows were lengthening and the west was growing golden, we dropped quietly down from our elevated position and found ourselves safely back again in Eastbourne, sun-browned, full of health, our minds stored with a host of pleasant memories and countless lovely pictures that will never be forgotten as long as life shall last. And now, kind reader, our pleasant summer wanderings "On Southern English Roads" are ended. I have to thank you for your good company for so far and for so long. Give me your hand. It only remains for me to say "Good-bye"—no, rather let it be "Till we meet again," for on another day, on other roads, I would crave anew your most welcome company. Before we part I propose a toast to our next enjoyable "Holiday on the Road."

APPENDIX

ITINERARY OF JOURNEY

	Stages in Miles	Total Distance in Miles
Eastbourne to Uckfield, *through Hailsham, East Hoathly, and Isfield*	25	25
Uckfield to Tunbridge Wells, *by Buxted and over Crowborough*	15	40
Tunbridge Wells to East Grinstead	15	55
East Grinstead to Crowhurst and back	14	69
East Grinstead to Cuckfield, *through Worth and Balcombe*	15	84
Cuckfield to Scaynes Hill and back by Lindfield	13	97
Cuckfield to Horsham, *by Slaugham*	12	109
Horsham to Storrington, *by Steyning*	$20\frac{1}{2}$	$129\frac{1}{2}$
Storrington to Arundel, *by Parham and Amberley*	10	$139\frac{1}{2}$
Arundel to Chichester, *by Slindon*	$13\frac{1}{2}$	153
Chichester to Fareham, *by Bosham*	20	173
Fareham to Southampton	12	185
Southampton to Stoney Cross, *through the New Forest*	12	197
Stoney Cross to Wimborne Minster, *through Ringwood*	19	216

	Stages in Miles	Total Distance in Miles
Wimborne Minster to Wareham	$9\frac{1}{2}$	$225\frac{1}{2}$
Wareham to Swanage and back *across the Isle of Purbeck*	20	$245\frac{1}{2}$
Wareham to Dorchester	17	$262\frac{1}{2}$
Dorchester to Sherborne, *up the Cerne Valley*	$18\frac{1}{2}$	281
Sherborne to Frome, *through Bruton*	24	305
Frome to Trowbridge	9	314
Trowbridge to Everley, *through Devizes and over Salisbury Plain*	24	338
Everley to Andover	12	350
Andover to Winchester	16	366
Winchester to Petersfield, *up the Itchen Valley and by Alresford*	22	388
Petersfield to Petworth, *through Midhurst*	16	404
Petworth to Worthing, *over the South Downs*	22	426
Worthing to Lewes	21	447
Lewes to Eastbourne, *through Seaford*	20	467

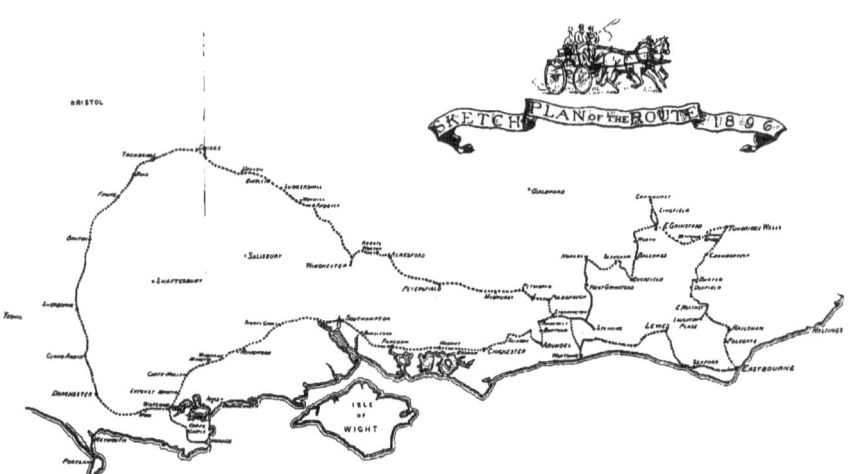

FOLDOUT BLANK

INDEX

ALFRED'S TOWER, 317
Alresford, 368, 369
Amberley, 194-197
Andover, 355-357
Arundel, 200-206
Arundel Park, 207-209
Ashdown Forest, 101, 104, 109

BALCOMBE, 143-145
Beachy Head, 78
Beckington, 324
Bindon Abbey, 280
Birling Gap, 416
Bishops Sutton, 370, 371
Bishopstone, 410, 411
Bosham, 217-224
Brambletye House, 104-107
Breeches Wood, 33
Broadwater, 395
Bruton, 313-316
Buckhurst, 98, 104
Bullington Cross, 359
Burpham, 199, 200
Bursledon Bridge, 231, 232
Buxted, 64-67

CADNAM, 235
Casterley Camp, 337
Castles—
  Amberley, 195, 196
  Arundel, 198, 208
  Corfe, 257, 259, 272
  Knepp, 177
  Lewes, 404, 405
  Ludgershall, 353, 354
  Maiden, 284
  Porchester, 227
  Sherborne, 310
  Warblington, 226
Cerne Abbas, 295-300

Cerne Giant, 300, 301
Cerne Valley, 291-302
Charlton, 338
Charminster, 288-291
Chichester, 209, 213-217
Churches—
  Amberley, 195, 197
  Arundel, 202, 203
  Bishopstone, 410, 411
  Bosham, 221-224
  Boxgrove Priory, 211-213
  Broadwater, 395-398
  Bruton, 315
  Buxted, 67-72
  Crowhurst, 124, 125
  East Grinstead, 115
  East Hoathly, 27, 28
  Fareham, 228, 229
  Frome, 319-323
  Hartfield, 101
  Headborne Worthy, 364, 365
  Isfield, 47, 53-58
  Lingfield, 118-123
  Old Shoreham, 403
  Piddinghoe, 409
  Seend, 331, 332
  Sherborne, 308, 309
  Slaugham, 165-168
  Sompting, 229, 400, 401
  Southease, 409
  Steyning, 179-183
  Titchfield, 230, 231
  Trotton, 375-378
  Wareham—
    St. Martin's, 255, 256
    St. Mary's, 271-273
  Wimborne Minster, 242-248
  Withyham, 97
  Worth, 138-142
Copthorne, 137

Corfe, 260-262
Corfe Mullen, 250
Cosham, 227
Cowdray, 380-383
Cowdray Park, 384
Creech Barrow, 258
Creech Heath, 258
Cripplegate, 176
Crowborough, 73, 80-85
Crowborough Beacon, 74, 82, 83
Crowhurst, 112, 123
Crowhurst Place, 125-132
Cuckfield, 146-151, 163, 164
Cuckfield Place, 149-151

DEVIL'S RACE, 32
Devizes, 332-335
Dicker Common, 20
Dorchester, 284-288
Dorman's Land, 134
Durlston Head, 263-268

EAST DEAN, 416
East Everley, 340, 341, 343-350
East Grinstead, 89, 107-116
East Hoathly, 19, 23-26, 46
East Mascalls, 151, 155-157
East Stoke, 275
Eastbourne, 7, 416
Emsworth, 225, 226
Eridge Green, 86, 87

FAREHAM, 227, 228
Felbridge, 136
Field Place, 175
Finden, 388
Fishbourne, 217
Fittleworth, 391-395
Forest Row, 102, 107, 109
Friston, 412, 413
Friston Place, 413-416

GLASTONBURY TOR, 318
Godmanstone, 293, 294
Groombridge, 91, 94
Groombridge Place, 91-93

HAILSHAM, 17, 18
Halland House, 26, 28, 32, 36, 37
Harewood Forest, 357
Hartfield, 100
Havant, 226
Haywards Heath, 152-154, 163

Headborne Worthy, 364, 365
Herston, 262
Holnest, 302
Horsebridge, 19, 20
Horsham, 172-175
Houghton Bridge, 197

ISFIELD, 46
Isfield Place, 50-52
Isle of Purbeck, 257, 258
Itchen Abbas, 367, 368
Itchen Stoke, 368
Itchen Valley, 364-367

KINGS WORTHY, 367

LANCING, 401
Langston Harbour, 227
Laughton, 43
Laughton Place, 26, 32, 38-42
Lewes, 403-409
Lindfield, 108, 158-163
Lingfield, 116-123, 133
Long Burton, 304
Longparish, 357
Ludgershall, 353, 354
Lychett Heath, 250
Lychett Minster, 252

MENDIP HILLS, 318
Midhurst, 374, 379-384

NEWHAVEN, 409, 412

OCKENDEN, 164, 165, 171
Old Shoreham, 399, 403
Otham, 14-16

PARHAM, 187-193
Petersfield, 373, 374
Petworth, 374, 385-389
Pevensey Bay, 8
Piddinghoe, 409
Polegate, 12, 14
Poole Harbour, 252
Portsmouth, 227
Pulborough, 395
Purbeck Hills, 258, 275

REVEL'S HILL, 302
Ringwood, 239, 240

INDEX

Rivers—
  Adur, 19, 401, 402
  Arun, 19, 195, 197, 201
  Avon, 239, 240
  Brue, 315
  Cerne, 291
  Cuckmere, 18, 19, 412
  Frome, 257, 276
  Itchen, 364
  Ouse, 19
  Rother, 19, 375, 384
  Stour, 249
  Test, 234, 357
Road, 324
Rogate, 374, 375
Rufus Stone, 237, 238

SACKVILLE COLLEGE, 113, 114
Salisbury Plain, 318, 336, 339-352
Scaynes Hill, 153
Seaford, 411
Seend, 330-332
Seend Head, 329
Sherborne, 305-310
Slaugham, 164, 165, 171
Slaugham Place, 168-171
Slindon, 209-211
Sompting, 400
South Downs, 10, 11
Southampton, 232-234
Southampton Water, 229, 234
Southease, 409
St. Leonard's Forest, 173, 174
Staplefield, 165
Steyning, 178-184

Stoney Cross, 236-239
Storrington, 186, 187
Stowborough, 257
Sutton Courtney, 359-361
Swanage, 262-264, 268-270
Swanbourne Lake, 207

TERRIBLE DOWN, 34
Tilly Whim Caves, 267
Titchfield, 229-231
Totton, 234
Trotton, 375-379
Trowbridge, 325, 326
Tunbridge Wells, 86-89

UCKFIELD, 60-62
Upavon, 339

WAREHAM, 253-257, 271-274
Warmwell, 282
Washington, 395
West Dean, 412
West Grinstead, 178
Westbury White Horse, 323, 324
Weyhill, 354, 355
Willingdon, 12
Wimborne, 242-249
Winchester, 361-363
Winfrith, 280
Winterbourne Came, 282
Wiston Park, 185
Withyham, 97
Wool, 277-280
Worth Forest, 142, 143
Worthing, 388, 389, 399

THE END

J. D. & Co.

Printed by R. & R. CLARK, LIMITED, *Edinburgh*

www.ingramcontent.com/pod-product-compliance
Lightning Source LLC
Chambersburg PA
CBHW022103300426
44117CB00007B/568